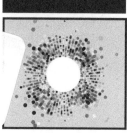

Minding the Machines

Building and Leading Data Science and Analytics Teams

Jeremy Adamson

WILEY

ISBN: 978-1-119-78532-3

ISBN: 978-1-119-78534-7 (ebk)

ISBN: 978-1-119-78533-0 (ebk)

For general information on our other products and services or for technical support, please contact our Customer Care Department within the United States at (800) 762-2974, outside the United States at (317) 572-3993 or fax (317) 572-4002.

Wiley also publishes its books in a variety of electronic formats. Some content that appears in print may not be available in electronic formats. For more information about Wiley products, visit our web site at www.wiley.com.

Library of Congress Control Number: 2021938292

Cover Image: © shuoshu/Getty Images
Cover Design: Wiley

SKY10027765_062421

to Melo

About the Author

Jeremy Adamson is a leader in AI and analytics strategy and has a broad range of experience in aviation, energy, financial services, and public administration. Jeremy has worked with several major organizations to help them establish a leadership position in data science and to unlock real business value using advanced analytics.

Jeremy holds a master's degree in transportation engineering and a bachelor's degree in civil engineering from the University of New Brunswick as well as a master of business administration from the University of Calgary. Jeremy is a professional engineer in the province of Alberta. He currently resides in Calgary.

Learn more at www.rjeremyadamson.com.

About the Technical Editor

Andrew McHardy is a strategic leader and advisor with over 25 years' experience in analytics and artificial intelligence, engineering, and management consulting. He has held roles ranging from field to executive level, working with asset-intensive organizations in Canada and internationally, across the energy, resources, manufacturing, transportation, and defense sectors. Throughout his career, he has focused on leveraging digital tools, predictive analytics, and artificial intelligence to drive improvements in workforce safety and productivity, capital project delivery, asset reliability and maintenance, quality, and production.

Andrew holds a master's degree in Statistics and Industrial and Systems Engineering from Rutgers University and a bachelor's degree in Chemical and Materials Engineering and master's degree in Defence Studies from the Royal Military College of Canada. He has also completed a business analytics specialization through the University of Pennsylvania, and is a certified Project Management Professional.

Prior to transitioning to the private sector, Andrew served in the Canadian Army and Special Operations Forces and has deployed on operations in Canada and internationally.

About the Foreword Author

A thought leader, change agent, and impact-focused innovator, Alfredo C. Tan is an industry professor in the Strategic Management faculty at McMaster University where he teaches at the undergraduate and graduate level and in The Directors College Innovation Governance program for board directors. He is also the senior vice president of Strategy, Data and Products at Rogers Sports & Media, where his team is helping lead the digital transformation of the organization.

Alfredo has led companies through changing digital landscapes and evolving consumer expectations and behaviors. Most recently he was the chief marketing officer and the first Chief Digital and Innovation Officer at WestJet Airlines. Alfredo is also a former Facebook and Instagram and Yahoo! executive, having worked in Canada, the United States, Asia-Pacific, and Latin America. Mr. Tan is a frequently requested keynote speaker at leading technology, media, marketing, corporate, and various other industry conferences. He has been profiled and quoted in *Forbes Magazine, Marketing Magazine*, the *Economist, Strategy Magazine*, the *Globe and Mail*, and many other leading industry publications. Alfredo currently sits on the Advisory Board on Innovation at McMaster University, is a member of the Leadership Council at the Perimeter Institute for Theoretical Physics, and sits on the Haskayne School of Business Technology Management Industry Advisory Council at the University of Calgary. Alfredo was recognized with the Desmond Parker Outstanding Young Alumni Award from the University of Toronto, has been inducted into the McMaster University Alumni Gallery, and is a recipient of the prestigious

Arbor Award for his service to the University of Toronto. Alfredo holds an HBSc in Forensic Science & Biology from the University of Toronto, an MBA from McMaster University, and an LLM from the University of Toronto Law School. He is a graduate of the Advanced Management Program at the Harvard Business School.

He and his partner, Jessica, are proud parents to five rescue animals and hope to own a large property one day where all their rescue animals can roam free.

Acknowledgments

I have been fortunate to work with many amazing people and organizations in the field of analytics. It was alongside them that the lessons of this book were learned. It would be impossible to list them all and their contributions, but to all my past and present colleagues, my sincerest appreciation for the support throughout the writing of this book, for your valuable feedback, and for your patience as we struggled together to figure out how best to build out a strong and value-driven analytics function.

Thank you to Devon Lewis, my acquisitions editor, who believed in this project and helped me to navigate the process of writing a book.

Thank you to Christine O'Connor, the project manager, and to Judy Flynn and Janet Wehner, the editors, for helping to wrangle my writing and keep me on track.

Thank you to Andrew McHardy for agreeing to be the technical editor for this project. His wisdom and experience really elevated the material and helped to focus the book on core concepts. He is the embodiment of parsimony.

Thank you to Alfredo Tan for his ongoing support and for contributing a foreword and sharing his experience in the field.

Finally, thank you to my wife, Melodie, and my boys, Finley and Wyatt, for all their patience and support through this project. My appreciation in particular to Finley and Wyatt for their careful review and approval of the swimlane and Venn diagrams that appear in the book.

—Jeremy Adamson

Contents at a Glance

Foreword		xiii
Introduction		xvi
Chapter 1	Prologue	1
Chapter 2	Strategy	17
Chapter 3	Process	69
Chapter 4	People	121
Chapter 5	Future of Business Analytics	187
Chapter 6	Summary	211
Chapter 7	Coda	213
Index		215

Contents

Foreword		**xiii**
Introduction		**xvi**
Chapter 1	**Prologue**	**1**
	For the Leader from the Business	5
	For the Career Transitioner	6
	For the Motivated Practitioner	6
	For the Student	7
	For the Analytics Leader	8
	Structure of This Book	8
	Why Is This Book Needed?	9
	Communication Gap	9
	Troubles with Taylorism	10
	Rinse, Report, Repeat	12
	Too Fast, Too Slow	13
	More Data, More Problems	14
	Summary	15
Chapter 2	**Strategy**	**17**
	The Role of Analytics in the Organization	20
	The Analytics Playbook	20
	Data and Analytics as a Culture Change	24
	Current State Assessment	26
	Readiness Assessment	26
	Capability Modeling and Mapping	28
	Technology Stack Review	32

Data Quality and Governance	34
Stakeholder Engagement	35
Defining the Future State	37
Defining the Mandate	39
Analytics Governance Model	40
Target Operating Model	42
Define Your Principles	43
Functions, Services, and Capabilities	43
Interaction Models	44
Organizational Design	48
Community of Practice	52
Project Delivery Model	55
Closing the Gap	57
Setting the Horizon	58
Establishing a Talent Roadmap	59
Consultants and Contractors	60
Change Management	62
Implementing Governance Models	64
Summary	65
Chapter 3 **Process**	**69**
Project Planning	73
Intake and Prioritization	73
Project Pipelines	77
Portfolio Project Management	80
Project Scoping and Planning	83
Scoping and Requirements Definition	86
Planning	92
Project Execution	96
Governance Structure and Communication Plan	99
Project Kickoff	102
Agile Analytics	103
Change and Stakeholder Management	106
Skeuomorphs	106
AI 101 and Project Brainstorming	107
Iterative Insights	110
Closeout and Delivery	111
Automation	112
Project Debrief	114
Summary	118
Chapter 4 **People**	**121**
Building the Team	122
Success Factors	123
Team Composition	128

Hiring and Onboarding   129
Talent Development   131
Retention   136
Departures   137
The Data Scientist Hierarchy of Needs   139
Culture   140
Innovation   145
Communication   147
Succession Planning   149
Potential Pitfalls   151
    Dunning-Kruger Effect   152
    Diderot Effect   153
Leading the Team   154
    Data Scientists as Craftspeople   157
    Team Conventions   160
        Formal Meetings   162
        Coffee Chats   164
    Managing Conflict   167
    Relationship Management   169
    Owning the Narrative   175
    Performance Metrics   177
Summary   181

Chapter 5   Future of Business Analytics   187
AutoML and the No-Code Movement   189
Data Science Is Dead   192
The Data Warehouse   195
True Operationalization   196
Exogenous Data   198
Edge AI   199
Analytics for Good   200
Analytics for Evil   201
Ethics and Bias   203
Analytics Talent Shortages   204
Death of the Career Transitioner   206

Chapter 6   Summary   211

Chapter 7   Coda   213

Index   215

Foreword

Data. There was a time when this word made reference to a *Star Trek* character or something professionals in the IT department who worked on databases would manage. Today *data, data science, data engineering, data analysts,* or any term including the use of *data* is pervasive across business, industries, and society. The use of the term *data* has practically become everyday vernacular in business; it seems to be the holy grail solution to everything. However, most organizations are still in the very early stages of their journey.

Many of the world's leading organizations can attribute their success to the fact that the practice of data science is increasingly becoming a strategic function. Analytics and data science enable consumer experiences that have become indispensable in our daily lives and deliver highly personalized recommendations and content, and this is now the expectation for almost everything else in our lives. The expectation of the customer has become immediate, personalized services that predict what it is they may want before they may even know it themselves. Data is what powers these great product experiences. Data science is no longer simply a technology function buried within IT or reserved purely for the tech giants in Silicon Valley. Data science and analytics will become increasingly indispensable in health care as it will improve diagnostic accuracy and efficiency. In finance, it will aid in the detection of anomalies and fraud. In manufacturing, it will aid in fault prediction and preventative maintenance. Whether you work in corporate strategy, research & insights, product development, human resources, marketing, technology, or finance, you will no longer be able to effectively compete without leveraging the talent and capabilities of the data science teams.

The need for knowledge in Data Science & Analytics, Algorithms & Artificial Intelligence is becoming evident in the sheer volume of online courses, degrees, and certifications available on EDx, Coursera, Udacity, and other online education providers. Top-ranked universities across Canada have introduced graduate degrees in data science and analytics. Two of the most prestigious universities in the world, the University of California, Berkeley, and Massachusetts Institute of Technology, are creating entirely new institutions within their campuses to come to terms with the ubiquity of data and the rise of artificial intelligence.

However, it isn't simply technical, mathematical, or scientific horsepower that is required by organizations in the data science world. In most organizations the premise is still that data science teams are over-indexed in the technical practice versus being embedded in the business to drive business performance. The most successful data science teams are those that have a focus on contributing to the strategy of hiring and retaining people who are focused on value creation and finding ways to democratize access to data and decision making. Because it is one of the newest functions in most organizations, there is little body of work to refer to on how to design and build the right data science organization. We are all learning in real time, across all industries and geographies. How do you hire? How do you structure the teams? What problems do you solve? How do you set up the culture of experimentation? How do you think about democratizing access? How do you evolve beyond reporting and move into prediction models and algorithms?

I have had the pleasure of being a senior leader to technology teams at organizations with widely varying analytical maturity, in industries ranging from Silicon Valley giants to aviation and from sports to media and digital. The key differentiator for those teams finding success using data science is not whether they have a data lake or are deploying neural nets and reinforcement learning. The winning teams are those that integrate into the organization, understand the business, build strong relationships, collaborate, align their objectives to the business, and see data science as a toolkit for solving business problems rather than an esoteric and technical field of study. They are integrated into the business and serve a strategic function with support at the highest levels of the organization, all the way to the president or CEO. The three pillars described in this book, people, process, and strategy, are every bit as important as the data and technology. The challenge, despite all the focus on the technical skills, is still a very human one. There is no doubt machines are helping drive more automation and the increasing power of data and algorithms to help make decisions. I would argue that the importance of the human element, the people responsible for building the models, doing the analysis and creating the algorithms, will becoming increasingly important. The need for leadership, empathy, and an understanding of organizational behavior is becoming increasingly important. It is essential for these teams to have the ability to deal across the enterprise with privacy and data governance, ethics, and bias, and to ensure that the capital and operational investments are solving the problems that really matter. As the field of data science advances, the human element and the team you build becomes even more important. The more important the machines become, and the data that powers them, the more the people element will be critical. Strategy, process, culture, and the human side of data science will be the next evolution of the practice to deliver on the promise of big data and business results.

Most data science leaders, focusing mainly on the technical aspects of their craft, have struggled to find successes in organizations and to unlock real business value. *Minding the Machines* helps to fill that gap and redirect these professionals to the things that matter. Blending the science of data and the leadership of people, process, and strategy is what Jeremy manages to do brilliantly in this book.

—Alfredo C. Tan

Introduction

Minding the Machines provides insights into how to structure and lead a successful analytics practice. Establishing this practice requires a significant up-front investment in understanding and contextualizing the initiative in contrast to better-understood functions such as IT or HR. Many organizations have attempted to use operating models and templates from these other functions, showing a fundamental misunderstanding of where analytics fits within an organization and leading to visible failures. These failures have set back the analytical maturity of many organizations. Business leaders need to hire or develop data-centric talent who can step back from analysis and project management to view their work through a lens of value creation.

Readers will understand how organizations and practitioners need to structure, build, and lead a successful analytics team—to bridge the gap between business leaders and the analytical function. The analytics job market is booming, and the talent pool has swelled with other professionals upskilling and rebranding themselves as data scientists. While this influx of highly technical specialists with limited leadership experience has had negative consequences for the practice, it also provides an opportunity for personal differentiation.

Minding the Machines is organized in three key pillars: strategy, process, and people.

Strategy—How to assess organizational readiness, identify gaps, establish an attainable roadmap, and properly articulate a value proposition and case for change.

Process—How to select and manage projects across their life cycle, including design thinking, risk assessment, governance, and operationalization.

People—How to structure and engage a team, establish productive and parsimonious conventions, and lead a distinct practice with unique requirements.

Minding the Machines is intended for analytics practitioners seeking career progression, business leaders who wish to understand how to manage this unique practice, and students who want to differentiate themselves against their technical peers.

There is a significant need for leaders who can bridge the gap between the business and the data science and analytics functions. *Minding the Machines* fills this need, helping data science professionals to successfully leverage this powerful practice to unlock value in their organizations.

How to Contact the Publisher

If you believe you've found a mistake in this book, please bring it to our attention. At John Wiley & Sons, we understand how important it is to provide our customers with accurate content, but even with our best efforts an error may occur.

In order to submit your possible errata, please email it to our Customer Service Team at `wileysupport@wiley.com` with the subject line "Possible Book Errata Submission."

How to Contact the Author

I would love to connect and hear what you thought of this book or to discuss opportunities to collaborate. You can reach me via:

Website: `www.rjeremyadamson.com`

Email: `jeremy@rjeremyadamson.com`

LinkedIn: `https://linkedin.com/in/rjeremyadamson/`

Twitter: `@r2b7e`

Instagram: `r2b7e`

Prologue

> How is analytics unique in a corporate context? What have other organizations done right? What have they done wrong? What are the expectations for a new analytics leader?

Building, integrating, and leading effective analytics teams is a business imperative. The organizations that are most successful overall are those that effectively leverage their analytics capabilities to build a sustainable competitive advantage. However, many organizations are simply not getting the return that they expected on their investments in analytics.

Does hiring an engineer cause the surrounding buildings to be more robust? Could hiring five engineers make those buildings even more robust? Would hiring a pharmacist make you healthier? Would hiring an actuary increase your longevity?

In the last 20 years, the once sleepy academic fields of statistics, operations research, and decision support have exploded and been rebranded using terms such as *data science, artificial intelligence, big data,* and *advanced analytics*, among others. These practices have matured, and they have entered the mainstream. Advanced analytics and AI have moved from being an investment in the future to a core component of corporate strategy and a key enabler for all areas of the business. Regardless of their size or the industry or sector in which they are used, these technologies are becoming an organizational necessity throughout the world. Organizations use advanced analytics and AI to develop new products, understand their customers, control their costs, and make better-informed decisions.

This new corporate function has been integrated in several support and core functions and has quickly become indispensable. Analytics is expected to add $16 trillion US to the global economy by 2030 and companies are eager to realize some of that value (PwC, 2017). As a result there has been a surge in demand for practitioners. There are approximately 3.3 million people employed in analytics in North America, and this is projected to grow by 15 percent a year in the United States over the next decade according to the US Bureau of Labor Statistics (2020). Educational institutions are eager to meet this demand.

Essentially every major college and university in the world offers some sort of analytics program or specialization, within multiple faculties such as mathematics, engineering, or business. There are several hundred books published in this space, and it enjoys a highly active online community. These resources are strong, edifying, and comprehensive and cover every new technology, framework, algorithm, and approach. With such an active community, new algorithms and methodologies are packaged and made publicly accessible for tools such as R, Python, and Julia, almost immediately after being developed. The best and brightest are choosing to enter the field, often called the "Sexiest Job of the 21st Century" (Davenport & Patil, 2012).

So, with overwhelming demand and a staggeringly capable pool of talent, why are there so many failures? Why are most organizations struggling to unlock the value in data science and advanced analytics? With so much executive support, so much talent, so much academic focus, why are so few organizations successfully deploying and leveraging analytics? In the 1980s, economist Robert Solow remarked that "you can see the computer age everywhere except in the productivity statistics." Why now can we see data science transforming organizations without a commensurate improvement in productivity?

The fundamental reason is in the opening questions. Clearly, having five engineers on your payroll will not improve buildings in the vicinity. Even if directly requested, ordered, mandated, or incented to "improve a building," they will struggle to do so. Replaced with any other profession, it is clear why this cannot work, but it persists as the typical furtive first steps into analytics. This is the essence of what most organizations have done with their data analytics team. They have hired talented, passionate, ambitious data scientists and asked them to simply "do data science." Advanced analytics and AI as a practice has been poorly defined in its scope, has been subjected to great overspending, and has been lacking in relevant performance measures. Because of this, it is failing to live up to its potential.

Effectively all organizations realize the benefits of analytics. In a survey by Deloitte in 2020, 43 percent believed their organization would be transformed by analytics within the next 1 to 3 years, and 23 percent within the next year (Ammanath, Jarvis, & Hupfer, 2020). Though most organizations are on board with analytics being a key strategic advantage, they are unaware of how exactly to extract value from the new function.

Short-tenured data scientists, employed in a frothy and competitive market, share stories of unfocused and baffled companies where they have been engaged in operational reporting, confirming executive assumptions, and adding visualizations to legacy reports. Uncertain what to do with the team, and in a final act of surrender, the companies no longer expect the function to "do data science" and transform the team into a disbanded group of de facto technical resources automating onerous spreadsheets in a quasi-IT role.

Contrasted with those organizations who have truly got it right, the differences are stunning. For several companies, well-supported analytical Centers of Excellence are a key team, perpetually hiring and growing, and are solicited for their input and perspectives on all major projects. In others, internal Communities of Practice encourage cross-pollination of ideas and development opportunities for junior data scientists. New products are formed and informed after a thorough analysis by data scientists, who are also supporting human resources with success indicators and spending Fridays pursuing their transformative passion projects. Theories and hypotheses are quickly tested in a cross-functional analytical sandbox. Individuals are sharing their work at conferences and symposia, building eminence, and gaining acclaim for the organization.

The irony is that while most analytics teams exercise great care in deconstructing a problem, modeling each of the elements, and developing robust simulations and marvelously elegant solutions, the business processes that they employ in their project delivery are often at best immature and at worst destructive. The challenge for any leader is to encourage and stimulate logical thinking from a lens of interconnectedness and value creation, and to direct that philosophy to execution as well. As the logician Bertrand Russell said, "What is best in mathematics deserves not merely to be learnt as a task, but to be assimilated as a part of daily thought, and brought again and again before the mind with ever-renewed encouragement" (Russell, 1902).

The title of this book, *Minding the Machines*, is meant to be an affectionate recursion. Those talented and creative practitioners, craftspeople, data scientists, and machine learning engineers, who create the algorithms that are transforming the way business is done, mind and care for those machines like a shepherd. Those machines need to be trained, informed, given established processes, encouraged to be broadly interoperable, and developed to be applicable to many different situations and problems. Similarly, the practitioners themselves need to be minded, cared for, cultivated, and encouraged for both the team and the individuals to be successful. This concept of recursion occurs throughout the book.

The second key theme is one of parsimony. Parsimony is a philosophy of intentionally expending the minimum amount of energy required in an activity so as to maintain overall efficiency. This is a key part of modeling; it is about keeping things as simple as possible, but no simpler. Similarly, and in the vein of recursion, teams themselves must be parsimonious. For analytics to mature as a practice while still delivering an accelerated time-to-value, teams need to be scrappy and lean.

At a foundational level, the objective of this book is to provide clear insights into how to structure and lead a successful analytics team. This is a deceptively challenging objective since there are no generalized templates from which to work. Establishing a project management office, information services, or human resources department is an understood process and does not vary materially between organizations. Establishing an analytics team, by contrast, requires a significant up-front investment in understanding and contextualizing the initiative. Many organizations have attempted to use operating models and templates from other functions—often IT and operations research. This fundamental misunderstanding of where analytics fits within an organization has led to visible failures and has set back the analytical maturity of many organizations. Business leaders need to hire or develop value-centric talent who can step back from analysis and project management to view their work as existing within a network of individuals and teams with competing priorities and motivations.

Corporations, without a template or a default methodology to benchmark against, have made expensive missteps in building these teams by installing the wrong leaders, copying other functions, positioning the function under the wrong executives, incentivizing destructive behaviors, hiring the wrong people, and committing to the wrong projects. They have contracted expensive consultants to provide roadmaps that do not consider the unique culture or competencies of their organization.

They have embedded disparate data science specialists throughout the organization and incurred enormous technical debt.

These issues are not insurmountable, however. Whether an organization is beginning its first foray into the analytics space or it is rebooting a failed team for the third time, the key is the creation of a carefully considered strategy, the establishment of realistic goals, and the full commitment of executive leadership. The advantages associated with analytics are too great to overlook, and the long-term cumulative impact of interrelated and interdependent models provides a powerful incentive for aggressive adoption.

This book was written for anybody who aspires to lead or be part of an effective analytics team, regardless of managerial experience. Every analytics leader, from a first-time team lead to a seasoned VP, has unique challenges to overcome.

For the Leader from the Business

Every new role is a challenge, regardless of ability, disposition, or motivation. This is particularly the case with a unique subculture of academic technocrats with whom it is difficult to establish credibility without enough time being "hands on keyboard." Without the respect of your team, it is impossible to get the buy-in required to establish best practices and ensure that the output of the team is not simply self-satisfying experimentation but can bring real value to the organization. As a corollary, every practitioner has experienced a manager who is out of their depth and who has compensated for their lack of self-confidence with authoritarianism and distrust, shifting the focus of the team toward an end they are more confident with, such as reporting.

For all but the most analytically committed organizations, there is a point along the chain of command where a practitioner reports to a nonpractitioner. This can be a challenging junction for both parties without clear expectations, transparent communication, and mutual respect. Catching up from a technical perspective isn't feasible or advisable, but by leveraging your business understanding and domain knowledge to become an intermediary, translating business needs into projects and analytical outputs into operationalizable processes, you can unlock the power of your new team and give them the opportunity to develop into more business-oriented individuals.

For the business leader, I hope that this book helps you to reframe and refine your current leadership abilities, and to use them in an analytics context in order to engage your team and find success together.

For the Career Transitioner

Those who transition to data and analytics mid-career have a key differentiator from those who have entered the field directly from university—breadth and context. The ability to leverage your multidisciplinary background from engineering, finance, sciences, and so on is valuable both to your career and the organization you join.

Though it would be almost impossible to compete with trained data scientists on a technical basis, it is the disciplinary and sector diversity of the team that drives innovation, and those who have worked in multiple industries and functional areas bring a unique perspective to the teams with whom they work. Rather than starting a new career as a new hire and individual contributor, with personal study and intentional self-reflection mid-career transitioners are often able to seamlessly make a lateral move. Having familiarity with the different AutoML and analytics-as-a-service offerings, combined with transferable managerial skills, can make for a powerful combination.

For the career transitioner, I hope that this book helps you to prepare for lateral movement into an analytics role and to use your transferable skills to add value in your new function.

For the Motivated Practitioner

It is an unfortunate truth (and perhaps an unfair generalization) that the skillset that makes a practitioner a competent data scientist is rarely the skillset that makes them a competent manager. Though there are certainly analytically minded people who have the natural inclinations toward leadership and bigger picture thinking, it is rare that in practice those people would have the technical depth to stand out as a candidate for management. Often, those with the natural capabilities required to enter management can appear to be less effective as individual contributors on a purely technical basis.

To make the leap to management is to leave an objective and predictable role with performance metrics such as p-values and ROC curves and exchange them for stakeholder management, workshop facilitation, and inherent subjectivity. Those able to successfully make this transition while maintaining the ability to downshift to provide analytical support establish themselves as leaders in the practice and are in high demand. Exceptional managers who have legitimate technical credentials are the unicorns of data and analytics.

For the practitioner, I hope this book helps you to understand what is required to move up the value chain and to prepare for leadership opportunities.

For the Student

When a student pursues an applied field such as business or engineering, the curriculum is generally developed in a way that seeks to balance between foundational academic elements and applied profession-specific education. The curriculum is updated and maintained such that it remains aligned with the changing needs of the field. For several professions such as accounting, law, and engineering, this takes place within a partnership between the administrative body of the professional practice and the educational institute, and through accreditation it's ensured that graduates of these programs are broadly educated and prepared to work in the field they have studied. This is unfortunately not the case with data and analytics.

Most North American universities have data science or analytics offerings, but having no natural home they are generally provided through multiple faculties such as business, mathematics, engineering, finance, or computer science. These programs provide instruction in highly simulated and well-defined problem solving, focusing on the improvement of a statistical metric. The data is often perfectly presented and accompanied by a well-articulated data dictionary, in great contrast to real life experience. Additionally, most curricula emphasize such topics as computer vision, natural language processing, and reinforcement learning, fairly esoteric topics that have little applied usage in industry. Finally, and most importantly, effectively none have mandatory coursework on the strategic and operational elements of an advanced analytics and AI team. Without this understanding, typical graduates have a thorough mathematic understanding, much in the way of raw horsepower, but require a significant investment in training before they understand how to leverage their education and apply it to a real-life scenario.

With so many new data and analytics graduates competing with mid-career transitioners and a global talent pool, they often seek ways to stand out as a potential hire. With the exception of highly specialized roles in technology companies, the key development opportunity for these new hires is the formation of leadership abilities in an analytical context. Reframing and focusing analytical concepts into a business context is an immediate and powerful way to differentiate yourself in a new role or in an interview, especially as the profession moves away from long-horizon highly technical solutions toward a focus on immediate value.

For the student, I hope that this book gives you the knowledge to stand out against your peers, to be seen as a strategic thinker, and to be able to add value to whatever organization you choose to work with.

For the Analytics Leader

Compared to other organizational functions, this exciting field has come about abruptly and without a blueprint for how to build or lead these new teams. Often playbooks from other functions have been used, with little success. The lessons that experienced analytics professionals have learned have been hard won. What further complicates the successful deployment of these teams is that they are so sensitive to the state of the organization, its immediate goals, and the technical maturity of its industry. While finance and human resources are largely the same between industries and individual companies, the number of factors impacting analytics are staggering.

Using a generalized, systematic, and sequential approach, adapted to the needs of the individual organization, is the best method to standing up a new team or restructuring an existing team. Once a base template has been established, careful reflection on organizational readiness and analytical maturity combined with regulatory requirements and immediate needs can help with developing a short-term roadmap in collaboration with executive sponsors. Though there is no approach that will work in every situation, these best practices can hopefully help you see a little further over the horizon.

For the current analytics leader, I hope that some parts of this book will challenge your views, other parts will confirm your experience, and the book as a whole will ultimately help you to build out a successful and engaged team.

Structure of This Book

The main body of this book has been organized within three key pillars: strategy, process, and people.

> **Strategy**   How to assess organizational readiness, identify gaps, establish an attainable roadmap, engage stakeholders, ensure sponsorship, and properly articulate a value proposition and case for change

Process How to select and manage projects across their life cycle, including design thinking, risk assessment, governance, and operationalization

People How to structure and engage a team, establish productive and parsimonious conventions, and lead a distinct practice with unique requirements

These pillars loosely follow the chronological and logical ordering of priorities with the creation or inheritance of an analytics team, with the understanding that this is an iterative and ongoing effort. The procedural requirements flow naturally from the strategy, and similarly, team structure and convention must be based on the processes that have been created.

Though this has been ordered to facilitate a front-to-back reading, subsections have been intentionally made self-sufficient to allow for ease of referencing, at the cost perhaps of occasional repetition.

Why Is This Book Needed?

It is my personal hope that this book will make creating and leading the function easier and help in some small way to advance the profession. Having been involved with or privy to rebooting these teams in several organizations, I have seen well-intentioned missteps repeated regardless of the maturity and sophistication of the company.

There are several underlying reasons why organizations and individuals struggle to get their hands around analytics.

Communication Gap

The business will rarely, if ever, have the analytics knowledge and vernacular required to clearly articulate its needs and to formulate a problem statement that naturally lends itself to an analytical solution. Whereas Kaggle competitions, hackathons, boot camps, and university assignments present problems with a well-formed data set and a clear desired outcome, business problems are fuzzy, poorly defined, and often posited without a known objective. As practitioners, it is our responsibility to find the underlying issue and present the most situationally appropriate and practical solution.

Advanced analytics and AI practitioners can often have the expectation that their stakeholder group will provide a solution for them. Just as a doctor cannot expect a patient to diagnose their own health issues and for the doctor's approval an analytics team cannot expect a business unit to suggest an approach, provide a well-formed data set and an objective function, and request a model. What the business unit requests is very often not even what the analytics project lead hears.

Early in the project intake process, an analytics lead will meet with a business lead to discuss an opportunity. The business leader (actuarial, in this example) may say that they want a model that predicts the probability that a policyholder will lapse. The outcome that the leader is hoping for is a way to reduce their lapse rate, but what the analyst hears is, "Ignoring all other considerations, how can I best predict the probability of an individual lapsing?" If the practitioner executes on this misapprehension, the deliverable will have little use for the business; a prediction model of this sort has no operational value. This model would only work on a macro scale, and even if it could be disaggregated, the business would be making expensive concessions in the face of perceived threats.

Empathizing with the underlying needs of the business, understanding what success looks like for the project, and leveraging the domain knowledge of the project sponsor would have highlighted that the value in the analysis was further upstream. The factors driving lapse behavior were where the value to the business was and where an operationalizable change in process was possible.

As with the doctor analogy, it is through deep questioning, structured thinking, and the expert application of professional experience that the ideal path forward is uncovered. That path requires collaboration and the union of deep domain knowledge with analytical expertise.

Troubles with Taylorism

For every decision to be made there is a perception that there must be one optimal choice: a single price point that will maximize profit, a single model that will best predict lapse, or a single classification algorithm that will identify opportunities for upselling. The fact is that in effectively all cases these optima can never be known with certainty and can only be assessed *ex post facto* against true data. In professional practice as well as in university training, the results of a modeling project are typically evaluated against real-world data, giving a concrete measure of performance, whether AUC, or R squared, or another statistical metric.

This has created a professional environment where analysts can confidently point to a single score and have an objective measure of their performance. They can point with satisfaction to this measurement as an indicator of their success and evidence of the value they bring to the organization. Certainly, performant algorithms are an expectation, but without viewing the work through a lens of true accretive value creation, these statistical metrics are meaningless.

In the 1920s the practice of scientific management led to improvements in the productivity of teams by breaking the process into elements that could be optimized. Through a thorough motion study of workers at Bethlehem Steel, Frederick Taylor created and instituted a process that optimized rest patterns for workers and as a result doubled their productive output (Taylor, 1911). He advocated for all workplace processes to be evaluated in terms of their efficiency and all choice to be removed from the worker. This brutal division of labor and resulting hyperspecialization led to reduced engagement and produced suboptimal outcomes at scale when all factors were considered.

Practitioners need to avoid those actions and policies that create a form of neo-Taylorism within their organizations. Models that fully automate a process and embed simulated human decision making remove the dynamism and innovation that comes from having humans in the loop. It cements a process in place and reduces engagement and stakeholder buy-in. Analytics should support and supplement human endeavor, not supplant it with cold efficiency. It is essential that analytical projects are done within the context of the business and with the goal of maximizing the value to the organization.

Model accuracy needs to be secondary to bigger-picture considerations, including these:

Technical Implementation   Is the architecture stable? Does it require intervention?

Political Implementation   Does it conflict with other projects? Will implementation create redundancies?

Procedural Implementation   Will this fit in with existing processes? Will it require significant changes to current workflows? What are the risks associated with implementation? Will it introduce the potential for human error? Does it have dependencies on processes that are being sunset?

Interoperability   Are there downstream processes depending on the results? What are the impacts of a disruption to these processes? Can it be shifted to another system? Does it create dependencies?

Extensibility   Can the output be upgraded in the future? Does it require specialized skillsets? Is it generalized enough to be used for other purposes?

Scalability   Would this approach work if the volume of data doubled? Tripled?

Stability   Has it gone through thorough QA? Has it been tested at the boundary conditions? What happens if data are missing? What happens if it encounters unexpected inputs? How does it handle exceptions?

Interpretability   Are the results clearly understandable? Does the process need to be transparent?

Ethics   Is it legal? Does it have inherent bias?

Compliance   Does it contain personally identifiable information? Does it comply with the laws of the countries in which it will be used? Does it use trusted cloud providers?

Without exception, effort is better spent in discussing and addressing the above considerations than in marginal improvements to model performance. Even a poorly designed model will work with strong phenomena, and a poorly performing model that is in use will outperform a sophisticated model that is sitting idle.

Rinse, Report, Repeat

One of the most memorable scenes from the 1990s classic *Office Space* involves the protagonist being chastised repeatedly by his coworkers and managers about an incorrectly prepared TPS report. The reason this was so memorable is that it reflects the experience of every office worker at some point in their careers. Bureaucracy is a self-propagating danger, and for many larger legacy organizations, entire teams are dedicated to the preparation and dissemination of unread reports. There are several compounding factors that have led to an explosion in the number of reports recently.

With legacy reporting tools, the effort required to create reports created a natural limit on the number that could be produced. This provided a control on the spread of new reports. Unfortunately, the strength and ease of use of reporting and visualization tools that are available today make creating new reports trivial.

In addition, as tenure at the management level falls over time, new managers arrive and request views of the data that are most conducive to their way of thinking. This, combined with a bias to action, can lead to a flurry of new reports, which are then promptly abandoned at the next reorganization but continue to be maintained.

Finally, a common rationalization for poor decisions by leaders is that they are due to a lack of information. In response to a personal error, and as a cover to their rascalities, it is not unusual for a new report to be requested, ostensibly to prevent the incident from recurring, but almost certainly as presentable evidence of their proactivity.

Despite all of these drivers of new reports, the organization could conceivably reach an isotonic point of stability where new reports are balanced by discontinued reports. Unfortunately, the process to sunset a report in most organizations is more onerous than the process to create a new one, leaving zombie reports that are diligently maintained by an army of analysts but unused.

For decision makers who have a more tenuous understanding of the value offering of analytics, and a desire to have better-informed decision making, the one-off choice to request that the team create a report can quickly become a pattern of distracting asks. At the expense of large transformative projects, more reports are created and maintained. Over time, the value of the analytics team is questioned.

How can this be prevented? Clearly articulating the value proposition of the team and ensuring from the start that it has executive support is essential to standing up a successful team. Respectfully pushing back against reporting and other non-value-add requests, though politically sensitive, must be done. Every member of the team must be empowered and given the autonomy to question the work that is being requested.

Too Fast, Too Slow

Understanding the first-mover advantage associated with data and analytics, many organizations of means yet with limited analytical maturity have hired dozens of practitioners to rapidly scale up and advance their data capabilities. After 18 to 24 months, these large technocratic organizations review the cost/benefit of the new $10M division and question the value of analytics to the enterprise. Moving too quickly, without the cultural or technical infrastructure to support it, can put an end to analytical ambitions before the first hire has been made.

Alternatively, many organizations have moved too cautiously and hired one or two early-career employees and placed them under a line manager with conflicting priorities and limited analytical understanding. The maturity of the data science team in this case often peaks with gentle scripting and automation, and executives are again left questioning the value of analytics.

It can seem that a Goldilocks approach of creating a mid-sized team could work, but the issue in both extremes has not been the number of people involved, it has been with a lack of a defined strategy. To prevent this situation, organizations need to have a clear objective in mind for the team, an understanding of what the field of advanced analytics and AI is, and the support that is required to make it a success. Further, organizations cannot look within to build out this strategy, as they thoroughly lack the capabilities to define this strategy. It is only by consultation with others and thorough benchmarking to industry and practice standards that this strategy can be developed.

More Data, More Problems

All organizations have some capacity for gathering data, and once the quantity of that data reaches a certain size, a data-centric team (whether business intelligence, data services, self-service insights, or general information technology) is naturally formed. The purview of these data teams in many cases has been confused with analytics and data science, to the point that the intersection of the two is very often considered the scope for both. Though there is certainly a strong mutually supportive relationship between these two functions, they exist in different spaces and with different incentives—one being a cost center and one being a profit center. Executives with medium-term ambitions to develop a next-generation analytical function will frequently prime the pump by engaging the data team and expanding their accountabilities.

The outcome of this is usually expensive, avant-garde data solutions such as data lakes, premature cloud migrations, and unnecessary latency reduction strategies. The organization, still in its analytical infancy, is unable to take advantage of these powerful technologies, the cost of which is allocated to the analytics team. Organizations need to learn to walk before they can run, and the burden of these data-centric initiatives, executed far too early, has weakened many emerging analytics teams who have had to justify their inheritance after the fact.

These issues are the result of a lack of strategic focus. Well-intentioned projects initiated from a mature data team, supported by an executive, and imposed on future analytics teams leads invariably to technical debt and a handicapped team. Analytical excellence needs to be the focus and the function to be optimized and not confused with the activities that enable it. Early holistic strategy development that considers the interactions between these different teams is essential.

Summary

These common issues all share similar root causes across the pillars of strategy, process, and people. Without exception, every failed attempt to build out the analytical function could have been prevented with some forethought, forbearance, and expert advice. Every externality in the equation supports the practice—there are new approaches and new technologies and success stories of analytics teams adding value, optimizing processes, automating, and increasing the bottom line to the organizations in which they work. To be successful, however, standing up these analytics teams needs to be a thoughtful and measured approach that leverages best practices and integrates with the organization while having a mind to the future.

Organizations and leaders need to follow three guiding principles to successfully build and lead advanced analytics and AI teams:

Start Early   The best time to have begun your analytics strategy was 10 years ago, but the next best time is today. Discuss with your colleagues in other industries, perform benchmarking exercises, and engage consultants where appropriate.

Go Slow   As the team is chopping their way through the jungle of legacy processes, vestigial data pipelines, and change management, ensure that they are taking the time to pave the way behind them by documenting, securing, understanding, automating, and training others in what they are doing. Moving between projects in a frenetic commotion gives the impression of positive activity at the expense of long-term sustainability. Considering the total project life cycle of each project ensures that future people and processes are not entangled in patchy solutions that had only a short-term view.

Commit Fully   Assume that the analytics function will not cover its own costs for the first two to three years and evaluate projects over a longer horizon. Integrate analytics into all functions and encourage a cultural change. Furtive deployments of analytics, starting with low-impact functional groups, leads to low-impact results.

It is my sincerest hope that this book helps you in your journey toward achieving analytics excellence in your organization. This practice can do great good in the world—it just needs to be allowed to succeed through planning and organizing and through minding the machines.

References

Ammanath, B., Jarvis, D., & Hupfer, S. (2020). Thriving in the era of pervasive AI. In *Deloitte's State of AI in the Enterprise*, 3rd Edition. Retrieved from http://deloitte.com/us/en/insights/focus/cognitive-technologies/state-of-ai-and-intelligent-automation-in-business-survey.html

Davenport, T. H., & Patil, D. J. (2012, Oct.). Data scientist: The sexiest job of the 21st century. *Harvard Business Review*. Retrieved from https://hbr.org/2012/10/data-scientist-the-sexiest-job-of-the-21st-century

PwC. (2017). *Sizing the prize: What's the real value of AI for your business and how can you capitalise*. Retrieved from http://pwc.com/gx/en/issues/analytics/assets/pwc-ai-analysis-sizing-the-prize-report.pdf

Russell, B. (1902). *Study of mathematics*. Cambridge University Press.

Taylor, F. W. (1911). *The principles of scientific management*. Harper Bros.

US Bureau of Labor Statistics. (2020). *Computer and information research scientists: Job outlook*. Retrieved from http://bls.gov/ooh/computer-and-information-technology/computer-and-information-research-scientists.htm#tab-6

Strategy

How to assess organizational readiness, identify gaps, establish an attainable roadmap, and properly articulate a value proposition and case for change.

Peter Drucker defined strategy in the 1950s as "a pattern of activities that seek to achieve the objectives of the organization and adapt its scope, resources and operations to environmental changes in the long term" (Drucker, 1982). This was updated in the 1960s by Alfred D. Chandler to "the determination of the basic long-term goals and objectives of an enterprise, and the adoption of courses of action and the allocation of resources necessary for carrying out these goals" (Chandler, 1962). There have been several academics and business leaders before and since who have offered subtly different definitions on what can be a nebulous field of study. Regarding analytics strategy, I offer the following simplified definition: strategy is a set of guiding principles for how to achieve a goal.

Strategy can be perceived, and not without some element of truth, as a precursor to the real work. This malignment has not been helped by the vapid vernacular and abstractions that can sometimes accompany discussions around strategy. Without a sense of drama or an appeal

17

to the emotional drivers in people, strategy can seem distant to many. Almost everybody has sat through dry strategy sessions and come away feeling neither compelled nor edified by the contents. New operating models, organizational designs, and 13-point plans come and go, but for most people in the organization, the daily work remains the same. Long-serving employees who have experienced several such reboots, strategy updates, disruptions, hacks, and Organization 4.0 sessions have soured to the concept and endure these initiatives silently before returning to their work as it has been.

There is a general devaluing of strategy, and in particular among the people within the organization who will be most accountable for implementing that strategy. Certainly, those early in their career will experience their first reorganization with a sense of optimism, but over time the compounding impact of failed strategic relaunches leads to cynicism and an active disengagement from the process. This is certainly a missed opportunity, as without an established enterprise strategy there is no consistency, and the aggregate output of the people throughout the organization is less a symphony and more of a cacophony.

The lack of confidence in strategy at the enterprise level is equally present at the business unit and divisional level—and is particularly clear with data science and analytics teams. For people involved in logical problem solving, abstractly articulated and poorly presented high-level guiding principles can appear to be a disturbance to their more engaging ongoing projects. The lack of harmony can detract from the elegance of a full orchestra, but for a string quartet, it is an unmitigated disaster when the performers have different song sheets. Without a clear and compelling vision for the future, a unified team, and a framework for decision making, the activities of a team will never be more than incoherent noise and a confused flurry of individual activities. The importance of establishing a strategy for a new or relaunched analytics team cannot be overstated.

The strategy for a data science and analytics team establishes the "how" and the "what" and provides a north star for future decision making. It serves as a constitution and provides guidance whether in six months or two years, a firmament from which they can assess the situation in light of new methodologies or technologies and plot a course that has narrative and logical continuity but maintains the flexibility to take new facts into account.

There are unique requirements for developing, articulating, presenting, and maintaining a strategy for an analytics team. Enterprise strategy, grand in scale, metaphysical in its language, in almost all cases will not gain traction with a group of analytics professionals. Likewise, checklists, decrees, mandates, and flowcharts will be too static and deterministic to encourage the flexibility that is required of an analytics team. The challenge, and the opportunity, lies in co-developing a future-oriented, concrete, and holistic strategy that will achieve the following goals:

Align Integration with enterprise strategy ensures the support of the executive and its overall stability along with clear identification of expected value. However, linking outcomes and success factors rather than approaches and methodologies creates a mutually beneficial conceptual junction, which allows some deviation between the two without causing inconsistencies or contradictions.

Substantiate Every element of the strategy must be defined such that it can be immediately applied to a situation without ambiguity. The development and presentation of such a strategy must include exhibits that lay out the practical application of principles so that it can be made real and show how daily tasks would be impacted.

Invigorate The vision needs to be captivating to the team and articulated in such a way that it appeals to their personal motivations. The goal of the strategy needs to highlight the overlap between the commercial and competitive objectives of the enterprise with the professional and personal objectives of the team.

Incentivize Each member of the team needs to have a reason to join in the journey, whether it is personal development, more interesting projects, increased autonomy, or compensation. In a competitive job market, individuals need to be pulled rather than pushed.

Scale In the course of an analytics project, opportunities for related projects are identified. No organization has reached the point where they have exhausted all potential avenues for extracting value from analytics. Expansion needs to be a component of the analytical strategy to keep pace with the demands of the organization and to provide continued growth opportunities for the team.

This section seeks to lay out the process involved in creating an analytical strategy by distilling it into three key questions that are sequentially dependent:

1. Where are we today?
2. Where do we want to be?
3. How do we get there?

People have studied strategy for centuries—from all perspectives, all belief systems, all moral frameworks. It has been studied in military, business, philosophical, and personal contexts. No single book could provide comprehensive coverage into this vast field of study, and neither is that the objective of this section. The goal of developing an analytics strategy should not be one that recalls and interprets the great thinkers of antiquity. The goal should be a parsimonious framework and flexible set of guiding principles for how to achieve the goal of analytical excellence.

This chapter is organized across three primary topics: current state assessment, defining the future state, and closing the gap. This structure follows the sequencing of the development of a strategy. Before that strategy can be defined, however, the role of analytics in the organization must be understood.

The Role of Analytics in the Organization

For many top-tier organizations, data science and analytics has become a core component of their strategy and an enabler throughout all functions. For many others, of course, it is an immature function or an aspirational goal. Given the cost and complexity of standing up an analytics function, it should not be undertaken lightly unless there are overarching goals or a vision, but often this is not fully developed or is absent. Without familiarity with analytics and an understanding of its capabilities, leaders can often be operating under an optimistic misapprehension.

The curse of knowledge is a cognitive bias that occurs when practitioners who are communicating with non-practitioners assume that they have more of an understanding than they do. Analytics practitioners, existing within a narrow niche, can overestimate the level of familiarity that executive sponsors have. Before determining how the analytics function will operate, it is necessary first to establish or explain in partnership with leadership what analytics is and what role it will play within the organization and within the stack where it sits.

The Analytics Playbook

There is a disagreement in the details as to what data scientists do as a profession. Data scientists in one organization may develop self-driving cars, in another develop loan-loss provision models, and in another may create dashboards. This lack of clarity has led to a proliferation in titles and definitions to differentiate the types of approaches and the level of complexity. Generally, however, analytics professionals gather, model, and interpret data to solve business problems.

In *Doing Data Science,* Cathy O'Neil and Rachel Schutt very accurately describe the work as follows:

> "[A] data scientist is someone who knows how to extract meaning from and interpret data, which requires both tools and methods from statistics and machine learning, as well as being human. She spends a lot of time in the process of collecting, cleaning, and munging data, because data is never clean. This process requires persistence, statistics, and software engineering skills—skills that are also necessary for understanding biases in the data, and for debugging logging output from code.
>
> Once she gets the data into shape, a crucial part is exploratory data analysis, which combines visualization and data sense. She'll find patterns, build models, and algorithms—some with the intention of understanding product usage and the overall health of the product, and others to serve as prototypes that ultimately get baked back into the product. She may design experiments, and she is a critical part of data-driven decision making. She'll communicate with team members, engineers, and leadership in clear language and with data visualizations so that even if her colleagues are not immersed in the data themselves, they will understand the implications." (O'Neil & Schutt, 2013)

This wonderfully covers the practice of data science, and what a career in the profession would entail generally, but it demands clarification in practice, particularly in the formative stages of a new team. The team could include these other broad accountabilities:

Data Engineering   Most organizations that are technically sophisticated enough to require an analytics function will already have an established business intelligence or data services team as well. While recurring reporting and dashboarding of insights should always remain with these teams, data preparation and engineering is often a responsibility that is shared. Larger-scale projects can also benefit from data engineers to ensure that operationalized models are performant in terms of their data pipeline.

Architecture   Though the main responsibility for defining enterprise architecture will remain with IT in almost all cases, analytics team members may serve in an advisory capacity on architectural review committees. Some technologies (stream-processing, cluster computing, MLaaS, etc.) may make demands on IT that they are unable to support independently and be the impetus for inclusion on these committees. This can often expand into joint accountabilities or in some unfortunate cases the formation of a shadow IT function.

Data and Analytics Governance   Typically the remit of designated groups or individuals within IT or business intelligence, governance can include the development of policies around model review or risk management with operationalized analytics models or with the implementation of data governance programs. Similar to architecture, this initial involvement can lead to a shared account-ability for overall organizational governance.

Organizational Change Management   Due to the lack of under-standing regarding analytics, many organizations will not provide organizational change management (OCM) support to data science projects unless there is a significant automation component or it is a function-led initiative. OCM plans can often be completed by the analytical function for review and approval by the OCM team.

Project Management   For projects with a significant cost or impact or those requiring coordination between different stakeholders, it can be beneficial to have a designated project management professional. Often large analytical projects can be exempt from the PMO cri-terion because the project cost and impact are difficult to assess using traditional methods. Project management for large projects in these cases can lie with the analytics team.

Product Management   At the successful conclusion of a project that involves a productionalized deliverable, there will almost certainly be iterative changes as the conditions change or as new features are required, as well as ongoing curation and mainte-nance of the models. With larger projects that touch multiple stakeholders, there will be competing and contradictory requests for new features and a lack of clarity around ownership. At some point, the support requirements can reach the point that it becomes designated a product and requires formalized prod-uct management. Because of the technical knowledge that is required, this can often lie with the analytics team supported by a product manager.

Vendor Management   It is important to maintain relationships with vendors and consultants to augment or enhance in-house data science capabilities and to maintain technical relevance, but for some organizations, the responsibility for vendor management can fall to the analytics team as well. Procurement, unfamiliar with analytics, will often delegate all but the most fundamental and operational parts of SCM.

Regulatory Compliance   For the public sector, financial services, aerospace, defense, and other highly regulated industries, there can be external reporting or audit requirements that must be adhered to. The coordination of these activities is typically done through an internal team, but in most organizations ensuring and communicating model transparency and interpretability lies within the analytics function.

Systems Support   Analytics-specific systems, packages, software, and frameworks can be alien to IT teams, who will sometimes resist supporting them. Further, the need for control and responsiveness in managing these systems can promote the formation of shadow IT functions and systems support. Though a balance should be found to make sure there remains alignment between the teams, the accountability weights can change over time and become an obstacle. Once established, and once critical tasks are dependent on them, all systems should move back to IT for long-term support.

Academic Partnerships   Research and development into areas without an immediate commercial application, or in support of academic institutions through the provision of data or models, can appear at first to be at the expense of more pragmatic projects. However, the benefits in terms of relationships, talent acquisition, and professional development for the team should not be dismissed. Expectations should be clear on how much time is dedicated to these partnerships and wherever possible opportunities for eminence building built into the partnership.

Eminence Building   It should always be a priority for individual analytics practitioners to give back to the profession and to seek opportunities for public speaking, but often it will be an expectation imposed by the organization as well.

Alignment of expectations with the executive sponsors of analytics teams is important to ensure that interactions are fully developed and that there are no overlaps in responsibilities. Fully defining the activities of the team in the ordinary course of business allows for the definition of a mission statement that covers the mandate of the team without being overly broad. Finally, it allows leadership to ensure that tertiary responsibilities do not overshadow the primary analytical goal of the team.

The role of analytics needs to be understood beyond the daily responsibilities and activities of the team. Data and analytics is a unique function that requires a culture change to fully integrate within the organization.

Data and Analytics as a Culture Change

The most talented and mature analytics team, with established and consistent processes, project management proficiency, and an understanding of the entire data and analytics value chain, will still not have any success within an organization if they are not working on the right projects and with the support and guidance of the business. Without strong relationships and mutual respect with the different functions and business units, these projects will be either non-operationalizable or isolated studies undertaken to confirm the intuition of leadership. It is only when the technical skills of the analytical team are combined with the subject matter expertise and operational understanding of the business that truly value-added projects can be identified and executed.

For this partnership to be created and maintained, analytics needs to be embedded into the culture of the organization. Analytics teams working in isolation, their efforts channeled through select managers and not interfacing directly with those who will ultimately be tasked with implementing the output of the work, will never be as productive as a fully integrated team. This cultural change does not come easily, but once established it is far more effective than depending on dictatorial decrees to effect organizational change. Once the organization realizes the benefits that the analytics team offers, they are more proactive in suggesting projects and are more able to identify appropriate use cases.

The concept of analytics as a culture change needs to permeate every interaction and deliverable. This integration can never be considered complete, and victory cannot be declared. It cannot be accomplished through a single email or presentation to stakeholders but must be a constant consideration for the team. Integration has several elements:

Intentional Relationships   Relationship building needs to be a priority and an expectation for every member of the team, regardless of level. In every project, one of the explicitly stated objectives should be stronger personal relationships with the stakeholder team and a deeper understanding of their role in the organization and the challenges that they face.

Community of Practice   Partnerships with technically savvy groups, citizen data scientists who are embedded within the business, data teams, and interested individuals should be cultivated and strengthened through the formal establishment of a Community of Practice. This loose association of practitioners within the organization serves as an enterprise platform for analytics and a way to maintain narrative control and consistency.

Accessible Technology   The technology stack that the analytics function depends on must be either the same as or interoperable with the conventional organizational stack. If a unique toolset is required, then the complexity of the tools should not greatly exceed the technical sophistication of the organization. Accessible and recognizable tools instill trust and familiarity with stakeholders.

Analytics 101   Providing training to stakeholders in data science fundamentals serves many purposes. It affords a high-level understanding of what analytics can enable to individuals in the business, it establishes the team as analytical leaders, it builds relationships and goodwill between teams, it uncovers potential projects with participants, and it provides a development opportunity to analysts. These sessions serve to make the practice more accessible and relevant for stakeholders and to reduce any potential anxiety.

Co-develop Projects   Projects that are proposed by the business will rarely be analytically coherent, and projects proposed by the analytics team will rarely be of practical use. Projects need to be developed in collaboration. Supporting the foundational technical training of the organization combined with facilitating Design Thinking and Art of the Possible sessions will reveal the most valuable projects and through the ideation process can populate the project pipeline.

Demystify   Perhaps most importantly, data science and analytics needs to be understood as a toolbox of techniques that can help improve life for the individual employees and the customers. Concepts should be explained in terms of outcome and requirements rather than jargon and theory. The function of the team needs to be presented and understood as parsimonious enablement rather than arcane automation. Stakeholders may not understand the mechanics, but they need to trust the insights that are generated, and practitioners need to avoid "black box" approaches.

For practitioners who work primarily with the left hemisphere of their brain, it can be a particular challenge to influence organizational culture. However, using the same systematic approach with which a practitioner would model a business problem can go some way toward this end. Considering the drivers of adoption, the indicators of success, and the distinct events that induce user acceptance can inform this plan.

Current State Assessment

Creating or refreshing the strategy for a data science and analytics team involves answering three deceptively profound questions:

1. Where are we *today*?
2. Where do we want to be *tomorrow*?
3. *How* do we get there?

As Terry Pratchett said, "If you do not know where you come from, then you don't know where you are, and if you don't know where you are, then you don't know where you're going. And if you don't know where you're going, you're probably going wrong."

The purpose of the first phase, the current state assessment, is to establish a fulsome understanding of the data and analytics function as it exists presently. This understanding needs to be across all aspects, including the capabilities, expectations, interactions, relationships, people, technology, processes, and data. The output of this review provides insight into where attention should be focused and an understanding of the strengths of the team and the opportunities for improvement.

The current state assessment is perhaps the most difficult of the three questions to answer because it requires a level of depersonalized introspection and for the assessor to avoid the defensive rationalization of the present condition. Separation of the individual decision makers from the decisions that were made requires a level of objectivity that insiders can struggle with. Though context is important, the prime objective of this phase of strategy formation needs to be impartiality. This impartiality can most easily be provided by an external consultant through a benchmarking or readiness assessment.

Readiness Assessment

The measurement of readiness is a methodical analysis of the capacity of an organization to undertake change by identifying challenges that might arise and quantifying the strengths and weaknesses across different criteria. Every consultancy has some assessment framework with which they evaluate the maturity of an organization and benchmark it against its peers across different criteria. One of the most enduring was created by McKinsey alumnus Tom Peters in the 1980s and remains relevant today (Peters & Waters, 1982). For an organization to be data and insight driven, these pillars need to be present and aligned. It is not solely about the technical proficiency; data science prowess is a necessary but insufficient condition for success.

Strategy   Is a coherent plan in place? Are goals established? What is the perspective on the future? What are the risks? How are they mitigated?

Shared Values   What are the guiding principles? What unites the teams? How do employees behave? What is the culture of the organization?

Style   How do leaders behave? How do things get done? How do people interact?

Staff   What are the demographics of the team? What are their capabilities? How are they recruited? How are they motivated? How are they rewarded?

Skills   What are the capabilities of the team? What are the capabilities of the organization? What is the technical proficiency? What is the general data and analytics maturity?

Structure   How is the corporation organized? Where does analytics sit? How do the entities interact?

Systems   What business processes are in place? What data and analytics processes are in place? What is the technology stack? Where does the data come from? How are decisions made?

Even for those with high levels of access and an excellent field of view it is difficult to have perspective into analytical best practices from within an organization. For that reason it is often beneficial to engage external consultants to complete a formal readiness or maturity assessment. Without the broad frame of reference available to external consultants, it can be challenging to objectively evaluate these elements against industry peers from an analytics perspective.

The primary focus of a readiness assessment is to understand what gaps exist that could impede an analytics deployment initiative. These gaps need to be understood to develop a bespoke strategy that works for the organization. Operating models need to consider the shared values and style of the stakeholders. The pace of change needs to consider the skills and staff. Alternatively, knowing the specific strengths of the organization can illustrate opportunities for building out a competitive advantage.

Once there is an understanding of the baseline that the analytics team will be working with, it is then important to fully comprehend the capabilities of the team.

Capability Modeling and Mapping

Business capability modeling is a way to decompose the abilities of a team into mutually exclusive but collectively exhaustive components. Once the model has been created, these individual components can be mapped to the strategic objectives for the organization, and any gaps in capability can be highlighted and addressed through a talent roadmap.

These capability models are visual representations of a hierarchy of abilities that describe everything that the analytical function will be expected to do. Creating these models involves first breaking out the key families of capabilities that are required, such as industry knowledge, functional knowledge, technical knowledge, and leadership. Each of the elements within these level-one capabilities are further broken down into level-two capabilities and reduced further in subsequent levels. The result of these multiple levels of detail should not be to define every potential capability and technology that could be required in the future but to illustrate what is generally required for the success of the analytical function and to allow for different fields of view depending on the application. Table 2.1 provides an example of a generic, industry-agnostic reference capability model.

Table 2.1: Capability model example

LEVEL	LEVEL 2	LEVEL 3
Leadership	Innovation	Strategy
		Eminence building
		People development
Leadership	Management	Project management
		Portfolio management
		Product management
		Stakeholder management
		Risk management
Leadership	Leadership	Relationship development
		Succession planning
		Communication

Functional	Governance	Policy development
		Policy enforcement
Functional	Operations	Recurring reporting
		Ad hoc reporting
		Vendor management
		Business advisory
Functional	Business Analysis	Project delivery
		Project intake and prioritization
		Facilitation
		Presentation
		Risk management
Technical	Data	Architecture
		Data engineering
		Data quality
Technical	Analytics	Data exploration
		Data preparation
		Data visualization
		Analytical modeling
		Analytics operationalization
		Automation
Industry	Varies	Varies

It is self-evident that a leader must understand the capabilities of the individuals on a team in order to understand what the team is capable of as a whole. This is necessary whether a new team is being formed or an existing team is being assessed. The most transparent and expedient way to accomplish this evaluation is through a systematic set of interviews with the individual team members. For many organizations, this exercise is considered supplementary, and group skillsets are inferred through tangential conversations and subjective observations. Rather than supposition, leaders should engage in frank and honest questioning with the members of the analytics team.

This exercise should take place after rapport has been established with the people on the team, and after the leader has seen them work enough to assess the validity of their responses. What they consider project management or data governance will often be from a narrow perspective, and they may simply not be aware what good looks like. There may also be resistance to the exercise itself for a new leader, as it can be seen by the team members as an assessment of fit and could affect the individual career trajectory. This can lead to a more liberal self-assessment or passive resistance. With relationships established, and a mutual trust and respect, it needs to be highlighted that this is a tool used in aggregate to identify opportunities for improvement for the entire team and not as a performance management tool.

There are several industry-agnostic reference capability models that can be adapted for use by any analytics function. The key feature is that they have equal emphasis on the strategic and foundational elements and are not solely dedicated to detailed analytical capabilities. Team members need to be interviewed on (what are or can be perceived to be) peripheral elements such as change management, policy and standards, eminence building, and vendor management.

At the beginning of the interview, put the individual at ease by restating the intention of the exercise, and be ready to acknowledge the discomfort that it may cause. Personalize the discussion by being willing to show vulnerability, and briefly share your own thoughts around areas that you need to work on and areas that you feel you are strong in. For each of the individual capabilities, ask the team member questions from the following three categories:

Current State   How confident are you in this area? Would you be able to lead a highly visible project that required this skill? What projects best highlighted this capability? Have you had any formal training in this? Do people seek your expertise?

Future State   Looking three years out, how much of your time would you like to spend in this area? How much does it excite you? Would you pursue training in this capability independently? Where do you think this fits into your personal development objectives?

Mandate   How important do you consider this to the success of the team? Is this something you think we should be accountable for? Who is currently accountable for this? Are you or the team ever consulted on issues from this area?

The interview should be kept as informal as possible to encourage candor but conducted in a guided and structured way. Allow the discussion to flow naturally between elements, ensuring that all are covered during the interview.

There are several benefits and uses for the results of the procedure. With a meticulous and systematic set of interviews with the individual team members, invaluable insights are revealed in the following areas:

Mandate Comprehension   Through the conversations it will become clear what capabilities the individuals consider important for their daily work and what they believe the team is accountable for. Often it can highlight cases where individuals are responsible for outputs that they have no control over, or that they are not suited to. This can present opportunities to improve the efficiency of the team and bring to light legacy processes that should be transferred or discontinued.

Personal Goals   Understanding of personal development objectives allows for better support of the individual and more effective resourcing. Though this understanding would occur naturally during one-on-one sessions, the conversations may be ambiguous. If the capabilities are properly deconstructed and articulated, a better-aligned set of mapped development goals can be created with the individual, resulting in a more personalized development plan and a more engaged team.

Evidence of Disengagement   The corollary of the above is that the person may be involved in work that they are strong in but have no passion for. The operational needs of the business must be met, but retention and engagement can become problematic unless opportunities for exploring areas of interest are available. By co-creating a transparent development plan with the individual, you can find a balance between leveraging the existing strengths of the individual and supporting them in developing the capabilities that they want to focus on.

Team Direction   Individual team members will instinctively gravitate toward areas that they are passionate about, and without a conscious effort to counteract, the team will naturally evolve toward those future state capability elements. This evolution should be allowed to run its course, while ensuring continuity of support, with a defined plan for filling the resulting skill gaps.

Talent Roadmap   Comparing the results to the future state goals for the team will highlight gaps that need to be filled and can inform a talent roadmap. Comparing these results to the personal development view of the results can help with the decision whether to source externally or whether the capabilities can be internally developed.

Individual Relationships   These conversations can rapidly accelerate your understanding of the team. Topics that would have taken months to emerge organically through coaching chats are discussed much earlier, establishing a mutual understanding and stronger relationship.

Individual Understanding of Capabilities   There will certainly be disagreement with team members on which capabilities are their strengths. This is a valuable insight, as it shows a misalignment in understanding of what good looks like. Typically this comes from individuals who have little experience outside the organization and are unaware of best practices. In cases where there is endemic overestimation of a certain capability, it can highlight the need for formal education sessions.

Once the capability model has been developed for the team, it should be aggregated into four views by counting the positive responses for all capabilities and dividing by the total number of participants, yielding the percent coverage in that particular capability as follows:

- Current Capabilities—What the team is currently able to do
- Future Capabilities—Where the team wants to go
- Perceived Mandate—What the team thinks they should do
- Future Gaps—The inverse of the future capabilities; those elements in which the team will not have coverage

These four exhibits can be shared with the participants to engage them in the strategy formation process, to confirm your understanding, and to discuss any inconsistencies. As a final step, the individual elements should be mapped to the key strategic priorities to ensure that the team is able to support those initiatives and that their perceived mandate aligns with the organization's expectations.

The output of this exercise is the primary source of data for developing a talent strategy. Using business capability models, one can quickly understand the strengths and weaknesses of a team in order to develop a strategy that is purpose-built and viable. This model provides a clear link between strategy and execution and a basis for hiring new talent.

Technology Stack Review

In the ordinary course of business, novel requirements or constraints will often lead to the onboarding of new tools. Processes depending on those tools are formalized, and as more modern tools are purchased, all future processes are based on them instead. Like an experienced tradesperson who has gathered tools over a career and finds that most sit unused, organizations often find that the list of vestigial frameworks and technologies they are supporting becomes exceptionally large. For the tradesperson, this can cause mild disorganization, but for an organization this can represent a significant cost in terms of maintenance, upgrading, vendor management, and cognitive friction. Just as a tradesperson needs to occasionally clean out their toolboxes, an organization needs to review its technology stack.

When viewed for the organization as a whole, the problem is exacerbated. Without oversight on which applications are being used, and what dependencies those applications have, software budgets, requisite hardware, and upgrading schedules can create undue cost for an organization. Citizen data scientists throughout the organization, with different approaches and preferences, can use different tools for similar projects, leading to onerous maintenance requirements and a significant amount of rework in the future when these tools are rationalized.

In order to have a parsimonious analytical function, the number of tools in use should be as low as possible, with as few special-purpose tools as possible. Industry- and function-specific software aside, using established and understood and broadly practiced platforms reduces complications in maintenance, hiring, and interoperability. The ultimate goal then of a technology stack review is in minimizing the complexity of the team by reducing the number of tools in the toolbox.

An assessment of the technology in use by the function needs to answer three main questions:

Is it being used?   Every technology that is in use needs to pull its weight. Having several tools available in case they are needed in the future increases maintenance requirements and reduces the productivity of the team.

Is there an overlap?   Changes in team structure, changes in practices, and legacy processes can all lead to situations where a team needs to maintain models and scripts across multiple platforms and languages. In order to accomplish this, many teams will implement model management solutions. Without the occasional pruning of dependencies, these processes can lead to inflated and expensive maintenance requirements. Surveying the tools, languages, reports, frameworks, packages, and so on that are in place and performing a functional mapping can highlight these overlaps and provide insight around rationalization opportunities.

Is it interoperable?   All the tools that are in use need to be able to interface with the enterprise technology stack. Often individuals will have personal preferences for development and translate to an enterprise standard as a last step. This reduces efficiency, introduces a failure point, and makes peer review more challenging. All technology in use should be evaluated against the enterprise standard.

Technology needs to support the needs of the team, align with their expertise, and be compliant. It needs to be viewed from a perspective of enablement and not solely as a qualitative assessment. Everybody has internal biases and preferences about programming languages and tools. Rivalries, friendly or otherwise, about different languages have existed for years, and almost every practitioner has a side. It is important that the technologies, frameworks, and languages that are in use are a means to an end, and that they add value.

Data Quality and Governance

Even though data governance is understood conceptually by most organizations, the execution differs greatly based on the culture, maturity, and expected outcomes of the organization.

Organizations without mature data quality and governance policies will have untrusted data sources, issues with reconciliation, confusion on ownership, and poorly defined metrics and measures. The Data Governance Institute defines data governance as "a system of decision rights and accountabilities for information-related processes, executed according to agreed-upon models which describe who can take what actions with what information, and when, under what circumstances, using what methods." The Data Management Association International (n.d.) defines it as "the exercise of authority and control (planning, monitoring, and enforcement) over the management of data assets" (DAMA International, 2017).

The importance of the interrelationship between data and analytics means that regardless of where accountability for data governance lies in the organization, the analytics function cannot extricate itself from involvement. Without a solid understanding and control of the underlying data, conversations that should be focused on outputs will be instead focused on the inputs.

Evaluating the state of data quality and governance needs to be across both the defined and the applied policies, realizing that in almost all cases there will be a significant disparity between the two. Well-intentioned individual decisions to provide immediate support to stakeholders, or provide alternate definitions to defined metrics, can lead to confusion and a proliferation of uncontrolled reports, data sets, and models.

For organizations with a relatively immature analytical function, it may be that there are no defined data governance policies and that it is treated in an ad hoc manner. Identify those individuals who are the de facto data owners and custodians and seek to understand their personal views around governance. This assessment should cover at a minimum:

Data Architecture   The overall structure of the data, including information on sources, policies, standards, collection, storage, arrangement, integration, major extract, transform, load (ETL) processes, technology, hardware, software

Data Quality   The policies and practices by which data integrity is monitored and enforced

Governance Structure   The degree to which related governance roles have been established (e.g., data custodians, owners, etc.) and their responsibilities

Metadata   The policies and practices around the collection and maintenance of reference, statistical, descriptive, administrative, and structural metadata, which provide "data about data"

Data Security   The policies and practices around access, personal information, applicable laws, and hashing and masking

Roadmap   The long-term vision for data within the organization

This assessment needs to review the strategy and policies and not be a simple inventory of current databases and tables. Though important from a technical understanding, the focus needs to be on the overarching principles and not on the outcomes. It is also important to divorce the assessment of the current state of data quality and governance from the individuals who have contributed to that state. Deviations from best practices will always happen, and the objective in identifying them is to fix them and prevent them from happening in the future, not to punish or single out the individual.

Stakeholder Engagement

Whether new to an organization, in a new role within a familiar organization, or building a new team, the first personal priority should be meeting colleagues and the deliberate development of relationships. In *The First 90 Days*, Michael Watkins (2003) advises that people seek to understand expectations, develop horizontal relationships, and build alliances. Though the style of the discussions can vary between casual coffee chats and more formal discussions depending on the culture of the organization and the disposition of the individual, these conversations do need to be toward the goal of understanding the culture, challenges, and politics of each of the different stakeholders. It should be made clear that the conversation will be used to inform the strategy for the team but that it will remain anonymous. At a minimum, the following topics should be discussed:

Past Interactions   The previous experience of the stakeholder with the team can give context to their outlook and speak to the current reputation of the team. Discussions surrounding the previous leader should be framed positively to build on their strengths and to avoid damaging perceptions. Asking in the third person, for example, "How did other teams perceive the analytics function?" can give the interviewee more license for openness by depersonalizing the feedback.

Analytical Maturity   Knowing the stakeholder's perspective on the analytical strength of the organization and of their individual team helps with understanding both the actual analytical maturity and the ability of that stakeholder to make an educated technical assessment. Be aware of the Dunning-Kruger effect, which can cause low-ability individuals to overestimate their skills due to a lack of knowledge. Try rather to infer based on the language being used and general topical confidence rather than stated ability.

Technology Stack   Understanding the technical dependencies and capabilities of all stakeholder groups ensures that solutions are appropriately designed. This can also highlight the potential need for rationalization.

Current Challenges   Understanding the current challenges provides an opportunity to pre-populate the project pipeline and understand the role that technology plays for that business unit. Be mindful that the individual may not be able to frame challenges in an analytical context or understand which problems may lend themselves well to an analytical solution.

Personal Ambitions   For all professional relationships it is important to understand the motivating factors and the private framework within which they make decisions.

Potential Champions   It is important to identify champions within the organization who can support and advocate for analytics. These can be enthusiastic amateurs, futurists, or other respected figures.

Potential Detractors   The corollary of the above is that any individuals who have misgivings regarding data science and analytics should be identified as early as possible. Ideally they will be won over after seeing the value that the analytics team brings to other business units, but the focus should always be on grooming champions and converting undecided stakeholders rather than engaging in negative interactions.

Citizen Data Scientists   Experts and existing go-to people within the organization need to be identified as early in the process as possible in order to ensure that the analytical narrative remains consistent and that technical debt does not continue to accrue. These embedded specialists should be engaged regularly, at first through informal chats to maintain awareness of analytics exercises across the enterprise and once possible through a formal Community of Practice.

At this point in the process, a vision for the team should be in a nascent stage. Once all new information has been gathered, it provides an opportunity to socialize certain aspects and to gather more specific input. This establishes a firmer bond with lateral business leaders and eases future buy-in when the strategy is promulgated.

These interviews provide a perspective on how analytics is viewed from the different business units and a sense of what challenges should be addressed in the formation of a strategy as well as an opportunity to begin to develop personal relationships. Without consultation with the future stakeholders, strategies will be ill-informed and poorly received. Once these lines of communication have been established, ideas and comments will flow more easily to the function rather than dispersed as informal and uncontrolled chatter.

Defining the Future State

The baseball philosopher and master of pithy quotes Yogi Berra said, "If you don't know where you're going, you'll end up someplace else." The future state of analytics is not a collection of important projects or key initiatives. It is also not a mission statement or inspiring vision for leadership among industry peers. The future state is how analytics will function within the organization to enable these initiatives and aspirations. It is explicitly defining what the team does, how they do it, and the tools they use.

There are several strategic frameworks for evaluating these future alternatives that provide systematic ranking techniques. One of the most well-known and straightforward assessment models is the SFA model, developed by Johnson and Scholes (Wu, 2010), which identifies three key criteria:

Suitable   Will this allow the group to achieve its goals? Does it address the opportunities and threats to the analytical function? Is it aligned with the culture of the organization? Is it aligned with the industry?

Feasible   Can we execute it effectively? Does it fit within the budget? Do we have the talent? Can we hire the right people? Does it overlap with other strategic initiatives? Are there any legal or technical constraints? Are there any dependencies? Would it integrate with the organization?

Acceptable   What are the risks? Are they acceptable? Does it meet the expectations of the stakeholders? Will it be positively received? Do the benefits outweigh the risks? Who will be impacted? How can we manage detractors? Who will be the biggest supporters?

These criteria are relevant for any organization and any function. For an analytics group to be successful, I would add one more particularly pertinent consideration:

Visionary   Are we looking toward the future? Does this create a sustainable advantage? Is it scalable? Does it inspire?

To be at its most effective, a data science and analytics function must inspire optimism in its stakeholders. Without a compelling vision of the future to draw the organization into a change-positive mindset, there are often challenges in gaining traction. Adopting established best practices as defined by an industry scan and benchmarking exercise ensures that the organization will consistently be several years behind the best-in-class. There is no question that a mature delivery model and sound project management fundamentals are essential for an analytics team, but they must also be purposely designed and communicated to excite people on a personal level.

Defining the Mandate

The first requirement for describing the future state is to define the role that analytics will play and the expected value to be delivered by the team. Through discussions with external stakeholders and leadership, the expectations for the team and individual deliverables should be abstracted to a broad mandate and played back to the same stakeholders for confirmation. Once the question on exactly what the team does has been answered, it will be much more straightforward to describe how they will do it. This mandate should be described in an arc, from current state to a future vision, and the roles that the team itself will hold. This could include the following roles:

Business Advisor   Acting as internal consultants, the team will engage with line and function managers to plan and execute on analytics projects.

Strategy Architect   Working with divisional or enterprise leadership, the team will define a strategy that advances the analytical maturity and capabilities of the organization.

Policy Setter   Creation and promotion of policies and guidelines around model management.

Analytics Champion   Promotion of the practice of analytics throughout a division or the enterprise.

Risk Manager   Development and maintenance of risk registers for all models and other operationalized analytical assets. In partnership with regulatory and legal groups, the team will ensure that models are compliant with extant laws and ethical frameworks.

Data Quality Owner   Owning accountability for the accuracy of the data for a certain segment of the division or enterprise.

Self-Service Enabler   Ingesting, transforming, staging, and making available data for the lightly supported consumption of other stakeholders.

Platform Owner   Providing control, training, and ownership over technologies such as version control systems, reporting and visualization software, or other function-specific applications.

Product Manager   Guiding the success of internal analytical products and leading the cross-functional team responsible for supporting and maintaining it.

Trainer Providing instruction in the use of products, foundational data science and analytics, or software.

Culture Ambassadors Building and leading a Community of Practice to support consistency in organizational analytics.

Change Agents Facilitating design thinking and art of the possible sessions with stakeholders. Model analytical thinking behavioral characteristics and encourage others to do the same.

Though all data and analytics functions will likely touch on some aspect of these accountabilities, the default orientation needs to be defined in advance, and so done with consideration to the analytical capabilities and the expectations of the team. Selecting too few roles can lead to a burdensome and overspecialized team that has dependencies throughout the organization and little control over their own success. Alternatively, selecting too many can lead to a fuzzy team, doing a little bit of everything but none of it very well.

Generally, the directive should expand over time, as the strength and credibility of the team grows. Newly formed teams should begin with core accountabilities, including the leading of advisory services, and co-developing policy and strategy. Over time, as credibility and capabilities grow and are recognized, new accountabilities can be brought online.

Once the mandate for the team has been unambiguously laid out and is understood by all involved, the analytics governance model that best supports that mandate can be crafted.

Analytics Governance Model

Without effective controls around methodology, peer review, data governance, and other standards, data science and analytics teams can deliver quickly on projects in the short term but over the long term have unsupportable maintenance requirements and disappointed stakeholders. Analytics governance is important, as it determines how decisions are made and how performance is monitored. Like a fire with too much oxygen, the function burns wildly and is destructive. Alternatively, if starved for oxygen, the flame fizzles. Overbearing and despotic policies stifle creativity and diminish the morale of the team. Governance needs to be in place to ensure the long-term and sustainable success of the function, but it must be in the interest of enablement and not control for the sake of control.

The first step in developing a governance model is a thorough understanding of the current state through interviews, cataloging, and assessing current practices. Though most organizations of size have a relatively mature data governance framework, often the standards and policies around analytics itself are informal and improvised, based on the skills and preferences of individual practitioners. Nonjudgmental yet candid assessments of these opportunities allow for the development of a strategy that balances between positive consistency and negative micromanagement.

The second step is the definition of principles that are in line with the strategy for the team and organizational best practices and are supported by stakeholders. These principles call out the intention and objectives behind the governance model and provide a framework for decision making. These principles should establish, in terms of priority and magnitude, the vision around usability, access, security, consistency, quality, costs, and other factors, noting that many are in direct conflict. As with the iron triangle in project management, you can have it good, cheap, or fast, but you can only pick two.

With the fundamentals established, an exploration and definition of all conceptual stages of the analytics function needs to be created, and these stages need to cover the entire project life cycle from ideation to sustainment. For each element, define the requirements around control, and evaluate the benefits of consistency over flexibility at an individual level. For each of those elements that need to be controlled, the following policies and guidelines need to be defined:

- Data acquisition
- Data preparation
- Analytical modeling
- Coding conventions
- Reporting
- Operationalizing

Governance needs to be a living function and reflect the changes in the business environment and the needs of the stakeholders. Changes in technology or regulation can happen quickly, and without conscious effort to maintain relevance, analytics governance can become ineffectual. Roles and responsibilities need to be defined and a regular cadence established for evaluating the analytics governance framework. There are four key roles that require representation:

Owner   Responsible for the direction of the policy and roadmap development and overall guidance.

Developer Responsible for the creation of the item for which governance is being defined and for compliance with policies.

Gatekeeper Responsible for day-to-day enforcement of the policy.

Business Owner Responsible for access decisions and ensuring that policies align with functional requirements. Approves or rejects access requests.

In larger organizations, especially those with decentralized analytics functions, these roles may also participate in governance forums that allow for representation from other groups. These forums provide an opportunity for the continued assessment of policies at an individual contributor level and ensure compliance.

Governance can be onerous. In developing policies, in defining accountabilities, and in enforcing minutiae and recurring reporting on SLA adherence, done poorly, governance can stand in the way of delivery. As with everything in analytics, regulations and policies need to be parsimonious and be designed to enable delivery rather than impede it.

Target Operating Model

The operating model for an organization or a function is an abstract representation of how the strategic aims are achieved in practice. It describes the underlying functions required to support the mandate of the team, the capabilities required to enable those functions, the avatars or personas who exhibit those capabilities, and the overall processes that translate effort to outcome.

Unfortunately, every large company has several expensive target operating models sitting unused. Most often, these models simply do not get traction. Leaders, recognizing that there are operational inefficiencies, engage consultants to perform operational studies and provide recommendations for changes. Those leaders review, agree, and commit to change, but the traditional way of doing things, the sclerotic inertia of older respected influencers, and a lack of consistent change management wins out in the end. For this reason, operating models need to be concise, exceedingly practical, and enforced with the highest discipline.

There are several frameworks that have been developed for building a target operating model. These frameworks tend to be comprehensive and generalized such that any function can leverage them. Analytics requires a parsimonious operating model that balances two competing priorities: flexibility and consistency. The function needs to establish firm guidelines around project intake, prioritization, delivery, and support.

It simultaneously needs to allow full creativity to the individuals on the team to design and implement a solution that has a short time to value and is sensitive to the needs of the stakeholder.

The following operating model framework attempts to distill the process into straightforward steps with key considerations and best practices.

Define Your Principles

Prior to laying out the operating model, it is important to establish the guiding principles and ultimate goals for the team. Discussing these priorities with leadership garners support for downstream decision making and can highlight disconnects between stated objectives. These goals exist on a spectrum and are in many cases in direct conflict:

- Better decision making
- Fastest turnaround
- Highest collaboration
- Lowest costs
- Most accurate data
- Most performant models
- Most explainable models
- Minimal disruptions to other groups
- Reduced duplication of capabilities
- Minimal key person risk
- Breadth of expertise
- Technical strength
- Communication strength
- Project management strength
- Eminence building

Functions, Services, and Capabilities

When the mandate of the team is clear, the framework for making decisions has been determined, and the principles for the operating model are established, the functions that are required to support the mandate and future vision for the team need to be clearly articulated. These functions are the individual services and tasks that the team undertakes in their daily work. They can be as specific as generating reports or as broad as project management. The most important factor in defining these functions and services is that the process is as exhaustive as possible and covers all potential expectations that may be placed on the team.

These functions should be defined and described in terms of how they fit within the defined principles. For example, a team that is expected to be high-speed may struggle with data governance, and a team that is expected to favor technical depth may struggle with vendor management.

The following list includes some potential functions and services:

- Data preparation
- Business advisory
- Vendor management
- Operationalization
- Master data management
- Research and development
- Data privacy and ethics
- Regulatory compliance
- Talent management
- Stakeholder management
- Data life cycle management

Once the services and functions have been defined, they need to be mapped to the requisite capabilities within a larger conceptual interaction model. This capability mapping exercise should be using the same capability model that was used previously in the team assessment in order to align expectations with the current strengths of the team. This alignment (or misalignment) can be used to develop a talent roadmap for the team.

Interaction Models

If an operating model is the methodology governing the flow of effort and capabilities to elicit an outcome, then an interaction model can be thought of as the rules that govern the flow of information.

When viewed from the field, interactions appear to be a series of touchpoints in the execution of a project, completed as necessary in the ordinary course of business. These touchpoints range from inconsequential emails to more ritualized milestone meetings. They are almost always in the support of a deliverable and are ad hoc based on the initiating individual, the recipient, their relationship, the preferences of the project sponsor, the complexity of the project, and several other factors. Without a defined interaction model, this inconsistency can lead to uncertainty on behalf of the stakeholder and can erode trust in the process.

Interaction models on a macro scale are used to define the inflow of resources and information from suppliers, the flow throughout the organization, and the outflow to the end customers. At the micro scale, it describes the relationships and interdependencies at a role level between the analytics function and all other groups, such as IT, business intelligence, data services, reporting, legal, and other domain-specific functions. It defines, for each activity within a project, what the expectations are around responsibilities and accountabilities.

One particularly efficient way to define these expectations early in the process is by repurposing RACI models to understand the flow of information. These models call out specifically which roles are Responsible, Accountable, Consulted, and Informed for each activity. Once defined, agreed upon, and put into practice, these remove all ambiguity from a process. When combined with basic service level agreements, it allows for confidence around level of effort estimations and greater efficiency in project delivery. Ultimately these models help with understanding the interfaces between these interdependent groups.

The second important piece in defining the analytical interaction model is the creation of illustrative swimlane diagrams, as shown in Figure 2.1. These deconstruct a generalized project into individual activities and place those activities in chronological order horizontally. Vertically, they are organized by the groups or roles responsible for execution. Last, arrows show the flow of information between groups as activities are completed. This process gives a visual representation of a project and provides clarity around accountabilities. The secondary purpose of the exercise is that through the process of discussing and constructing these swimlanes, potential weaknesses in the proposed model such as areas of excessive handoffs or a lack of load balancing can be seen. These exhibits should be developed in consultation with all groups to encourage a consistent understanding.

Owing to their heavy reliance on data, analytics functions exist almost always on the periphery of data provisioning and in some cases have specific accountabilities in that area. For most aspects of an interaction model, flexibility in light of operational considerations is important, but

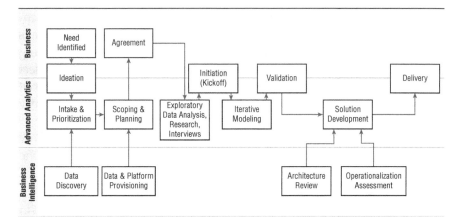

Figure 2.1: Swimlane diagram of analytical interaction model

in developing interaction models for data provisioning, it is necessary to firmly and explicitly lay out all responsibilities at a data-set level. The potential for conflicting information or irreconcilable data is such that these should be kept separate if at all possible, and individuals should be coached to avoid the circumventing of the provisioning process.

Outside of these formalized methodologies describing the flow of information, an analytics team needs to have a consistent character and style of communication, which should be considered as part of the strategy development. Every interaction with others in the organization, such as informal requirements gathering, polished presentations, and curt emails, set a tone for the team and have direct repercussions on the reputation and overall reception and success of the team. Though individuals within the team should have the autonomy to define their personal brand and be given the flexibility to be authentic to their character, it needs to take place within defined boundaries. Because analytics teams typically operate fluidly and cross-functionally, those individuals who are upstream dependencies in one engagement may become the client in following projects. Every interaction (email, deliverable, document, coffee chat, phone call, etc.) should be treated as an important event and an opportunity to positively showcase the team.

Analytics is unlike other functions within the organization, which practice a traditional exercise of authority and provide solutions from a place of control. Individuals seek advice from IT or human resources, and in most cases they accept the results as truth. Analytics exists within a gray area, where the results of a study or project can almost always be ignored if so desired. Because of this, the function needs to practice fundamental openness and act from a place of cooperation and mutual respect. Operating as a traditional technical authority in character or practice can derail initiatives and engender distrust.

There is a great deal to be learned in observing the way in which consultants interact with an organization. Every piece of work must be courted and won, and every interaction is treated as an opportunity to strengthen relationships and solicit additional projects. There are fundamental differences between an in-house advisory function such as analytics and an external consultancy; the best of the consultative mindset can be had simply by encouraging practitioners to consider stakeholders to be clients rather than colleagues.

Interaction models provide direction and guidance to the analytics team and promote alignment between interdependent technical and functional teams. This gives consistency and a cognitive fluency that lets practitioners focus more on projects and less on procedural issues. Developing these interaction models at the required level of abstraction requires the development of avatars and personas.

Avatars and Personas

The purpose of creating personas is to craft a realistic representation of the makeup of the team that will execute on the vision. Conceptually, this requires a complete divorcing from the current team makeup, and a review of the required functions and services in isolation, by working backward from the primary mandate of the team toward defining those avatars best suited to delivering against it.

These personas should have distinct responsibilities and characteristics. They should have independent drivers and challenges and be relatively homogenous internally. These should not be job titles, or levels, but rather a set of characteristics best suited to support the assigned functions and capabilities. It can be easier to conceptualize these personas by prefacing each one with *The* and thinking in terms of archetypes. Some common personas are as follows:

The Data Scientist   Develops, trains, customizes, and deploys sophisticated models and algorithms

The Data Modeler   Creates conceptual models and database designs by translating business needs

The Advisor   Provides professional advice to the business at a strategic level

The Business Analyst   Interfaces with the business stakeholders to determine needs and facilitate information gathering sessions

The Product Manager   Plans the maintenance, design, and governance of analytical products

The Architect   Designs data pipelines and processes for maximum performance

The goal of personas is not to represent all members of the team but to focus on the major needs. For any team, it is best to focus on three or four personas to allow for a concise determination of needs and development of a talent strategy.

Mapping to Function

As a last step, the connections between the services and the individual need to be considered by determining which roles have the capabilities that have been previously mapped. This is done at an abstract level using the defined theoretical personas or avatars. This can be challenging with an existing team, where individual skillsets are known.

As a final step, each of the personas must be reviewed in terms of how they will support the functions that in turn support the mandate of the team. Each of the personas must be mapped to one or more of the functions and services.

For a fulsome review of these mappings, it needs to be considered in the opposite direction as well. For each of the personas, consider the number and nature of services that have been assigned. When personas have a large disparity in the number of responsibilities, consider leveling them through reconsidering the personas that have been developed or reallocating the services.

Organizational Design

The organizational design (OD) of an enterprise includes all the structural components such as lines of reporting, span of control, and degree of centralization. It influences the relationship between management and employees, the style and flow of communication, and the focus and form that oversight takes. The OD impacts the culture, formality, and agility of an organization or function through the level of control and range of accountabilities. Large multinationals, for example, can often have rigid and strictly defined OD, where teams have a narrow purpose and little visibility into other teams. Alternatively, startups can have so loose an OD that an individual feels lost and without clarity on their main objectives.

Enterprise-level OD typically takes one of four forms, with varying implications for the analytics function:

Functional   In this most common form, the enterprise is divided into smaller groups based on their function, such as finance or human resources or operations. In most organizations, analytics will exist either in a business unit or within IT. Regardless of where the analytics function lies, there is a tendency in this form for groups to operate in silos and for communication to be "up and over" rather than lateral. Groups have the tendency to be deeply specialized in their capability but have little visibility into other groups or the organization as a whole. In order to be successful in this paradigm, it is important that analytics be as cross-functional as possible.

Divisional   The organization is split into a number of smaller divisions, each consisting of several functional groups. These divisions are aligned to an individual product or geography and act much like a separate organization. This is beneficial for an analytics team that is able to focus their efforts to a more specific goal, but when viewed at the enterprise level, it can lead to inefficiencies. Problems solved in one division can persist in another. Creating an informal cross-divisional Community of Practice can mitigate many of the negative effects.

Matrix   This form is a combination of divisional and functional, in that everyone lies within two lines of reporting simultaneously, often having both a functional manager and a region or product manager. This alleviates the silo issue with functional reporting but introduces complexity and a potentially high level of unhealthy conflict due to opposing priorities. Whenever possible, projects should be focused on those lines that have strong analytical champions, and there needs to be a focus on relationship building.

Team   Temporary or permanent teams are formed for a single purpose or project within an organization that has one of the above predominant structures. This is one of the ideal forms in theory, as there is less hierarchy and more ability to deliver innovative solutions without being hindered by political inheritance. In practice, the lines of reporting align the group to a specific leader, who often has priorities within a certain function; as such it can often operate as a de facto functional team. There is also the additional challenge of enacting change without formal authority.

Typically, whether divisional, structural, or matrix, analytics will structurally lie within a decidedly nonanalytical function. In terms of best practices, there are three competing views on where the data and analytics function should reside within an organization. No one view is better than the other; all have different positives and negatives and should be considered within the context of the culture of the organization and to the perceived challenges the team may face.

One side of the argument has it that analytics should reside in a specialized group under IT in order to be closer to the requisite machinery and to avoid the aversion to sophistication that can lie within a business unit (Davenport & Harris, 2007). Adjacency to IT can allow for greater autonomy in building solutions and reduce the amount of IT bureaucracy that an analytics team faces, such as promotion cycles and code reviews. Consequently, however, the team will be further from the business and is often confused with IT itself. Intake, prioritization, and delivery models can be constrained to align with IT models, which are often burdensome and favor conformity over consistency. IT leadership often perceive analytics as a slightly more sophisticated Business Intelligence function and may favor reporting engagements over more value-added data science projects. IT is also a cost center and subject to understaffing for cost savings. The temptation to reallocate broadly capable data science talent during peak periods to support Business Intelligence can be difficult to resist. For analytics groups situated within IT groups, it is of primary importance to establish autonomy and an intake and prioritization model based entirely on business value and to soundly reject the notion of it being a pure cost center.

The other side of the argument has it that analytics should be embedded within the business so that it can be closer to the stakeholders and have a better understanding of the challenges they are facing. This is the most natural evolution of the analytics function and usually emerges as a specialized group after a cluster of citizen data scientists has received attention for the value they have brought. Analytics groups within a business unit tend to specialize within that function (e.g., finance, marketing, etc.) and may struggle to deliver on projects for other units. Highly technical requests may be rejected by IT for noncompliance and require frequent executive approval (and pressure) to advance larger projects. Managing the relationship with IT can be important, as well as ensuring that there are not shadow analytics functions in the organization pressing in different directions. Owning the narrative around analytics and establishing a Community of Practice to understand cross-enterprise analytics is essential to avoiding technical debt and implementing best practices.

Finally, for organizations of significant scale, and who have made a full commitment to enterprise-level analytics, the function can report directly to a chief data and analytics officer. There are several benefits to this, including more visibility around analytics and the advocacy that can often be needed with large and challenging projects. Even though it is highly beneficial that a push toward data-driven decision making is happening at the highest level, the cost of supporting so large a team requires significant and consistent value generation. Once a group has grown to the point that they must manage their own P&L, they can often find that projects are scheduled and sequenced (and in some cases, creatively completed and closed) to reduce variability and ensure targets are hit. This gamesmanship takes focus from delivering value.

The second key aspect of OD is the amount of centralization that exists within analytics. The centralization often depends less on the actual analytical sophistication of the organization and more on the time in which the function has existed. The natural march toward centralization and bureaucratization needs to be counteracted with a conscious push toward agility and innovation.

Centralized   When the practice of analytics occurs through a single function it ensures consistency and control. Costs are controlled due to quicker assimilation of knowledge and a concise toolbox, and processes can be more easily standardized. Bottlenecks can occur, however, due to staffing, and a lack of domain knowledge can lead to project overhead and, without great care and teamwork, inappropriate solutions.

Center of Excellence   Centralized specialists interface with citizen data scientists throughout the organization or division to promote standardization and collaboration. The domain knowledge of the business can be translated by the embedded analytical resource and projects executed in partnership with the centralized analytical function. This model provides opportunities for the internal flow of talent and with more scalable resourcing due to the broader allocation of personnel costs. Possible negative aspects are similar to a matrix OD including conflicting priorities for citizen data scientists and complexity around relationships. There are problems around prioritization, and in some organizations, cost allocation as well.

Federated or Decentralized   Citizen data scientists are empowered to make unilateral decisions around methodology and technology. This is the natural first step into analytics and allows for maximum agility and ensures context-sensitive solutions. Technical debt accumulates the longer this model persists, and without opportunities for peer review, solutions may be suboptimal, or at worst damaging. The solutions that are developed are often not supportable and are tied to the individual.

Leaders seldom have control over the OD of the analytics team and need to work within existing constraints in terms of where the team lies, the reporting structure, and the amount of centralization. With consistent successes, these teams will find opportunities to increase in their remit and potentially have opportunities for influencing reorganization to serve more stakeholders. Analytics leaders need to press to be involved in these discussions.

The OD of the analytics function should be an outcome of careful deliberation on the mandate of the team and how it fits into the organization. Though it is a valuable and important step in strategy formation, it should not be relied on in isolation to lead to meaningful change. As Colin Powell said, "If people really followed organizational charts, companies would collapse. In well-run organizations titles are pretty meaningless" (`https://govleaders.org/powell.htm`). Flexibility needs to be maintained and the OD and structure created in such a way as to enable the work of the individual practitioners. Status, title, and OD should never stand in the way of project execution.

Community of Practice

Over time, the individuals in an organization whose roles have analytical aspects will naturally be introduced and collaborate on projects. With decentralized data and analytics functions, this can be quite common, while with nascent or undefined analytics functions it may be more haphazard. Once analytics becomes a material and consequential part of the organization, however, it is important that the leaders be aware of the projects and priorities of the individual citizen data scientists in the organization. The best way to maintain these relationships is through a Community of Practice (CoP).

The CoP is an informal affiliation of individual data scientists or business-embedded analytical teams who gather to share best practices, discuss challenges, and offer mutual support. When effectively deployed, a CoP has the potential to quickly accelerate the analytical development of the organization and to motivate the practitioners who are involved. These coalitions let people who are passionate about analytics gather and build relationships and share ideas. Data and analytics practitioners are not quite in IT, not quite in the business, and there is a common sense of isolation, especially among embedded individuals. Providing an avenue for fellowship and the forming of positive personal and professional relationships can make a qualitative difference in the working lives of those involved and go some way toward addressing that isolation.

These relationships are best served through a purpose-driven CoP charter that lays out the mission of the group, highlighting the benefit to the organization, and that defines measurable goals. These goals can be material benefits in terms of value delivered through collaborative projects or less tangible aspirations around attendance at events and eminence building activities. Formalizing this group through a charter that clarifies the benefits to the business garners the executive support required to dedicate the time and resources needed to make it successful.

One of the primary benefits of a CoP is in facilitating the engagement and education of the individual practitioners as well as the larger organization. This can be accomplished by hosting relevant industry and professional lunch and learns with external speakers, which also provides an opportunity for fellowship and professional development. When attended by nonpractitioners, this also presents an opportunity to actively promote the work of the CoP and the individual teams and data scientists. Another approach is through joint attendance at conferences, hackathons, and bootcamps, which serves to strengthen relationships and find opportunities for collaboration. Focusing on joint education also encourages parallel and consistent professional development, which reduces discrepancies in project approach and delivery.

The more formal expression of this group is through regularly recurring forums, where leaders and senior practitioners meet to discuss the practice across the organization. These forums typically have a standing agenda:

Eminence Building   Providing development opportunities for individual practitioners within the organization for professional development through partnership with local groups and universities. Often requests for speakers come informally and throughout the organization. Sharing these requests with the broader group can ensure that the speakers are best situated to deliver, and to best represent the organization.

Data Assets   CoPs provide an opportunity for the sharing of data and the development of communal assets. These assets can include such things as analytical sandboxes and code repositories. The use of these assets encourages consistency in delivery and reduces time in reconciliation. While managed primarily through data governance forums, the data roadmap should be widely circulated and understood by the CoP forum as well.

Project Pitching   Practitioners who roll up to a function that is outside of an area of interest can experience difficulty in gathering support for projects. Proposing projects to the CoP can encourage the sharing of talent between business units, which make support for these initiatives more likely. Larger cross-functional projects that have broadly attributed benefits can be difficult to gain support for from within a business unit, as project selection hurdles may not reflect the total benefit to the organization. These forums with cross-functional representation are best suited for proposing these projects.

Feedback and Support   Often colleagues throughout the organization have had experience with particular data sets or processes and can be relied on for assistance with challenges. These forums provide a venue for raising technical and professional issues for support.

The other goal of the forum, and the CoP as a whole, is that it provides the chair the ability to control the narrative around analytics in the organization. Any measure of decentralization, over time, will lead to a disparity in approach and technology. Independent practitioners, urged on by the pressure of their business unit, run projects without the benefit of professional oversight or peer review. These projects result in ad hoc solutions, which are typically quick to value but are difficult to maintain and rely on unique transformations or tools. This short-term concession has long-term consequences, and the net effect is a disorganized whole and technical debt.

Most organizations will eventually, as analytics becomes more of a focus, adopt a more centralized Center of Excellence. This evolution is supported by the presence of a Community of Practice. Often at this developmental step, the main challenge is addressing this legacy of disunity. From outside the function, this can have the appearance of a sudden drop in productivity, at the exact time that expectations have increased. This can be disastrous to the support of the team and put analytical leaders in the position of not addressing the technical debt in order to maintain pace. For these reasons, it is important to proactively work toward unifying the function, even if no one group has the clear authority to do so.

Developing a network of practitioners throughout an organization, supported by IT and Business Intelligence, provides several benefits in advancing the status of analytics, stimulating learning, and encouraging sharing and alignment of approaches and best practices. It improves retention and the internal flow of talent by making opportunities available for movement within the organization.

Project Delivery Model

The success of an individual project depends on several factors, only some of which can be controlled. Because of that lack of control, the best way to ensure positive outcomes is through consistency around project delivery, alignment on expectations, and always seeking the buy-in of stakeholders. Adhering to a systematic approach ensures that project management fundamentals are followed, business leads are involved, and team productivity is maximized.

The processes and structure around delivery enterprise-wide is reflective of the operational maturity of an organization. The delivery maturity of analytics can often be distinct from the organization. Often, mature organizations with a robust project management and capital planning function are reactive and improvisational when it comes to analytical projects. Without a communicated and understood delivery model, projects differ wildly between practitioners and stakeholders and can miss the mark in terms objective, timing, or cost.

Analytical project delivery can be broken down into four key phases:

Scoping   This phase involves the formation of the project team and the explicit definition of the purpose of the project as well as the expected outcome. The schedule and budget are defined, and all procedural aspects are clearly described.

Design Thinking   This allows for the exploration of novel solutions to the defined problem through a facilitated discussion with the stakeholders.

Statement of Work   This formal document is the charter for the project and includes such items as the scope (timelines, deliverables, limitations, exclusions, costs), the acceptance criteria, the risks and their mitigations, and the individuals that will be involved in the project.

Project Roadmap   This describes key milestones and anticipated completion schedules for discrete activities as well as their interdependencies. The roadmap is typically organized as a Gantt chart with supporting detail.

Risk Analysis   The issues that could potentially arise negatively affect the project as well as ways to mitigate or avoid those risks.

Steering Committee   The list of all involved individuals (executive sponsor, department sponsor, project lead, project manager, core team, etc.), their interactions, and the project communication plan, including meeting cadence, the format and frequency of status updates, and decision-making authority.

Planning   This second more detailed phase involves the creation of a detailed and sequenced list of activities required to execute the project.

Project Kickoff   This ceremonial meeting is an important psychological bookend to a project and allows for all team members and stakeholders to meet and discuss their role on the project and confirm the mutual understanding and acceptance of the statement of work.

Interviews   As the first step in most analytics projects, interviews and requirement gathering should be scheduled at the planning stage.

Epic Planning / Workstreams   Owing to the dynamic and unpredictable nature of analytics projects, traditional waterfall-style project delivery is normally not possible. Defining larger strategic objectives at the planning phase allows for adaptive sprint planning during execution.

Execution   The third phase is the carrying out of the agreed-upon plan in order to deliver on the outcome defined in the scoping phase. Execution often follows an Agile approach, where the scope varies within constraints in response to new information.

Sprint Planning   Sequenced epics or workstreams are broken into discrete tasks and assigned to individual practitioners for a period of days or weeks.

Plan / Build / Review   Through a cycle of execution and peer review, user stories are completed.

Approval   As required, individual components or features are provided to stakeholders for user acceptance testing.

Communication   As defined in the statement of work, progress, upcoming items, and required decisions are communicated to the stakeholders and steering committee.

Delivery   In the closing phase of a project, all deliverables are finalized and formally transferred to the stakeholder. In a data science and analytics project, continued post-delivery support is often required.

Transition The deliverables are formally transferred to the stakeholders.

Debrief The stakeholder and project partners are solicited for feedback after the formal close of the project.

Retrospective The execution team review the results of the debrief and reflect on potential future improvement to process.

Training All requisite training is provided to the stakeholders to allow for the use of the deliverables.

Roadmap Update In cases where the project was part of a larger overarching program or portfolio, learnings and timelines are reflected in the project roadmap.

Delivery models need not be viewed as a burdensome process to be followed. Ultimately the purpose is to ensure consistency and cognitive fluency so that practitioners can focus on the project and not struggle with uncertainty on the project management elements. At the same time, flexibility needs to be considered, and for smaller projects, aspects of the delivery model can be discarded. The philosophy of parsimony should be followed, in that the minimum structural elements required for success are included and all that is nonessential is removed. The model itself can also be adapted over time to meet the needs of the organization. Analytics practitioners need to commit to relentless self-questioning and self-investigation to ensure that all processes are balanced and adding value.

For consistency and the benefit of the project team, delivery exhibits can be pre-made and made available. Some helpful exhibits and templates include steering committee updates, debrief scripts, ideation placemats, and statement of work documents.

Closing the Gap

Having laid out the vision for the analytics function, and in full understanding of the current state of analytics within the organization and the target state, the final conceptual step is the development of a roadmap to achieve these goals. This roadmap is an expression or visualization of the strategic plan and acts as a guide to direct activities in a way that serves the longer-term vision.

Unlike a project plan, which is a series of concrete activities to deliver on an objective, a strategic roadmap lays out such items as the implementation timeline for a target operating model and the business rollout of a new governance framework. These initiatives take place in parallel to daily project-based activities and influence all other work.

For an organization to successfully adopt and support the analytics function, it also needs to have the appropriate resources, processes, and values:

Resources   Often, people and platforms were selected to meet the challenges that the organization had in the past. The capabilities and education of most of the organization were attained prior to the advent of analytics, requiring reevaluation in order to keep current and reflect the present competitive environment.

Processes   The processes that are in place have made the organization successful to date, and the individuals likely believe they will ensure success in the future.

Values   Novel, disruptive organizations embrace innovation and new approaches. With time and stability, organizational values become more conservative (Christiensen & Overdorf, 2000).

Establishing a roadmap is like charting a long-term course through an unknown and unknowable future, filled with distractions and competing priorities, arriving ultimately at a state that was designed in a different environment. Because of the time involved in attaining the target state, it is important to reassess the goals and desired outcomes as new technology and industry best practices are revealed. It is also important that the roadmap is set against defined horizons.

Setting the Horizon

When a person is driving their daily commute, it requires little planning. It is along an established path between two points and within familiar enough an environment that mitigation plans for every eventuality are implicitly known, and a road closure or other event can be easily resolved by adjusting the route. Longer, unfamiliar cross-country road trips, on the other hand, require a combination of careful planning on the large scale and flexibility on the small scale. Preparations are essential, but if one were to plan for every potential issue, they would never get on the road. The objectives and environment could both change midtrip or the driver may change their priorities and set a new destination. Similarly, the descriptiveness and flexibility of a strategic roadmap must reflect the horizon that is being planned for.

Short-term tactical roadmaps are concerned with the unveiling of an initiative or the hard cutover to a new process. These roadmaps need to be comprehensively defined and have risk mitigation plans in place for any issues from change management to technical. Every stakeholder needs to be identified by name and all aspects socialized in advance. In execution, they need to be perceived and be presented as solid, defined, and inevitable. These short-term deployments of strategic initiatives will at this point have been discussed extensively and all stakeholders aligned on approach and outcome.

Medium-term operational roadmaps are concerned with the less immediate yet still definable transition to a new model or the implementation of a new policy. As with tactical initiatives, there must be alignment in terms of approach and outcome, but because of the challenge in considering all potential issues, flexibility needs to be maintained in all aspects. These initiatives need to be presented as aspirational, beneficial, and collaborative journeys taking place in a consultative partnership with the stakeholders and practitioners involved.

Long-term strategic roadmaps are concerned with cultural or otherwise transformational long-term initiatives for which a detailed plan is impractical and inadvisable. Full flexibility needs to be maintained, with a view toward opportunistic activities that support the larger initiative.

It bears repeating that this roadmap exists as an overlay to the recurring activities of the team and the project delivery schedules. Rarely will there be surplus resources available to dedicate to these activities. With some exceptions, these roadmaps should be less overt—a thematic influence on all subordinate activities, and as a change in tone set by leadership.

Establishing a Talent Roadmap

One of the key outputs from the reference capability modeling exercise is an understanding of what capabilities are lacking in the team, both in the current state and those anticipated in the future. This list of gaps is the basis for the development of a talent strategy including training, hiring, and outsourcing. For each identified gap, leaders must determine where they will do the following:

- Transfer accountability
- Hire new people with that capability
- Partner with academia
- Provide training to current people

- Build alliances and partnerships
- Engage consultants or contractors

This talent roadmap should be informed by the capability mapping and framed by the future state definition as well as key strategic initiatives for the team. The roadmap provides leverage in receiving talent requisitions and training budget.

Consultants and Contractors

The first choice to execute projects in the majority of cases should be to utilize internal resources. Due to the mobilization time and domain knowledge gaps combined with higher hourly wages, it is rarely cost effective to use external resources to deliver on a typical project. Externally delivered projects are also more challenging to maintain or modify in the future because they are often developed outside the regular conventions of the team. Also, the opportunity to develop individuals on the team is lost.

However, there are cases where it is advantageous to use contractors or consultants.

Unique Projects   For one-off projects that require a very specialized skillset, it can be better to hire a contractor to complete the work. Upskilling existing talent can be time consuming, and hired resources who are able to deliver will be difficult to keep engaged over the longer term. These externally led projects provide an opportunity for training in-house practitioners when using a joint team, which also has the benefit of reducing the risk of unconventional practices.

Independence   In cases where the project requires an external perspective, there is little choice but to leverage a consulting firm. Analytics teams embedded within the business can find it challenging to extricate themselves from the political environment and can often find their deliverables challenged by stakeholders. Consultants, even engaged in a supporting or auditing role, can add credibility to a politically sensitive project.

No Resources   Resource-constrained teams may find that employing contractors to support demanding projects can be net positive when viewed against the costs of deferral.

Strategy Refresh   Group analytics strategy should be regularly evaluated against the enterprise strategy and should be evaluated independently by those who have a broader industry or practice perspective. Without an independent assessment against current norms, a group can become stagnant and archaic.

Benchmarking   Similarly to a strategy refresh, without regular benchmarking exercises an organization can significantly lag its peers without their awareness. Competitive information can be gathered informally through published articles, publicly available earnings reports, and interviews, but for a comprehensive industry scan, consultants have a better vantage point. It should be stated, however, that benchmarking only provides a baseline to be competitive and that a truly visionary team needs to look beyond current trends and best practices.

Owing to several misperceptions, there is a common distrust in the motivations of consultants, despite an acceptance of their expertise, that can prevent organizations from realizing the maximum value from the consultants' work. From an adversarial posture, clients push consultants to close out projects quickly, ostensibly to maximize value and reduce the cost of the engagement. This is a missed opportunity because once consultants and contractors have been engaged, there are great opportunities to develop in-house talent. The exposure to the practices and techniques of multidisciplinary management consultants who have a wealth of implicit knowledge is invaluable.

When deciding who to dedicate to support the engagement, it is important to choose the most capable on the team. Unfortunately, usually the opposite happens; managers often pick those who simply have availability, which is both a drain on the project and a missed opportunity for the development of the strongest team members. Consultants, with their strict focus on process and systematic problem solving, can provide informal training opportunities, which are hugely beneficial. Weaker or more junior team members will also not have the knowledge or confidence to provide guidance to the consultants, leading to unplanned changes and a less effective overall project.

Last, start with the end in mind. While this is important for any project, it is particularly so for expensive consulting engagements. Many bookshelves and hard drives are full of unused target operating models and resourcing plans. Take an active role in the development of the terms of reference and ensure that the projects are structured in such a way that the deliverable can be operationalized, and with the honest intention of implementing the outcome.

Consultants and contractors should be viewed as an opportunity for internal development and for executing projects outside of the capabilities of the team. Unfortunately, emotional responses based on pride and distrust can often get between the analytics function and a successful project. Well-meaning scope reduction can prune a project's budget but also reduce its impact. Committing to the project, and entering a consulting engagement with a positive and growth-oriented mindset, can have benefits that last far beyond the delivery date.

Change Management

The development of a strategy for the data science and analytics function has, up until this point in the process, relied almost entirely on technical know-how and a logical progression from problem definition to solution. All of the precursor activities can be accomplished through research and deep quantitative analysis. Once changes begin to impact people, however, change management principles become essential to ensure that the strategic aims can be achieved. There is a common statistic that between 50 percent and 70 percent of change initiatives fail, due mainly to a lack of consideration for the human factors associated with the program. Understanding the underlying causes of this high failure rate is important to ensuring the success of a strategic transformation.

For the most part, people are naturally change averse. It is a part of our DNA that has allowed us to avoid danger and be successful as a species. What has worked for an individual in the past will be their default approach in the future. Leaders cannot move people between roles and expect changes. Leaders cannot give raises or adjust performance objectives and expect changes. People are hard wired against change, and without an enemy at the gates or a sense of threat, most people will not change.

There are unique considerations to analytical change management in that typically the function operates without express authority. Outside of operationalized models, or activities that have automated processes, the work of the team is usually in an advisory capacity. Given this lack of authority, leaders cannot enact change through mandate or decree without losing the support of the team. Rather, leaders should aim to be what Debra Meyerson calls a "tempered radical," an informal leader who challenges the status quo and provokes change without fanfare or trumpets or banners but through leading by example (Meyerson, 2001). These leaders should be firm in their commitments but fluid in their methods. They should also seek to manage change using positivity rather than negativity, and rather than challenging the methods of detractors, they should seek to build alliances and develop strong relationships with analytical champions.

It is not possible to convince everybody in the organization of the benefits of analytics. Science fiction and the media have given many a distorted view of data science and analytics, and the threat of automation causes feelings of anxiety and alienation in many. It is a losing battle to convince everybody of the benefits of analytics, either as a whole or for an individual project. The secret is not to convince everybody, just the influencers within an organization. These well-situated champions are essential to the success of the function, and relationships with them should be purposely cultivated as early as possible.

Enterprises of a certain size will most likely have an organizational change management (OCM) group able to support larger initiatives. Engaging this team early in the process of a strategic refresh can ensure alignment with organizational best practices and the support of the OCM team in the execution of the strategy. Unfortunately, due to a lack of general understanding in analytics, OCM will often be unavailable unless it touches on automation or is a function-led initiative. OCM plans should be completed by the analytical function for review and approval by the OCM team.

Analytics professionals naturally default to the programmatic and the logical. Problems are approached from a mechanistic and stochastic perspective where behaviors are modeled and uncertainty minimized. Once a project is operationalized, the practitioner moves to the next project. This systematic approach is at odds with what is needed for successful change management. The John Kotter 8-step process for leading change is a great resource for a holistic view of change management, which serves to inform the following primary analytical requirements (Kotter, n.d.):

Never declare victory. The promulgation of the strategy cannot be confused with the execution of the strategy. Further, the execution of the strategy cannot be confused with the successful arrival at the defined "future state." The strategic vision for the analytics function must permeate every project, every new hire, and every interaction. Declaring victory can only lead to complacency and the revival of negative behaviors.

Establish a sense of urgency and drama. Individuals want to be part of something larger than themselves, and to be involved in vicarious competition. Improvements in productivity, no matter how drastic, do not compel people at a personal level. Whenever an opportunity to discuss the strategy arises, use storytelling rather than bar charts to inspire people. Describe the future as one of either subordination to the technical superiority of competing firms or dominance through cunning. Seek to overcome the ennui and indifference of more moderate team members and stakeholders through the judicious application of stressors.

Find short-term wins.   Seek opportunities to showcase measurable results of the strategic refresh such as engagement scores or productivity or stakeholder comments, and frame it as part of a larger narrative arc that everybody is a part of. Create the opportunity for those involved to personally feel and celebrate successes.

Remove obstacles.   Difficult relationships, detractors, technology, and legacy processes can all be used as evidence against the function. Wherever possible, remove or reallocate these from the mandate of the team, and do not allow negativity to follow the transformation.

Change management is a complex field that combines elements from psychology, sociology, and management. The subject has been an area of study for over 60 years, and there are numerous comprehensive resources available. While a comprehensive overview of the topic is not feasible in this work, the most important thing from an analytical perspective is that it is specifically and intentionally addressed. By disposition, practitioners focus on the technical aspects and frame value propositions by their technical aspects. Analytical change management is about considering the human implications of the work, the underlying human motivations, and reframing the value of the practice in a human-centric way.

Implementing Governance Models

The implementation of analytical governance models is almost always responded to with a NIMBY-like opposition. Everybody involved is in violent agreement that it is an essential activity but only wish it to be applicable for other groups in the organization.

The fundamental change that comes from most governance models among analytics practitioners is around coding, commenting, approved frameworks, and peer review. These practices are well established in more mature organizations, in particular those in the tech industry or those with large numbers of software engineers or computer scientists who are used to this level of programmatic rigor.

For all others unfortunately, this often feels like an invasion into their work and a commentary on their ability. Like a previously independent craftsperson who is now accountable to a manager, it can feel like a demotion or a violation of this autonomy. When considered from a distance, most practitioners would agree that there is little to support absolute autonomy in terms of execution. In practice, however, moving from having absolute sovereignty to being accountable to a group of peers is always a difficult transition. For some, the arrogance of logical supremacy can tempt leaders to sanctimony and blind them to the anxieties of the team. Leaders need to remember that companies are formed of individuals, each with individual sentiments and motivations, and be sensitive in the implementation of these governance models.

These governance policies need to be deployed slowly in the beginning and need to be planned so as to create positive associations. Individuals need to be praised for their participation and encouraged to share the positive results of their experience. This can be achieved through integrating parts of each practitioner's personal toolkit. Individuals will have different areas of strength, and this provides an opportunity to use the best of each person's style as the team convention and gain support.

In most organizations, depending on the culture, the introduction of competitive behaviors by providing scoring mechanisms can have a great impact in adopting new practices. For example, quantifying the number of bugs found by a peer reviewer (without naming the originator) or the number of snippets in a repository can give an individual a marker of success and a metric for achievement. Though it should be managed to avoid negative behaviors, friendly competition can enshrine positive governance.

All will agree that analytical governance is theoretically important. It allows for interoperability and the easier reuse of code and codifies peer review processes that reduce errors. That it involves some sacrifice in professional independence, however, can be difficult for many. However, through positive framing, the tactical and consistent application of pressure, and the introduction of competitive behaviors, it can be adopted by all teams.

Summary

It needs to be remembered and communicated that analytical transformation is a process and not an event. It is change in culture, processes, and conventions, which cannot be accelerated or forced. It is a long-term gentle and intentional nudge toward a more analytical future. This new and compelling vision cannot be communicated in a single email or a meeting, but rather through all channels, in every meeting, in every email, without allowing people to forget the direction in which the function is going and the benefits that will be realized.

Change management is difficult. People are unpredictable, and each one has individual goals, drivers, and fears. Despite the difficulty, however, change management is essential to the successful launch or refresh of an analytics function. There are countless resources and materials dealing with change management, but they all boil down to a single maxim: the strategy that has been developed has consequences for individual people. Consider, consult, and genuinely care for those people, and the process will be much easier.

Change management is the customary conclusion of any discussion on strategy and the natural bookend to the current state assessment that began this phase of the discussion. Strategy is essential to defining the goal of the analytics team and to provide a set of guiding principles on how to achieve that goal. But strategy alone does not make an analytics team strong. That strength comes from the processes and the people.

References

Chandler, A. D. (1962). *Strategy and structure: Chapters in the history of the industrial enterprise*. MIT Press.

Christiensen, C. M., & Overdorf, M. (2000, March–April). Meeting the challenge of disruptive change. *Harvard Business Review*. Retrieved from https://hbr.org/2000/03/meeting-the-challenge-of-disruptive-change

DAMA International. (2017). *DAMA-DMBOK: Data management body of knowledge*. Technics Publications.

Data Management Association International. (n.d.). *Data governance definition*. Retrieved from http://datagovernance.com/adg_data_governance_definition

Davenport, T. H., & Harris, J. G. (2007). *Competing on analytics: The new science of winning*. Harvard Business School Press.

Drucker, P. F. (1982). *The changing world of the executive*. Routledge.

Kotter, J. (n.d.). *8-step process for leading change.* Retrieved from `http://kotterinc.com/8-steps-process-for-leading-change`

Meyerson, D. (2001, Oct.). Radical change the quiet way. *Harvard Business Review.*

O'Neil, C., & Schutt, R. (2013). *Doing data science* (1st ed.). O'Reilly Media.

Peters, T. J., & Waters, R. H. (1982). *In search of excellence.* Harper Collins.

Watkins, M. D. (2003). *The first 90 days: Critical success strategies for new leaders at all levels.* Harvard Business Review Press.

Wu, T. (2010, Spring). Strategic choice—Johnson and Scholes suitability, feasibility, and acceptability model (relevant to paper p3). *Learning Centre.* Retrieved from `http://tolobranca.nl/wp-content/uploads/2020/07/SFA-Matrix-learning_strategic_choice.pdf`

Process

How to establish productive processes that enable the effective planning, delivery, and sustainment of analytical projects, programs, and products.

W. E. Deming, the guru of quality, said of process, "If you can't describe what you are doing as a process, you don't know what you're doing." Paradoxically, while practitioners are highly skilled at breaking down a business problem into their individually optimizable components, the processes by which they operate internally have the tendency to be ad hoc and reactive. It is critical for practitioners to maintain flexibility and adapt their working style to support the stakeholders they are engaged with; however, having deficiencies and inconsistencies in intake, delivery, and communication will invariably lead to poor stakeholder experience and ultimately to poor project outcomes. Maintaining structure around these elements reduces operational friction, improves cognitive fluency, and lets the focus remain on the work; the processes must be managed before the people.

Process simply describes how things are done, a series of actions or steps taken to accomplish a distinct goal. When fully described and sequenced, processes lay out how people and equipment produce a product or service. Once a process has been deconstructed into discrete actions, those actions can be more easily optimized. Scientific management took this idea to the extreme in the 1920s. Frederick Taylor, the leader of the efficiency movement, demonstrated the efficacy of the philosophy through mandating rest patterns for workers who were loading railcars with pig iron (Taylor, 2006). After close observation, the individual movements made by the workers were defined, and the rest patterns were compared to the productivity for each worker. This exercise yielded an optimal routinized process that, when consistently executed, doubled the number of bars that could be loaded by an individual during their shift. Because these processes are completed so frequently, small changes can quickly reap huge rewards. Similarly, in a business context, these small adjustments to process can reduce the amount of time spent in superfluous activities and allow the practitioner to focus on the value-added work. Small time savings in aggregate lead to much greater productivity.

When a person is new to a role, they need to rely on their education and direction from management. As the individual onboards, they will at first make several mistakes but will hopefully receive feedback from their peers and managers until they are able to reach a semi-coherent synchronicity with the rest of the group. In the absence of well-articulated processes, this stage of development is the evolutionary ceiling of the natural analytics function. Though they are capable of executing smaller projects, the team will struggle with more complex initiatives. Without deliberate procedural models, the activities of the group will be variable and reflexive, changing in style and character as new people join and leave the firm and as new projects are undertaken. Process must consider explicitly the environment in which the activities take place. It should not be so explicit that innovation is stifled through a lack of variability or that practitioners are not empowered to deviate from norms if a project requires it. Process should be ultimately about defining and enforcing the tangential features of an engagement and creating a framework to ensure the successful creation and delivery of the final product.

Well-defined processes encourage cognitive fluency both in the analytics team and with the involved stakeholders. Beginning a project with a mutual understanding of all procedural elements brings focus on the problem being solved rather than administrative activities. However, the impact of having well-defined processes goes beyond productivity improvements and can have a positive effect on the emotional frame of the stakeholder. In the 1980s, psychologist Robert Zajonc (1980) laid out his Affective Primacy Theory that said initial judgments are often made without active cognitive processing and rather are based on familiarity. Through a series of experiments, Zajonc proved that animals and people are more likely to have positive feelings toward stimulants they have experienced in the past. What this means in practice is that for an analytics team, executing novel solutions within a familiar delivery framework can have a huge impact on the mood of the stakeholders and reduce the challenges that can arise from their natural resistance and apprehension toward unfamiliar situations. Alternatively, too many surprises will promote defensive behaviors in stakeholders.

Analytics teams can certainly operate in the absence of either business processes or analytics execution processes, and they may even have some measure of success. Many organizations have loose amalgamations of individual data scientists who independently run projects under the nominal guidance of a nominal leader. After enough time, stakeholders will express satisfaction with the deliverable and consider the project closed. The model or script will chug along indefinitely with regular intervention by the analytics team. Without a basis for comparison the organization will generally believe things to be fine and carry on in this manner for years, never truly unlocking the potential for the function. Process is necessary to move the team from being a disorganized group of individuals to a cohesive whole, allows the execution of larger projects, and improves the experience for both the practitioners and the stakeholders.

One overarching philosophy that is essential to the running of a strong analytics function is that of parsimony. Parsimony has several synonyms that are more commonly used and familiar to people. Using a memorable five-dollar sesquipedalian word that does not have ingrained meaning to people on the team allows them to own it and make it part of the team vernacular. *Cheap* implies inferior quality, *simple* is associated with a lack of vigor, and *plain* is rude. What a successful analytics team needs to be is *parsimonious*.

There is a real danger in well-intentioned standardization leading to burdensome bureaucracy. Approached in steps, successful improvements in productivity can lead to a "more is better" rationalization, with the inevitable outcome being that more time is spent in planning, documenting, and reporting the work than in doing the work itself. It is self-evident but worth mentioning that every hour spent on procedural items such as documentation and process is an hour taken away from the core work of an analytics project.

Organizations and teams have a natural tendency toward becoming more bureaucratic over time. As the number of small tasks a group implements and is responsible for grows, checklists and oversight become necessary. Ensuring that there is coverage for those checklists requires cross-training and process documentation. Maintaining that documentation requires governance frameworks and regularly scheduled document reviews. Eventually, without sunsetting vestigial processes, the support becomes Kafkaesque and the energy of the team declines.

Parsimony is a philosophy of intentionally expending the minimum amount of energy required in an activity so as to maintain overall efficiency. It is about keeping things as simple as possible, but no simpler. There are three key ways to encourage parsimony in teams:

Define Limits   During the planning stage of a project, stakeholders should be included in determining their involvement, the communication cadence, style, and project updates. The analytics function should have a minimum and maximum amount of administration that they are able to provide, which should scale with the scope of the project. The minimum should be presented as the default communication plan, with the group being amenable to increases up to a certain point.

Operationalization   The long-term maintenance requirements of any project should be a major consideration when planning an approach. When evaluating the return of the alternatives, labor costs associated with recurring tasks should be on the cost side of the ledger, and the risks associated with that failure point should be explained and mitigated. Each process, deliverable, and report should be held to this standard.

Accountability   Project leaders should be evaluated on their ability to plan and run an efficient project and individual contributors on their ability to develop efficient solutions that are resilient and minimize requirements around ongoing support. Clear expectations need to be set to encourage the proper behaviors in the team by highlighting the associated labor costs at every opportunity.

Parsimony should be a key theme for any analytics team, used in their model designs, in their project planning, and in their communication style. It needs to be embedded into the culture of the team to be most effective, and there should be few status meetings where the parsimony of a project is not challenged.

This chapter is organized across two primary topics: project planning and project execution.

Project Planning

Effective analytics project delivery requires the definition of a comprehensive group of processes that includes intake and prioritization, project planning and scoping, planning, execution, and the final handover required to complete a project. The overarching purpose of a project delivery model is to provide a parsimonious supporting framework within which practitioners can execute a project, which promotes collaboration and improves the likelihood of success. These models should not be burdensome, imposing time-consuming reporting activities or recurring poorly attended and nonproductive meetings. The goal should be a minimal set of guidelines that allows the stakeholders visibility and input into the project, while giving the analytics team freedom to progress without ambiguity.

These models deal with uncertainty around such questions as, How should we structure steering committees? When should we meet? How do we deal with scope creep? How do we estimate timelines? When should we engage the project management office? How do we operationalize? How do we hand off the product? How do we support and maintain our work? While these questions are essential to the project, they can cause unnecessary churn and uncertainty among those involved.

These models need to be contextualized to the organization, with culture and overriding processes taken into consideration. In many organizations, projects with a budget above a certain threshold will require oversight by a project management office (PMO), which may have its own reporting requirements. Projects that impact multiple business units may even require the involvement of an external change management professional who may have impact assessment guidelines that need to be considered throughout the project life cycle. The delivery model should remain flexible enough to account for these external requirements but rigid in the core aspects of transparency and communication.

The following sections attempt to provide generalized and sequential project framing in an industry and function-agnostic setting.

Intake and Prioritization

Intake and prioritization includes the processes and procedures centered around the receipt of new work, its evaluation and acceptance or rejection, and its preliminary assessment of urgency. These models ensure that there is organizational clarity and that resources are being efficiently deployed in the way that creates the most value. All project management functions begin with this foundational first step.

Typically, as nascent data science and analytics teams are formed, they are effectively individual technical resources who are shared among stakeholder teams. These developing teams respond to requests in an ad hoc way, prioritizing based on seniority of the requestor and urgency of tone. This reactive process will continue until the workload exceeds their capacity and the projects will get prioritized by somebody more senior, and potentially new data scientists will be brought on to the team. This natural evolution of a data science team in a medium-sized nontechnical organization leads almost always to a small team of highly technical specialists who have little experience in project management or other foundational management capabilities and struggle with independently balancing competing priorities. For these teams, the most important process to establish is around intake and prioritization.

Project intake falls on a spectrum, from the reactionary, where emails, verbal requests, and direct messages are ordered by recency, to the abominably administrative, where onerous forms are filled and approved by senior leaders. Intake models should provide a structured way for the business to submit a well-formed and concise request to the analytics function that enables rather than prevents and fits within the culture of the organization. In the absence of a formal process, there will arise naturally one of many implicit prioritization models, none of which are able to support an effective analytics practice. The following list includes some of these models:

Seniority   In hierarchical organizations, projects that are endorsed or requested by senior leaders are often prioritized. Though this can ensure alignment to strategic priorities, it is subjective and can mar the team with political resourcing struggles.

Urgency   Stakeholders who can better articulate a sense of urgency will often receive more support from analytics teams, leading to a negative feedback loop where all requests are presented as being immediately required. This negates the possibility for any planning or prioritization.

First In, First Out   The most utilitarian approach, but for a successful analytics function that has more incoming projects than discharged, it will inevitably lead to large delays. Many organizations use FIFO as a baseline and overlay prioritization by seniority or urgency.

Preferential   Organizations with well-funded but poorly understood analytics functions can in some cases defer to the analytics team to prioritize projects. Without business guidance, projects tend to be selected based on technical interest rather than on their substantive value.

Corporate   Mature organizations with an established PMO or BA function will have an external project approval process that can be imposed on the analytics function. Cost-benefit analysis, internal rate of return, and payback period are the traditional metrics by which projects are evaluated. This approach provides a well-structured starting point but ignores key elements of the function and can lead to transformative projects being delayed indefinitely, supplanted by incrementalist projects.

The primary consideration is that projects need to be prioritized and assessed on their value to the organization. Whether this is through top line revenue growth, cost savings, or a combination of the two, all projects need to be assessed consistently to prioritize them on the same basis. As with any optimization algorithm, there needs to be a response variable. This value can be calculated in several ways. The first method should be a logical assessment of the outcome, such as projected revenue growth or cost savings associated with automation using existing and accepted metrics. For many project types, such as independent studies, it will be difficult to assess the actual monetary value to the business. In this case, the secondary approach of determining the value of the insight through cost avoidance can be used, determining approximately how much it would cost for consultants to undertake the project, or an assessment by the requesting leader on how much they would hypothetically be willing to pay for the project.

The following questions need to be addressed during the initial analytics intake process:

- What is the desired outcome?
- What is the background?
- What is the perceived priority by the sponsor?
- What is the requested delivery date?
- What is the absolute deadline?
- Who is the department sponsor?
- Who is the executive sponsor?

- What groups or individuals are impacted?
- What is the initial value of the insight—how does it help the business?
- What is the strategic area of focus?

The ideal analytics project intake and prioritization framework uses these traditional corporate project evaluation criteria augmented with considerations around human factors and provides flexibility to allow for immediate action on breakfixes, regulatory, or executive requests. Analytics projects must necessarily create value for the organization, but consideration of these less tangible human factors creates a more sustainable practice.

There are three key human factors to consider in prioritization: projects need to inspire, align, and challenge.

Inspire   The analytics function is at its best when it inspires people and is seen as an innovative team that expands the potential for the organization. This leads to more opportunities and encourages stakeholders to think bigger. This optimism for a better future, however, can be slowly eroded if the team focuses only on delivering quality of life improvements such as new visualizations or marginally improved processes. Some projects simply need to be inspirational.

Align   Projects that support a larger initiative should receive priority attention even if their individual value creation is lower. These enablement activities provide a larger sense of purpose and a narrative arc for the team. It prevents projects from becoming a flurry of individual unrelated tasks, rather directing them to a larger cohesive end.

Challenge   Projects need to be challenging and to support the career growth of the practitioners. Most practitioners have made the decision to pursue data science and analytics out of passion for the practice. If in the interest of efficiency, each project uses only a few simple tools and approaches, the more creative individuals will become disengaged. Practitioners must be challenged and given the opportunity to grow their skillsets to be at their best. Though the laws of parsimony need to apply, stretch projects need to be present for the development and engagement of the team.

The level of rigor present in an intake and prioritization process needs to reflect the size of the analytics team, the maturity of the organization, the typical project complexity, and the number of stakeholders and dependencies involved. For smaller functions, or those teams servicing a single business unit, a simplified algorithmic approach may suffice, while for a larger team with an enterprise mandate, a more robust process based on portfolio project management principles may be required.

For analytics teams who have previously only had informal project intake, this can be a challenging transition. Stakeholders who previously had back door access to an analytics team will almost always push back against the introduction of formal intake processes. From their perspective, something has been lost, and there will be concerns about a lack of responsiveness or of having to queue for simple requests. Analytics leaders need to highlight the benefits of the process, share them broadly, and ensure that there is support from stakeholders. Once established, the intake process needs to be formalized without allowing for circumvention or exemptions. This represents as much a culture change as a process change, and without monitoring and continual reinforcement teams will invariably revert to old habits.

For those old habits to persist requires the involvement of both a requestor and a requestee, and avoiding this backsliding needs to address both of these parties. Within the team, assigning ownership over the intake process to managers or senior individuals provides a sense of shared accountability and serves to discourage their tacit acceptance of direct requests. Ensuring as well that there is a single avenue for requests, either a group email or an intake form, prevents confusion and provides less confident practitioners an objective way to reject noncompliant asks. On the side of the rebellious requestors, transparency into the current prioritized list helps to replace negative sentiments with positive visibility. Stakeholders, aware that their peers and leaders have visibility into the prioritized list, and aware of the impact of their attempts to butt ahead in line, are more apt to maintain and mind the pipeline.

Mature project intake procedures set the stage for future project success and are foundational to sound project management. When the project life cycle begins with a systematic and objective process, it is much easier to progress in a structured way.

Project Pipelines

After intake and prioritization, projects will exist within a pipeline before being fully scoped and planned for execution. The concept of a project pipeline is based on the idea that prior to a project being kicked off, there is a significant amount of work and time involved in scouting, scoping, planning, discussing, waiting for resources, waiting for technology, waiting for approvals, and so on. Analytics teams that are in their infancy, or individual citizen data scientists, can often be entirely transactional, having no managed pipeline. They perform their daily operational duties until clear instructions are received. They execute the plan that has been provided, deliver the outcome they have not designed, and return to their daily operational activities. It is a logical approach, and quite safe both professionally and psychologically; if the instructions are ever wrong, they are protected from accountability.

In sales, it could be several years between an introduction and a revenue-generating sale. If the salesperson did not have an active pipeline, and waited for a sale before pursuing another opportunity, they would have little success. Just as in sales, analytics teams should be looking for new projects far in advance of their current work being completed. Thinking in terms of a project pipeline is about getting mentally away from the workface to plant seeds and to cultivate budding projects that are at different preliminary phases. This is accomplished through fostering relationships within the industry and organization, in purposeful eminence building, in networking and developing the capabilities of the individuals in the team.

The minding of the project pipeline is not the sole responsibility of analytics leadership, but it should be an expectation of each individual on the team. Even the most junior member of the team should, within their first few months, be aware of key groups, or the interrelations between teams, and be vigilant in the scouting of potential projects for the team.

Conceptually, the analytics project pipeline can be considered a funnel, with each step having fewer items than the previous. The different phases of the project pipeline, the considerations, approximate duration to kickoff, and the proportion of projects that should lie within this phase for pipeline health are shown in Table 3.1, which loosely follows the traditional sales pipeline.

Table 3.1: The analytics project pipeline

PHASE	DESCRIPTION	TIMELINE	PROPORTION
Relationship building	The intentional founding of relationships with future project sponsors and participants within the organization, the industry, and partners. Eminence building to support such relationships.	Several years	Hundreds of prospects

PHASE	DESCRIPTION	TIMELINE	PROPORTION
Discovery	The direction of existing relationships toward collaborative opportunities in the analytics space within the organization who have a perceived expectation to convert.	Years or more	Dozens of prospects
Pre-qualification	Exploring and understanding the situation of the stakeholder, including their challenges and motivation, both professionally and personally.	Months or more	30% of pipeline
Qualification	The identification of discrete potential projects that have been suggested by stakeholders or the analytics team or as future phases of past projects.	Several months	10% of pipeline
Solution	Aligning with the stakeholder on a solution to the defined problem either directly or through a design thinking session.	1–2 Months	5% of pipeline
Scoping	Investigating the implications of the solution, including all resourcing requirements.	1 Month	5% of pipeline
Planning	Completing all items in the statement of work, including a work breakdown structure.	Weeks	5% of pipeline
In progress	Projects that are under active execution.	N/A	<5% of pipeline

Healthy pipelines with proper proportions ensure that the analytics function will always have high-impact projects to work on and is able to confidently articulate their value within the organization. It also allows for more conscientious resource planning and can be used to build support for continued growth. Conversely, poorly maintained pipelines lead to boom and bust cycles, projects undertaken out of desperation, and difficulty in planning.

After project intake, through formal channels, a brainstorming session, or a design thinking exercise, the potential project exists within the pipeline until the situation is such that it has the highest marginal benefit to execute or it is required to support a larger initiative. Often the time between intake and execution can be long, so the environmental factors need to be reassessed, including employee availability, constraints, limitations, or parallel projects. The preliminary plan developed during the intake phase needs to be considered in light of all current variables. During a planning and scoping session, the analytics function and the sponsoring stakeholders align on a solution and consider the high-level workstreams involved and the level of effort involved for each workstream.

Portfolio Project Management

Project management guru Bob Buttrick said that project management is about doing projects right, while portfolio project management (PPM) is about doing the right projects. In a data and analytics context, portfolio project management is concerned primarily with the sequencing and organizing of multiple related projects to achieve a larger goal and establishing value much earlier in the process. The next developmental step for analytical leaders who have led projects and workstreams is to take a broader view of the project pipeline and to determine how to orchestrate them to maximum benefit. The effective prioritization and coordination of individual projects can improve productivity and reduce resource requirements. Establishing processes based on PPM is the fullest expression of intake and prioritization models.

Portfolios exist within a broader project management hierarchy, according to the Project Management Institute (2008):

Project   A temporary endeavor undertaken to create a unique product, service, or result

Program   A group of related projects managed in a coordinated way to obtain benefits and control not available from managing them individually

Portfolio   A collection of projects and programs that are managed as a group to achieve strategic objectives

The Standard for Portfolio Management from the Project Management Institute (2006) describes five steps in the process of PPM:

Clarify Business Objectives   Determine what the stakeholder ultimately wants from this project and assign a value to that outcome.

Capture and Research   Scope the proposed projects more thoroughly and build a list of candidates.

Select the Best Projects   Rank the candidate projects by value to the organization, constrain by resources, and ensure that they are balanced.

Validate and Initiate   Ensure feasibility by conferring with line managers, analytics team, and leadership.

Manage and Monitor   Execute the plan and establish regular monitoring points to view the portfolio as a whole.

These steps can give the illusion of a deterministic procedure that can be implemented immediately and to great effect. In practice, this is a subjective and nuanced process that requires a great deal of intuition and emotional intelligence. The preceding list advises that the portfolio be balanced, and this is where the challenge lies for an analytics team. There is no systematic way to determine balance, but some considerations are as follows:

Strategic Alignment   Enabling projects and those that support the strategic objectives of the enterprise should be prioritized, even if they do not have an immediate and quantifiable value.

Stakeholder Balancing   All business units should have at least some representation in the portfolio, even if the ranking does not explicitly support it.

Moonshots   Passion projects should be encouraged, even if success is not guaranteed. This improves team engagement and inspires others throughout the organization, leading to increased visibility and awareness.

Development Objectives   Every individual within the analytics team has personal objectives that should be respected and considered when portfolios are established and staffed. The short-term benefit of higher productivity will be offset by long-term stagnation and reduced team engagement if this is not a part of the decision process.

Parallel vs. Serial   Projects with shared inputs or resources should be completed in parallel when possible. Serial projects, which take longer when executed in isolation than when executed with sister projects, should be avoided unless deferral would have an associated opportunity cost.

Synergies   Less tangible than opportunities for parallel execution are synergies. Often groups or individuals encourage and support each other such that the effect of their collaboration is greater than the sum of their separate parts.

Time to Value   Longer-term projects should be structured such that they have the shortest time to value possible. If deferring a project to establish joint or parallel workstreams will improve the time to value, this should be done.

Dependencies   Projects with support requirements from other teams need to align with their availability and be scheduled accordingly. Inter-project dependencies and the impact of delays need to be understood and the risks managed.

Politics   Realistically, the social implications of the inclusion or rejection of a project needs to be considered. While politics should never be a primary driver behind portfolio planning, a sober assessment of the effects on relationships and standing in the organization is always prudent.

Portfolio project management plays another key role for a team in ensuring resource leveling through the proper sequencing of long- and short-duration projects. Analytics teams delivering exclusively on large transformative multiyear projects will have many idle practitioners between the phases of these projects and will face dwindling success as their momentum drops between project deliveries. Similarly, an analytics team that executes exclusively short-turn projects will have limited impact, be burned out from transitioning between small projects, and be disengaged from the lack of large appealing projects. Teams and individuals need a combination of short-duration quick wins and longer-duration meaty projects. The team needs to experience these successes to remain engaged, and the team itself needs to be able to showcase continued value creation.

In practice, less-mature analytics teams will often be reactionary to incoming projects. The stated priority of the stakeholders will be respected, and there will be little control over the sequencing or prioritization of the projects. As analytics teams grow, it is important that this control be established. Without a structured approach to portfolio project management through systematic intake and prioritization, teams can quickly become overwhelmed and less productive.

PPM, as a second-order project coordination, ensures that related initiatives can be aggregated for the benefit of stakeholder planning to manage dependencies and understand how it fits with other organizational priorities. It is remarkably challenging for an organization to understand and control all of the projects that are in flight. Even with dedicated project management offices, often projects with overlaps and redundancies will be done in parallel, leading to conflicting outcomes. For an individual group to understand all the changes and ongoing initiatives within the enterprise that will impact their own group and projects is all but impossible.

One of the best ways to achieve this is through a simple philosophy of alignment at the top and autonomy at the bottom. In a similar way to how an individual project is broken down into individual tasks, large transformative initiatives are broken down into discrete projects, each of which adds iterative value and gets the team closer to the end goal.

For example, organizations in several industries are seeking to offer personalized pricing to customers by modeling their willingness to pay. The inherent risk of a knife-edge cutover to a new pricing model combined with the technical complexity of such a transformation would require months of planning, coordination across the enterprise, and likely years of development and testing to ensure that the solution was stable and worked as expected. However, by splitting the larger initiative into a series of steps, where components of each project can be used in subsequent projects, there is a much lower time to value and new technology and opportunities that arise in the life of the initiative can be deployed.

This larger personalized pricing portfolio can be shared with stakeholders in marketing, IT, sales, and digital to align on support requirements and timelines. Without this second-order planning, projects are at risk of duplication of effort and suboptimal outcomes.

Portfolio and program management is often associated with traditional command and control style management, and when exercised to its full capacity introduces unnecessary bureaucracy and control. In an analytics context, this second-level strategic project planning is a way to structure and communicate larger plans to leadership and should be employed in the most noninvasive way possible. Small, self-organizing, and highly independent teams who are executing individual projects, lightly directed to ensure alignment to interrelated projects, provide efficiency gains and ensure assets are shared.

Project Scoping and Planning

One of the clearest ways to assess the overall maturity of an analytics function and its position in an organization can be in seeing how active a role they play in creating a project plan. For recently formed teams or more junior practitioners, the greatest comfort comes from a clean data set, detailed instructions on how to proceed, and clarity on the desired outcome. For stakeholders who do not understand the function well and want to exercise control, it can appear to be a beneficial arrangement as well. This combination of, on one side, a desire for clear instruction and, on the other, a desire for control over the unknown, is the usual first iteration of an analytics team. While it provides stakeholders with comfort initially, this is a missed opportunity in the longer term for both stakeholders and practitioners; the value of collaboration is lost, and the team devolves quickly into a group of technical resources. For an analytics team to be truly valuable to the organization, they must be considered, and consider themselves, as business advisors and not as a pool of order takers.

Another less common arrangement is that of an experienced analytics practitioner and a less secure stakeholder. In this scenario, the more assertive analytics lead will reframe the problem statement into one that is more technically solvable, but unfortunately often providing a deliverable that cannot be implemented. This likely is the result of the practitioner insisting on tweaking the approach to incorporate advanced methods and tools such as natural language processing or neural nets where a more parsimonious tactic would suffice, usually in the direction of their personal interests. In this way it is worse than the first—as though the output may be impressive in its design, it is developed without business context and can rarely be implemented without significant changes to the existing processes. Whether the analytics team is operating as order takers or autocrats, the solution lies in the educated empowerment of the stakeholders through focusing on effective communication.

In several studies, it has been shown that outsiders perform better than experts when problems are framed such that no domain knowledge is needed (McAfee & Brynjolfsson, 2017). This idea is not a modern breakthrough; in the 1940s creative destruction advocate Joseph Schumpeter (1983) said, "It is not the owners of stagecoaches who build railways." Incumbents have an interest in the status quo and are less innovative than outsiders who can apply their multidisciplinary background and fresh perspective to the problem. Understanding attrition models in a marketing context, for example, can be helpful to improve lapse models in an insurance setting or churn models in a sales function. Without the exercising of analytical expertise to inform a project, the best that can be expected is tepid incrementalism.

Project planning must then begin with two crucial questions—what is the stakeholder truly asking for, and can a solution be implemented?

When a stakeholder asks for an attrition model, what they genuinely want is an operationalizable process that reduces attrition. If a practitioner answers the mail and provides a predictive model, it will not add value, regardless of the R^2 or other statistical measure of model performance. In this case, the stakeholder truly needs is to know the drivers of attrition. Similarly, when a stakeholder asks for a customer segmentation model, it is essential to understand the business limitations on what features can be included. Passion for the craft and an ardent desire for performant models can lead to segmentation along unavailable or in some cases illegal dimensions. Stakeholders, for their part, without an analytical corpus of knowledge to draw upon, struggle to articulate their precise need.

The business decision maker must be involved in the problem framing and push to understand the proposed approach to arrive at a solution. Stakeholders can often recuse themselves from the process, relying solely on the analytics team for creating and executing the solution and not committing the time and resources to support the project from the side of the business. Decision makers need to impress the importance of the project upon the team, to attend all meetings, and to learn enough about the inherent assumptions to be able to point out where one might be invalid or require clarification. Conversely, analytics practitioners need to be comfortable asking stakeholders pointed questions to be able to understand the problem and be able to frame it analytically. There are several aspects that may not have been considered by the business leaders (Davenport & Kim, 2013):

Data   What is the source of the data? Have there been any quality issues identified? Has there been any transformations applied?

Statistical   Is the sample representative? What is the impact of outliers? What conditions make it invalid? Is this correlation or causation?

Procedural   Have other nonanalytical approaches been considered? If they were rejected, why?

The solution must be contextualized to both the organization and the individual. Actuaries, engineers, and other highly skilled professions tend to be averse to innovation and have little exposure to business functions (McQueen, 1985). In contrast, marketing and technical functions tend to be more open to creative approaches, more collaborative, and more accepting of uncertainty. Regardless of the veracity of the model, if it is not accepted or trusted by the department sponsor it will not be implemented, and a poorly performing model is always preferable to an excellent but inoperable model. Similarly, the solution needs to be interoperable with the technical framework that is available and able to be maintained with a minimum of manual processing.

Scoping and Requirements Definition

Prior to planning the execution of a project, it is essential that the problem being addressed is deeply understood and is appropriate for an analytical solution.

Design Thinking

There is an adage in marketing that nobody needs a quarter-inch drill bit, what they want is a quarter-inch hole. Understanding that underlying and implicit need is essential to creating and executing a meaningful project. For analytics professionals who generally exist in a world parallel to the business and have few opportunities to develop a deep knowledge of any one division, understanding to any depth the motivations and limitations of stakeholders can be difficult.

Design thinking seeks to obviate these challenges by employing contextually new principles of solution development. Design thinking originated in the 1950s as a mental shift from finding customers for your product to developing products for your customers. This shift toward human-centered design was a new way of thinking about product development and ultimately sought to remove preconceptions of what the product should be and focus instead on what the end user wants. This small but revolutionary paradigm switch was adopted in the business world as a new decision-making framework and in the technology space as new fields in customer experience, user interface design, information architecture, and so on.

The philosophy of user-centric design or design thinking is most effective in scenarios requiring collaboration between mutually uninformed groups. The developers behind MS-DOS and classic MacOS likely had similar capabilities, but the products they created varied greatly based on the needs of the users. MS-DOS was created for people who liked computers, while classic MacOS was created for people who just wanted to use their computers. In a similar way, the understanding of the desired outcome is an integral step in forming an analytics project that truly adds value and is ultimately pleasing and usable for the stakeholder.

Design thinking follows a formalized process regardless of the domain or industry. This process can be adapted as needed, but in general the process in an analytical context is as follows:

Determine Personas   Develop a depersonalized archetype of the end users, including those who generate, manipulate, and consume the final output. Understand the capabilities, limitations, and priorities of the personas.

Empathize   Understand at a personal level what problem the persona is facing and why it is important to them that it be solved. Set aside all assumptions and approach the engagement as an uninformed outsider. Consider questions such as these: What outcome are they hoping to achieve? What have they been doing about the problem until now? What are the process, technology and data constraints? What are their personal motivations? How often is the problem faced? What is the potential value of the fix? Who initiated the request? How urgent is this? Consider using an empathy map and record specifically what the stakeholder said, felt, thought, and did.

Define   Using everything that was learned in the empathize stage, define the problem statement. This should not be a broad goal such as improved operational forecasting, but specific and human goals such as helping to reduce uncertainty in staffing levels. This problem statement should be played back to the stakeholder along with all caveats and limitations discovered during the empathize stage.

Ideate   During a facilitated session between individuals from the analytics team and from the stakeholder's team, brainstorm on ideas for addressing the problem statement. Encourage both sides to start from a blank slate, and look for solutions that are novel and avoid exclusively incremental quality of life improvements that build off existing tools. There is a common issue at this stage where groups will focus on technical solutions. As assumptions on the solution arise, redirect the group to the problem statement and encourage people to reflect on the outcome and to work backward to a solution. The goal during the ideation phase should be breadth and not depth. Several ideation frameworks can be leveraged for this, including morphological analysis, SCAMPER, and crazy eights (Cotton, 2016).

Evaluate   Consider each of the ideas against the caveats and limitations and discuss from a business and analytics perspective how each would be developed, implemented, operationalized, and maintained. Select those top few solutions that have a balance between efficacy, operationalizability, and time to value for rapid prototyping.

Prototype   Derive wireframes, minimum viable products, or mock-ups for each top solution. In partnership with individuals from the business, create a conceptual end product including all data flows, business processes, algorithms, and future accountabilities in a high-level flowchart.

Test   As with the empathize stage, present the problem statement and prototypes to the stakeholder as well as individuals on their team who would be responsible for implementing and maintaining the solution. Quickly remove any prototype that does not solve the original problem. Iterate, adapt based on feedback, and refine the solution.

Implement   Once the ideal solution arises, create a fulsome project plan to develop and launch an operationalizable version of the prototype

Involving the stakeholder, their team, and front-line people in the design phase of a project ensures that the solution they will be accountable for maintaining will be positively received and will take into consideration any operational constraints. This reduces the potential for issues throughout the project, improves relationships, and leads to less risk in the change management stage.

Design thinking requires skills that are often underdeveloped in analytics professionals, including facilitation, ideation, and visualization. There can also often be resistance to these sessions, which are seen as superfluous by more logical practitioners. Detractors warm to the idea quickly if they are encouraged to participate, as the insights gathered in these sessions are invaluable in developing a solution. Formal requirement gathering invariably misses key elements, and stakeholders are often unaware of how their unstated assumptions can impact an analytics project. Facilitated sessions with everybody in the same room allows for a depth of understanding that simply cannot be achieved any other way.

Regulatory

In most jurisdictions and industries, the limits on model complexity are enacted by internal convention and stakeholder comfort. If they are governed by best practices and a general philosophy of parsimony, this allows the function to apply the best approaches and algorithms for the task. In the financial services industry, however, and increasingly other high-impact arenas, models are required to meet criteria of transparency and explainability.

For example, in the United States, under the Equal Credit Opportunity Act, creditors are required to notify applicants of the rationale behind declining applications:

---

(2) Statement of specific reasons. The statement of reasons for adverse action required by paragraph (a)(2)(i) of this section **must be specific and indicate the principal reason(s) for the adverse action.** Statements that the adverse action was based on the creditor's internal standards or policies or that the applicant, joint applicant, or similar party failed to achieve a qualifying score on the creditor's credit scoring system are insufficient (Equal Credit Opportunity Act).

Similarly, for customers from Europe, the General Data Protection Regulation (GDPR) states that

---

1. The data subject shall have the right not to be subject to a decision based solely on automated processing, including profiling, which produces legal effects concerning him or her or similarly significantly affects him or her. (EU GDPR, n.d.)

In practice this means that any analytics project that involves credit decisions has a high standard to meet in terms of explainability, and the function must be capable of identifying, at an individual level, the features and criteria that have led to a decision. In the case of GDPR, the standard is even higher, and fully automated decision making is disallowed in cases where it may have a significant effect on the impacted person's livelihood, health, or reputation.

At first glance this can appear an onerous burden for an organization to bear. In the interest of avoiding ambiguity, analytics practitioners had until recently limited their toolkit to the most elementary models to avoid any legal exposure. This ensured that auditors and regulators are familiar and comfortable with the techniques being deployed in these sensitive areas. Recently, however, tools such as SHAP and LIME have been gaining traction and allow for the use of more sophisticated models while retaining transparency.

Many stakeholders, especially those in highly specialized and technical areas such as engineers and actuaries, have an aversion to using novel and nondeterministic approaches to solving problems. These professionals can have in particular great difficulty in accepting black box solutions, regardless of the potential business value they may offer. The lessons learned around explainability as a regulatory requirement can be redeployed to garner support and provide confidence to these colleagues.

Regulatory requirements are, at present, a concern for a subset of practitioners. As automated decisions based on machine learning algorithms become more impactful in people's lives, it is likely that the number of industries subjected to this standard will increase. Familiarity with the methodologies that facilitate this transparency can both prepare a team for future regulatory changes and give them the tools to better describe their output to stakeholders.

Operationalization

One of the best pieces of advice to both novice and experienced data scientists is to always consider the last mile because often your stakeholders have not. Whether it is an attrition model, an attribution model, or a simple regression, it is meant to fill a need and provide value to the organization. Every model not in use, regardless of its splendor, accuracy, and elegance, has been a detriment to the organization that has invested time into its development. Poorly performing models that have been implemented are vastly more valuable than well-performing models that have not been implemented.

Projects should always be formed around a concrete objective, with the end in mind. From inception, each member of the project team and the steering committee should know what the deliverable will be and how it will be implemented. Trying to operationalize a model by shoehorning it into processes and data pipelines that it was not designed for can lead to interoperability problems, a lack of scalability, and long-term maintenance costs. Ensuring that there is a concrete outcome also naturally filters out those projects that are at their core an attempt to statistically justify an extant heuristic. Stakeholders, if pressed to justify a project they would not pay consultants for, will often abandon these low-value projects.

There are several considerations surrounding operationalization that a project team should address prior as part of normal scoping:

Data Pipeline   The interdependent data processing elements, which provide the source data for the asset being developed.

Where does the data come from to feed the model? Does the output need to be redirected to another process? Has this been put through an architectural review? Is it subject to any data governance requirements? Do we understand its lineage? Will it reconcile? Has it been transformed upstream?

Procedural Changes   The impact of the project on the daily operational processes and tasks for people in the organization.

Does this change the daily work for any frontline employees? Does it introduce or remove tasks? Has training been considered? Does it eliminate the need for any other processes? Can we adjust the output so that it does?

Usability   The ease of use and future portability of the proposed output.

Are the results easy to understand? Are they formatted in the most appropriate way? Do they align with existing policies or best practices on formatting and presentation? Can the results be used in other processes without modification? Does it introduce the need for any new tools with the users?

Impacted Stakeholders   Those people who will directly or indirectly be affected by the project.

Has everybody who will be impacted by this project been consulted? Are we aware of all constraints on the output? Does it require formalized change management?

Change Management   The approaches around identifying and implementing changes within an organization.

Have the leaders of all impacted stakeholders been informed and cascaded the messaging to their teams? Has a case for change been established from the perspective of all impacted parties? Has a risk register been compiled?

System Requirements   The technical infrastructure that is needed to support the project.

Can the existing systems support the deliverable? Does it delay existing processes? Do we have adequate disk space and memory to support the deliverable even if demands increase? Does this change the organizational hardware upgrade schedule? Does this introduce any proprietary software that we cannot replace in the future?

Introduced Constraints   The intentional or inadvertent change in operational constraints for a group through the introduction of new artifacts or processes.

Does this change the criticality of any systems or processes? Does this use resources that were scheduled for sunsetting or upgrading?

Introduced Dependencies   The intentional or inadvertent change in dependencies for a group through the introduction of new artifacts or processes.

Will the software or frameworks in use introduce new dependencies in the team? Does it involve new packages or software? Who will be responsible for maintaining and upgrading these frameworks and packages? Which budget will it roll up to?

Maintenance   The assignment of responsibility for the ongoing continuance of the project from a technical perspective.

Who will own the long-term maintenance of the deliverable? Will it need to be refreshed? How much support will be required? Do parameters need to be updated regularly? On what cadence?

Ownership   The assignment of responsibility for the ongoing continuance of the project from a business perspective.

Who will own the long-term development of the result? Where will the requests for changes come from? Who needs to be consulted?

Assumptions   All presuppositions surrounding the project, including conceptual simplifications.

What needs to be true for the operationalization to be carried out? What degree of confidence is there in the simplifications? Is accepted expert opinion available? Is there a cumulative impact of interacting assumptions?

With the exception of independent studies, operationalization is essential to a project having any value to the organization. Analytics teams should never let a desire for a perfect outcome stand in the way of a solution. Confucius said, "Better a diamond with a flaw than a pebble without." Shakespeare: "Striving to be better, oft we mar what is well." The modern equivalent is that one should not let "perfect be the enemy of the good." Great thinkers have opined on this natural human tendency, and analytics leaders should convey this wisdom to their teams.

Being mindful of the last mile can ensure that even an imperfect project can add value and can act as a stopgap until more fulsome solutions can be developed. It is in the end much more straightforward to update a model with existing connectors than it is to develop new connectors for a model created in isolation.

Planning

Once the scope has been defined, and all business requirements understood, an appropriate plan can be designed.

Statement of Work

The statement of work serves as the plan for the project, laying out in detail what is to be done and how it will be achieved. For external engagements, this is a legally binding document and should be exhaustive in both what is in scope and what is not, but for internal clients, its goal should be alignment between the analytics function and the stakeholders; as such it needs to be jointly developed, ensuring that all involved understand the project. The level of detail should be such that it avoids ambiguity but is not arduous. This document includes the following elements:

Summary   One or two sentences that capture the purpose of the project and highlight the value being captured.

Scope   The high-level timelines, deliverables, limitations, and exclusions. For iterative projects, this feature, which will be delivered in future phases, should be specified.

Business Requirements   The ultimate change in capability that will result from the successful execution of the project. The features or functions that need to be implemented in order to enable the stakeholders to achieve their desired outcome.

Technical Requirements   The individual solutions for how each of the project requirements will be satisfied, and the items necessary for successful execution, including environments, software, data, and systems.

Acceptance Criteria   The necessary conditions for the project to be considered successful. Objective criteria such as time-boxing should be used wherever possible rather than a blanket approval by executive sponsor, in particular for projects that have a large modeling component as they can often be indefinitely improved.

Project Team   Named list of those who will be involved in the project, including their roles and responsibilities. For longer-term projects, key persons should have named delegates This may include a RACI but should at a minimum include role descriptions and accountabilities.

Governance   Who has approval authority, and how decisions will be made throughout the project.

Project Plan

The project plan is the method for completing the project, including all items described in the scope of work.

Workstreams / Work Breakdown Structure (WBS)   Each general phase of an analytics project (interviews, data discovery, data preparation, design, modeling, operationalization, handover) should be broken down into discrete pieces of work organized around mutually dependent components. Each workstream should be detailed in the required inputs and outputs, the individuals responsible for execution, and the expected duration.

Schedule   The workstreams are visually organized along a timeline based on their duration in a Gantt chart. Wherever possible, based on resourcing and dependencies, workstreams should be organized in parallel.

Milestones   Important achievements in the project life cycle, including high-priority tasks, checkpoints, or deliverables. These milestones serve as performance targets throughout the project.

Deliverables   Specifying at what point the individual deliverables (models, reports, environments, scripts, etc.) will be completed during the project.

Budget

The budget is the overall cost to the organization to undertake the project. Projects supported at an enterprise level tend to have a formal process for establishing and monitoring the budget, but many smaller analytics projects fall outside of the needs of an enterprise PMO. Internally budgeted projects, in particular those reporting to a business line, have the tendency to consider labor a sunk cost and as a result undervalue the time invested in projects. Presenting fully allocated personnel costs in this stage can protect against this and serve to avoid future scope creep. The following items are typically included in the budget:

Costs   All relevant and incremental costs for software, licensing, consultants, contractors, forecasted cloud consumption charges, systems, etc.

Resourcing   Individual forecasts for each workstream by the number of hours per individual involved. This should also include a blanket wage plus fringe estimate of the labor cost involved for the analytics team, all partner functions, decision makers, and technical support in IT, Data Services, and BI.

Maintenance   The ongoing cost associated with upkeep and maintenance of the project or subsequent product. This can include time spent in manual processes, cloud usage, storage, BI/IT support, software licensing, etc. For PMO-managed projects, this maintenance is typically separate from the project budget.

Risks and Limitations

The risks and limitations are potential issues that could arise, which would negatively affect the project as well as how the risks will be dealt with. This should be collaboratively developed with all involved stakeholders and IT/BI. Executive sponsors should be aware of all risks and provide explicit signoff on the risk mitigation plan.

Risk is inherent with any project, and it is essential that the practice and the stakeholders discuss and describe thoroughly all foreseeable environmental changes, market events, technical failures, or personnel changes that could lead to a positive or negative outcome for the project.

As part of a project planning and scoping exercise, every task within the WBS should be discussed from a risk perspective, seeking to exhaustively list the potential events that could impact the project. Developing categories in advance can support this discussion.

Once each risk has been identified, they are evaluated by their impact and likelihood, and once those have been discussed the team determines and documents the mitigation plan for each risk, selecting one of the following responses:

Acceptance   Proceed without modification to the plan, accepting that the low impact or likelihood is such that mitigation is not justified.

Mitigation   Invest resources to prevent the impact or the likelihood of the event.

Transfer   Move the risk to a third party, either through insurance or using contractors and consultants to deliver that item.

Avoidance   Do not execute that part of the project, determining that the likelihood and impact are too great and that the cost of mitigation cannot be justified.

For longer-duration projects, it is also important that the risk management plan be reassessed in light of the current environment. Without revisiting and refreshing the plan, events that have become more impactful or more probable can cause the preferred mitigation approach to change without the awareness of the project team.

Many less-mature analytics functions allocate little time to risk planning, and some no time at all. The lack of a risk mitigation plan is simply the acceptance of all risks, obvious and hidden, and a tacit acceptance of all that entails.

Project Execution

Once a project has been kicked off and is being actively worked on, it should be supported by established analytical processes, guided and governed by the steering committee and working against the statement of work and communication plan. Frameworks should support the engagement, not supplant it; the project team should not lose sight of the ultimate objective of the project. At each step, every individual should look for disconfirming evidence and ask themselves how their assumptions could be biasing their work. Leaders should be actively surveying the organization and the industry and aware of how environmental changes could support or detract from the approach that was originally decided upon. Analytics practitioners, and the experienced leaders on the steering committee, can easily change from objective-based thinking to process-based thinking once a project plan has been developed. Cognitively it is easier to follow instructions than to be actively reassessing.

To facilitate project execution, participants are typically working under an Agile, or hybrid-Agile, methodology (explored in greater detail in this chapter), having the following major components:

Sprint Planning   Sequenced epics or workstreams are broken into discrete tasks and assigned to individual practitioners for a period of days or weeks, depending on sizing (e.g., T-shirt sizing or planning poker), dependencies, and the successful completion of the previous sprint. Individual project leaders typically coordinate priorities with analytics functional leadership, who serves as the scrum master and reviews the sprint plan at the opening of each new sprint. This gives the team a shared understanding of what they will work on for that sprint and a high-level plan on how they will approach the work. As a general rule for the depth of planning required, *The Scrum Guide* advises that a month-long sprint should be planned within eight hours, while a one- to two-week sprint should be completed within one to two hours (Schwaber & Sutherland, 2017), with the general rule that one hour per sprint-week be allocated.

One of the guiding principles of Agile (specifically Scrum) is the relative autonomy of the individual practitioners or squads and their involvement in sprint planning. Because they are closer to the work and end user, they have a better understanding of capabilities and estimates and can pull in their colleagues as required. This empowerment also improves engagement and engenders a sense of accountability.

Sprint Execution   Immediately following the sprint planning session, practitioners self-organize to deliver against the objective for the sprint. During this phase, project and team leaders (and, in some cases, dedicated Scrum Masters) facilitate and remove roadblocks. Product owners or business sponsors should be available to answer questions as required. There are numerous techniques available for organizing subtasks, visualizing progress, which can be leveraged depending on complexity of the sprint/ project, team conventions, and individual disposition. Sprint execution can vary across organizations, but typically follows a PDCA cycle:

1. Plan—Deconstruct individual tasks required to deliver on the larger sprint.

2. Do—Carry out those tasks.

3. Check—Evaluate the results against expectations, or a known source of truth.

4. Adjust—Identify all nonconformities, inefficiencies, or opportunities for improvement. Determine which activities need to be repeated, and which can be deferred to a future phase.

Approval/Communication   As defined in the statement of work, project leaders communicate all results of the sprint to the stakeholders and steering committee. This should include all progress, upcoming activities, and required decisions. Progress against milestones, any required decisions, and any adjustments to the risk register should be included.

Review/Retrospective   Though formally they are different aspects of the Scrum process, sprint reviews and retrospectives can in practice be combined in an analytics delivery model to encourage parsimony. During the review phase, each practitioner reports on what they have accomplished during the sprint, provides observations, and shares outstanding items and roadblocks if appropriate. During the retrospective phase, the sprint itself is assessed, similar to a project-level debrief, with the goal of understanding what went well and what opportunities exist for improvement. Attendance should be encouraged, and active participation rewarded, so as to promote a culture of continuous improvement.

Every project needs to be prioritized on the basis of its value to the organization, but within each project the time spent honing and perfecting models must be evaluated as well. The first day of model tuning is more impactful than the last 10, and the marginal benefit of each additional day of effort should be evaluated against the total backlog of projects, not just the current project. This phenomenon of suboptimization is particularly present in those who have formal training in data science and analytics. When their work is evaluated against statistical metrics, that mindset is carried forward in their view of what success looks like in a corporate setting.

This paradigm of optimization does not sit well with a large proportion of data scientists—in particular those more junior team members who, with the best of intentions, want to produce high-quality work but in practice damage the function. There are a number of practical ways to help these team members to self-govern in regard to evaluating the marginal benefit of continued iterations:

Project Involvement   Ensure that even the junior team members understand the context of the project, including the original request, how the results will be used, and any constraints on the project in terms of deliverables or timelines.

Sensitivity of Results   As part of every project with a measurable output, assess the sensitivity of the results with the stakeholders. If the results were 10 percent more accurate than a baseline, what would be the net impact on revenue, EPS, or cost?

Performance Management   The work of the team, both individually and collectively, has to be assessed in terms of its contribution to the business results. When this is ingrained in each team member, they will naturally gravitate to the work with the highest benefit-cost ratio.

Transparency   Leaders should openly discuss their decision-making process with the team and encourage them to attend decision-making sessions with the steering committee when appropriate. Individual practitioners should have the opportunity to hear directly from the stakeholders what their priorities are.

Governance Structure and Communication Plan

The governance structure and communication plan sets clear guidelines for how information will be shared throughout the project.

The steering committee is a group of senior people, normally assembled for larger or more impactful initiatives, that provide guidance during the life of a project. Typical members include the executive sponsor(s), department sponsor(s), project lead, project manager, and potentially subject matter experts from the organization.

When a line manager in service functions such as human resources or IT loses sight of the end customer, the mission of the organization, or the products that it creates, the result is relatively inconsequential. Likely, if their organization pivoted from consumer retail to pharmaceutical overnight, these functions would be unaware and could continue uninterrupted. The processes, mandates, and daily tasks vary little between companies and between organizations. An analytics team losing this high-level view, however, can be detrimental to the productivity and prioritization of the team. The analytics function can never forget that except in very rare cases, the function of the enterprise is not to sell analytics models—these models are solely in the support of a broader mandate. The presence of a steering committee encourages this higher-level view of the project and encourages coherence.

Projects that cross divisional boundaries and require the collaboration of multiple teams face the challenge of competing priorities and incentives. In a typical analytical engagement, the regulatory department will consider it a success if no privacy laws are violated, the IT group will consider it a success if compliance is maintained, the data services team will consider it a success if the solution uses existing data pipelines, and analytics will consider it a success if the model is highly predictive. Without effective oversight, each of these groups can interpret the project as a success without any actual progress being made toward the stated objective. Establishing a strong steering committee with appropriate representation can ensure that these group-specific priorities are met within the context of the larger project mandate and direct the efforts of the teams toward a common end.

Projects of materiality, especially those requiring the cooperation of multiple teams, need executive sponsorship and departmental oversight to be successful. These groups act as advisory bodies to guide the project and provide decisions and direction on overarching issues such as strategy, interrelationships with parallel initiatives, and budgeting. Though it varies based on the organization, the type of project, and the significance of the project being undertaken, a steering committee for a typical analytics project requires the following key people to be involved:

Executive Sponsor   Ensures that the project is aligned with the overall company strategy and offers support in overcoming resistance from other executives. Typically a senior member of the company, they manage resources and own the results and budget.

Departmental Sponsor   Typically a report of the executive sponsor and leads the group for which the end deliverable is intended. They and their team are most impacted by the results and provide signoff on the results. They provide support and ensure that the goal of the project is maintained.

Technology Representative   Usually a senior manager from IT, BI, or Data Services. They ensure solution compliance and assess the approach from a data and technology perspective.

Project Manager   The project manager leads the meetings, distributes minutes, and provides the agenda and all relevant materials. In collaboration with the project lead, this role facilitates discussions with the stakeholders and monitors and reports on project progress.

Project Lead   The analytics practitioner responsible for the delivery of the project. This person represents the analytics function.

Subject Matter Experts   Senior technical advisors who provide technical information in terms of operationalization or requirements.

Steering committees need to be deployed judiciously so that they find a balance between guidance and overinvolvement. Comprising senior members of the enterprise, each meeting is costly and has the potential to lead to conflict and confusion without the presence of a strong project manager. These steering committee meetings tend to take place at project kickoff, key milestones, and regularly occurring intervals. Meetings that are too frequent can lead to burnout, while those that are too infrequent can lead to misalignment. The ideal interval tends to be between four and six weeks but can vary based on the magnitude of the project and the conventions of the organization.

The agenda for these meetings should be consistent and facilitated by a mature and experienced project manager from the analytics function. Supporting materials and presentations should be presented and circulated among the members in advance. These materials should also be consistent, both within the broader analytics function portfolio of projects and between steering committee meetings for an individual project. Project managers and project leaders should socialize all the content from the agenda with the stakeholders in advance and should not allow any person from the steering committee to be surprised in the meeting or to receive new information there. The meeting should lead to alignment between stakeholders. As another benefit, socializing the content and ensuring that committee members are well informed can prepare the manager for what questions will arise.

Parsimonious preparation of the materials is important. With each topic presented, the project manager needs to consider its relevance from the perspective of the steering committee and present it in a way that is most appropriate given their level of understanding and priorities. Though the project manager and lead need to understand the project in full technical detail, this should be brought up only at the prompting of the committee. Likewise, the planned portion of the agenda should be at an appropriately high level. The following topics are typical of those covered in these meetings:

Progress Update   Where are we currently on the project timeline?

Major Achievements   What milestones have we hit? What successes have we had?

Issues or Changes   Are there any changes to the cost or schedule that need approval? Are there any issues blocking the project?

Next Steps   What are the current and immediate tasks and work-streams? Who is responsible for these?

Decisions   What decisions are needed from the steering committee?

At the conclusion of every meeting, detailed minutes that include outstanding action items, responsible persons, and timelines should be circulated. Maturity and care around these minutes, as well as other supporting materials, improves confidence in the project and the general stakeholder experience and reduces the probability of unexpected requests or scope changes.

One unique characteristic for steering committees on analytical projects is that typically the members have a limited understanding about the practice, and often an implicit distrust. Steering committee members with a high degree of technical expertise, such as actuaries, may in particular want to understand an approach from basic principles. Care must be paid to ensuring that concepts are explained at an appropriate level for the audience.

There are inherent risks involved in having a steering committee. Each presentation is an opportunity for a senior person in the organization to ask a question the team is not prepared for, or a chance for embarrassment. There will be very few meetings, regardless of how much effort is spent in pre-planning and preliminary discussion with stakeholders, that do not have some unforeseen event. The benefits, however, far outweigh the risks. The broader field of view and wealth of experience brought by these senior stakeholders, as well their ability to control resource availability and advocate for cross-functional support, ensures that projects maintain perspective, are delivered effectively, and do not have barriers to implementation that should have been known earlier in the project. Analytics teams should welcome the chance for increased understanding of their practice, and actively seek the feedback and input of others in the organization at all levels.

Project Kickoff

The project kickoff meeting is the official start to the project and often the first time the entire project team will be together. The agenda should be to provide an opportunity for introductions, review the statement of work and schedule, and confirm that everybody understands the expectations around performance and deliverables.

Prior to the kickoff, every individual should be intimately familiar with the project, as most will have been involved in its scoping and planning. There should be no surprises or objectives at this point in the project life cycle. For some projects, there may have even been a "week zero" workstream, and in practice the project is already underway. The main purpose then for these internal project kickoff meetings is social and psychological.

This meeting provides a clear demarcation on when the project begins and aligns with day one on the project plan. It makes clear to all involved that each passing day moves the current date line in the Gantt chart one notch to the right, and there is an expectation of performance. Similar to a football huddle, a pregame speech, or an empowering routine before a speaking engagement, this event should leave participants with a sense of optimistic anticipation.

Given the importance of the meeting and the unique objective, kickoffs should include involvement by somebody with the appropriate disposition and level of authority to get the teams excited about the project. Dry reviews of the already understood statement of work are a missed opportunity. While the project manager or team lead should drive the agenda, it is very beneficial to have either the executive sponsor or a departmental sponsor present to speak to the importance of the project and the benefit to the organization.

Agile Analytics

Agile began in 2001 with the Manifesto for Agile Software Development, a terse yet transformative document that called for a more human way to do development. This manifesto (provided in its entirety below) called for less documentation; less up-front planning; more responsiveness; and a deep, almost singular, focus on user needs. This was revolutionary at the time when traditional multiyear all-or-nothing projects were the norm. This new philosophy and project management approach toward value-focused iterations was applicable to almost all industries. Given its origins in software development, however, a field not generally known for innovative thought in management processes, people were slow to recognize the value that it brings.

The Agile Manifesto

We are uncovering better ways of developing software by doing it and helping others do it. Through this work we have come to value:

      Individuals and interactions over processes and tools

      Working software over comprehensive documentation

      Customer collaboration over contract negotiation

      Responding to change over following a plan

That is, while there is value in the items on the right, we value the items on the left more.

© 2001 Agile Manifesto Authors

This declaration may be freely copied in any form, but only in its entirety through this notice.

Though it began as a new philosophy for software developers, it has expanded into a broader set of tools and processes that are in broad usage in other fields. There are several terms that most practitioners will have heard: *Scrum, Kanban, Scrumban, sprint, stand-up*. These terms often take on different meanings depending on the organization, and as a result the Agile approach to project management is often misunderstood.

Agile was developed in contrast to the traditional waterfall approach, where a project would be broken into discrete and sequential tasks, individually resourced and costed, and executed serially to achieve a single goal. This traditional approach comes from construction and manufacturing, where long detailed plans with a single timeline are developed and changes are expensive, hence there is a need to ensure scope-freeze early in the project. This has the benefit of being reproducible, and it seeks to achieve certainty around scope, budget, timeline, and deliverables, which is essential in physical projects.

For contemporary knowledge workers, however, the traditional waterfall approach simply does not work. The pace of change in analytics is such that through the project life cycle, the best practices and tools available may change, leading to a deliverable that is obsolete before it is even delivered. For a physical project, we can be relatively certain that concrete and steel will be the appropriate building materials once the project is completed, but in data science we cannot be so confident. The second difference is that for an analytics team, deliverables absolutely need to be focused on outcome rather than approach. The ideal path toward achieving this outcome may change through the life of the project as challenger models are developed and as business sponsors are presented with interim results. Last, the nondeterministic nature of data science is such that in an applied setting, there is no singular solution to a problem, there are only algorithmic processes for arriving at a solution, which can and should change over time. This contrasts with the physical deliverables for which waterfall was designed. The deliverable needs to be adaptable, modular, and dynamic—requirements that make Agile methodologies the only realistic approach in most cases.

In *The Age of Agile*, Stephen Denning aptly describes three laws that are necessary for success using Agile methodologies (Denning, 2018):

Law of the Small Team   The use of small teams that are self-governing, work in short cycles, and have fast feedback from the end users or customers.

Law of the Customer   Solutions are designed to the needs of the user, not the other way around.

Law of the Network   Impact increases with penetration. Minimizing the interfaces between Agile groups and the traditional hierarchical groups leads to performance improvements as Agile usage increases.

Agile teams, working in small autonomous squads, reward trust with performance as the bottlenecks surrounding constant leadership input are removed. These teams are able to interface directly with the end user and rapidly move toward a solution within a predetermined procedural framework. Beyond the speed that this autonomy provides, there is a tertiary benefit in that it has the effect of motivating underperforming team members. In traditional hierarchies, performance is managed mainly through the individual's manager, and the visibility into that performance is limited. In Agile teams, with daily standup meetings and peer-to-peer accountability, there is nowhere for underperformers to hide. Self-organizing teams that require the active participation of each member will not abide people shirking their responsibilities and can lead to a quicker resolution.

DevOps is a set of practices that is related to Agile and serves a complementary role in an analytics function. *DevOps*, a portmanteau of *Development* and *Operations*, is a policy of combining software development and IT operations responsibilities within the same group. This provides an environment where there is end-to-end accountability, which leads to an improvement in quality. For analytics practitioners, this is applied by ensuring that the developer of a model or script is responsible for the support. For larger products, new work is shut down if the amount of noncritical bugs reaches a certain level. DataOps, the combination of data engineering and data quality with operations, serves a similar role though is focused more on data provisioning.

Traditional legacy organizations have a deeply embedded command and control mentality, and as such it can be challenging for a single team to lead the change toward a new delivery methodology for the organization as a whole. The Law of the Network shows that the gains are greatest when Agile teams work with other Agile teams. Even though the analytics function, which is typically a shared service, does not have the authority to define operating models for the organization, it is beneficial to operate internally in an Agile manner and to encourage stakeholder teams and teams with whom the analytics team is collaborating to work within this framework for the duration of the project. This can have the impact of increasing the awareness of Agile and planting the seeds for future improvement. Even in the absence of a formal application of Agile approaches, the basic establishment of the ideals of continuous communications, active feedback, and collaboration makes for a much more productive partnership.

Every well-functioning team, with some exaggerated bravado and camaraderie, thinks themselves a cut above other teams within the organization. This pride, directed productively, can be healthy in building a spirit of teamwork and shared purpose. Those teams can work effectively for or alongside other teams with different skillsets and objectives, using a different language and even seeking contradictory goals. As with different tradespeople coming together to construct a house, as long as they are well orchestrated by an experienced and savvy contractor, their differences can become a strength. However, if these groups have different delivery models and attitudes toward decision making, construction will be slow, expensive, and of poor quality. In the same way, if an Agile team is working on a project involving collaboration with multiple traditional command-and-control teams, there will be no benefit to the project and a great deal of friction between the teams. In these cases, analytics leadership should seek the explicit delegation of authority by the partnering team leaders for the routinized portions of the project and for the explicit approval of the scope and approach in advance of the project kickoff. This can go some way toward reducing the time spent in deliberation and awaiting instructions.

There are innumerable Agile accreditations, books, courses, and derivatives, but it is worth recalling that it all comes from only four precepts. Though it is certainly beneficial to explore Scrum, Kanban, and other Agile solutions, any analytics function can benefit simply by basing priorities and decision making on these elements.

Change and Stakeholder Management

Data science projects often introduce new processes or ways of thinking about problems, and often for individuals or teams who have little familiarity with data science and analytics. Stakeholders must be supported at each stage of the project life cycle in order to gain buy-in and for the project to be successful.

Skeuomorphs

One of the best approaches to minimizing apprehension and making a new approach more amenable to stakeholders is by keeping all the tertiary elements the same and reducing the outward appearance of change. This concept of skeuomorphism, from the Greek *skeuos* for tool and *morphê* for shape, comes from the user design philosophy of maintaining traditional design elements to improve user acceptance and adoption.

The resistance of impacted stakeholders when presenting or deploying an analytical solution can be easily empathized with at an individual level. The processes and approaches that the business leader has relied on and in some cases implemented themselves are being changed by people who do not share their expertise, background, or personal motivations. Even the more progressive business leaders will want to have a significant level of understanding before they approve changes.

The amount of time and effort that will be dedicated to ensuring this understanding is a nonlinear function of the change in sophistication in methodology. The greater the change in solution complexity, the more difficulty stakeholders will have in accepting those changes. For example, adjusting lapse predictions from historical averages to a single-factor linear regression may require no additional explanation, whereas advancing directly into a more sophisticated gradient-boosting approach could cause the project to stagnate due to a lack of understanding and trust. Analytics practitioners must be able to find a balance between using the most effective technique while making sure it gets the approval from the project sponsor. Some examples of skeuomorphs include the sound of a digital camera used on a smartphone, the icon of a floppy disk to represent file saving, the page-turning animation on modern e-readers, or even nonfunctional shutters as an architectural feature on modern windows. All of these elements are unnecessary, but by giving the user a feeling of safety and familiarity, they engender positive feelings and encourage adoption.

For analytics teams, this could mean maintaining existing reports and simply replacing the algorithm that generates the results. It could also mean adapting existing user interfaces to work with new processes or labeling metrics in a more familiar way. The fewer changes that the user needs to accept, the more willing they are to accept larger changes. By ensuring that the tertiary elements are familiar to the user, there will generally be more leeway to use more sophisticated models.

AI 101 and Project Brainstorming

Donald Rumsfeld said, in a remark that came to be his most famous, "As we know, there are known knowns; there are things we know we know. We also know there are known unknowns; that is to say we know there are some things we do not know. But there are also unknown unknowns—the ones that we don't know we don't know" (Defense. gov, 2003). For most business professionals, analytics represents an unknown unknown. There is a loose awareness that data science is a field of practice but no knowledge of what the function actually does. When they then have the opportunity to collaborate with these teams, there is not the mutual understanding necessary for it to be an effective exchange. Like a ferrier soliciting the support of a mechanical engineer, requests are constrictive, misguided, and biased by perspective and lived experience. The requests tend to be either overly simplistic, as in the development of retrospective reports, or sweetly misguided, such as using reinforcement learning to automate budgeting.

AI 101 and project brainstorming is a structured approach for giving stakeholders in the organization a rudimentary knowledge of data science and analytics so that they can identify opportunities that are suited to an analytical solution and making it a known unknown. The intention is not to provide a thorough education in programming or statistics but to present broadly applicable use cases and an overview of general approaches. This provides the stakeholders with the base understanding and vocabulary necessary to craft requests and effectively ideate.

These sessions are typically two- to three-hour facilitated and highly interactive discussions with first- and second-level managers as well as representative individual contributors. The typical agenda varies depending on industry and level of interest but generally includes the following elements:

Introduction   Set expectations for the session and introduce the attendees.

What Do You Do   Discuss, at a tactical level, what the recurring deliverables, activities, and expectations on the team are. This should not be aspirational or strategic, but concrete daily tasks. Avoid framing the section in such a way as to elicit defensiveness but rather to understand what the critical activities are.

How Do You Do It   Discuss the approach that the team takes and all of the dependencies. Understand the tools involved, the amount of manual intervention, how decisions are made, and who the consumer of their outputs is. Develop conceptual flowcharts to guide the discussion.

Art of the Possible   Present two or three use cases from the appropriate function to highlight successes that other organizations have had leveraging analytics. Use primarily examples from other industries that do not elicit defensiveness or a comparison to competitors.

Identify Opportunities   Review the flowchart and earlier discussions and solicit input from the attendees on where opportunities exist for using analytics. Using any brainstorming methodology, seek to identify as many as possible.

Proof of Concept (POC) Identification   Together, select one or two of the possible projects that have the highest chance of success and a material benefit.

Closing   Plan on follow-up meetings to scope the POCs that have been selected and set a regular cadence with the functional leadership and the more enthusiastic attendees.

It is important to frame the discussion in such a way that it is the analytics team providing information to the business unit and not the reverse. Information gathering on the part of the analytics team should be done in advance to curate relevant use cases, to understand the function, and to understand their role in the organization. The underlying goal needs to be edification and building excitement around the potential applications for analytics. Selecting POCs with a high probability of success cements that enthusiasm and helps to develop analytics champions within the organization.

This is beneficial for the analytics function primarily because it builds cross-functional relationships and establishes the analytics team as the source of data science expertise that is important for controlling the narrative around analytics in the organization. The POCs selected at this stage are typically low-value projects, but they are necessary for the long-term successful collaborative relationship with the business unit. What is often more valuable is the list of rejected ideas created during the opportunity identification part of the session, which during an internal debrief can be whittled to a few potential high-value projects to be pursued once the team is ready.

These sessions require a lot of up-front work to be effective, which invariably takes attention away from in-flight projects. Facilitating discussions and prolonged interactive workshops is also not typically within the skillset of analytics professionals. For these and many other reasons, sessions such as these are often overlooked, with the unspoken hope that senior leadership will take care of all advocacy work. This is a missed opportunity, as most of the automatable tasks exist at the workface. Frontline employees and individual contributors know firsthand what repetitive work they do and are a wealth of information for automation opportunities. Similarly, first- and second-level managers are often tasked with making tactical business decisions guided by well-understood logic—scenarios that are well suited for prescriptive modeling. The projects identified in these sessions have a high likelihood of success and a high likelihood of employee buy-in and provide the analytics team quick wins, insight into longer-term bold plays, and stronger relationships with business stakeholders.

Iterative Insights

When data science and analytics was in its infancy, it borrowed heavily from the processes of its two main predecessors, operations research and statistics. These highly research-focused, and academic forebears relied on a "collect, analyze, and report" structure. In the beginning, this approach made a lot of sense.

The problems that data science or advanced analytics teams were tasked with solving originally were typically deterministic and numerical. For example, the analytics team at a real estate investment trust (REIT) may be asked to determine which locations will have the highest rent growth in the future. The team would gather relevant internal and external data, work (normally in isolation) on models that would provide the highest predictive values, and report back to the project sponsor on which locations they should focus on. If particularly novel, the approach may be shared in an academic journal or at an industry conference.

This approach is largely obsolete in the face of more dynamic techniques that deliver a highly reduced time to value and integrate into existing workflows. Considering the REIT example, by the time the report has been delivered, it is based on months-old historical data and is likely answering a question that the sponsor has moved on from. At best, it serves to confirm a decision that was already made and acts as a gut check.

The analytics function has moved in terms of approach from its operations research ancestors to Agile principles. Analytics needs to be an iterative process, delivering a minimum viable product as quickly as possible and building subsequent features into the product in order of stakeholder priority.

Using the REIT example, a hypothetical modern team would first build connections between a geographic information system (GIS) and the enterprise resource planning software to ingest current and historic rent data to provide a real-time summary of current trends to the stakeholder. Using exogenous data sets, acquired through an operationalized web scraper or API, a ranked feature list can be added in a subsequent phase to show in real time what the current drivers of rent growth are. Using externally generated socioeconomic data sets, projections of growth as a function of population flows can be developed and linked to external government forecasts. At each phase, the product is improved, pushed to production, and shared with stakeholders. Stakeholders in kind can influence the direction of the product as their priorities and vision change.

The archaic approach of working in isolation provides a high-quality, well-considered, and defensible response, but it is to a question that is no longer relevant due to either stale data, changes in underlying assumptions, or stakeholder interest.

Iterative thinking is a challenging transition for new practitioners because it is in direct opposition to the formal training process. In university, courses provide a question, a clean data set, and a deadline. In practice, the question changes, the data is anything but clean, and the deadline was yesterday. Building this capacity for pace in a team is essential to a modern analytics function.

Closeout and Delivery

The final phase of a project is the formal recognition of its completion, and the transition of all project documentation and deliverables to the business sponsors. This should not be considered simply a project management formality but rather a crucial process from a professional and psychological perspective to ensure that all loose ends are tied up, all deliverables in the statement of work have been addressed, all processes have been documented, and the receiving team is ready and able to accept and use the results of the project.

Depending on the nature of the project, there are four key ways that closeout and delivery are handled:

Model Operationalization   For pure data science projects with a resulting model, that deliverable should be live in a production environment and integrated with existing business processes. The maintenance of that model should be planned for and any subsequent phases or features developed. Accountability for all aspects of the model needs to be documented and understood.

Process Operationalization   For projects that have led to a change in existing business processes or introduced a new process, a change management plan needs to be in place, which is developed in partnership with the business and the analytics function. Regular reviews of the process for compliance and effectiveness need to be in place. If the process is to be run in parallel with a legacy process for a time, there needs to be a firm decision date for the sunsetting of the existing process and a plan for switchover.

Product Transition   This includes those projects that constitute a new product for the business, such as a predictive model, or a script that cannot be automated, or a customer-facing tool. These products require long-term ongoing maintenance and monitoring. During project closeout, a product governance team that includes representation from the business and data science and analytics needs to be in place. Next steps and opportunities identified during the project should be included in a formal feature backlog.

Presentation   For those projects that can be classified as an ad hoc study, the final delivery is usually in the form of a document or presentation.

The final presentation should not be a retelling of what happened, simply recounting the sequence of activities. Rather, using high-quality visualizations, and with a perspective of a storyteller, share the value that was captured and work backward through the project, considering always the priorities and motivations of the sponsor (Davenport & Kim, 2013). People are rarely inspired by statistical metrics and documented evidence of completion. Speak instead to the business value that has been created and how it will personally impact those that are receiving the work.

With the delivery of the project, the project is formally marked as completed. Immature analytics teams can often neglect the closing of a project, even going so far as to not inform the stakeholders that the project is done. This has the effect of leaving the door open to unexpected iterations and requests for projects that have been effectively closed out and can impact future schedules for the team.

Most projects will involve some aspect of training that will allow the recipients and their teams the use of the created deliverables. This training should, wherever possible, be in the form of a "train the trainer" session, including detailed documentation, a frequently asked questions document, and a trainer presentation. Without fully transferring ownership over training to the recipient business unit, the analytics function can find themselves in a position of supporting learning and development of analysts throughout the business for numerous projects, which can become burdensome over time.

Finally, for those projects that are part of a larger overarching transformation goal, governing roadmaps should be updated to incorporate learnings and update any estimates regarding timelines. Typically the executive sponsor will also be the sponsor of the larger transformation, and the project closeout provides an opportunity for planning and soliciting involvement in the next phase.

Automation

At the conclusion of each project that has an operationalized outcome, a decision needs to be made as to how much of the business process can or should be automated. Opinions vary between the authoritarian position of automating all aspects of a model to the more laissez-faire position of casually resolving to revisit a process if it becomes necessary. There are reasons for and against each approach, which can either support or hinder the adoption and ultimate success of a project.

The key consideration is what Marc Vollenweider (2016) calls the efficiency frontier of automation. Each project will have an optimal combination of automation and manual intervention, which will provide the most efficient long-term solution. Depending entirely on automation can create a process without safeguards, while depending entirely on analysts to perform rote tasks increases costs and opens the door to human error.

Many groups, in an effort to establish systematic and objective criteria for automation, make the decision based on what amounts to a net present value of time calculation. The time savings created through automation needs to be greater than the time invested in automation. Though on the surface it is a perfectly logical and consistent approach, this ignores several less tangible considerations. The creation of a decision model around automation needs to include the following:

Human Error   Every human touchpoint, such as moving files, copying and pasting cells, and updating parameters, is an opportunity for error. Without exacting peer review, these errors are difficult to detect and debug.

Support Cost   Human touchpoints have an associated labor cost. Even though the marginal cost of a minor process can seem low, these support tasks can quickly consume the time and productivity of a team. Documentation, cross-training, after-hours support, mobilization, technical limitations, file transfers, and Internet connectivity can all add to the true cost of ongoing support.

Resilience   For processes with multiple potential failure points, developing a programmatic solution that can tolerate and adapt to these failures can be challenging. Processes tend to find new and interesting ways to fail that had not been considered by the project team. Embedding resilience against these one-off failures creates a patchwork solution that needs to be holistically reviewed over time.

Auditability   Real-time evaluation of the results of fully automated and operationalized processes can only be done if exceptions can be defined in advance. The criteria that identified a result as an exception changes over time and imposes the need for recurring reviews.

Stakeholder Comfort   In the early developmental stages of a data science and analytics team, there may be fundamental distrust or discomfort with automation. Stakeholders may be more comfortable with a "human in the loop" business process requiring the step-by-step validation of interim results. Staggered deployments that take into account the characteristics of the people involved will be far more successful in the long term, regardless of short-term additional validation work.

Deliverables and routinized processes that have been purpose-built for automation are much more straightforward to automate than those meant to simulate the existing processes. For example, the use of robotic process automation to simulate interactions with a website by a stakeholder group can in most cases be replaced with application programming interface calls or direct web requests.

As it is normally the last step, automation can be rushed without the care given to other parts of the project. Automation should be planned for from the beginnings of a project and discussed with all of those involved. This includes the amount of automation that will be completed and the associated risks and limitations. Including features in a model that introduce an external dependency and require sensitive web scraping, for example, may not be justified and can require a more easily acquired set of inputs.

Project Debrief

Debriefs, separate from the post-sprint retrospectives that are often completed in Agile project execution, are an opportunity after the delivery of a project to consider and discuss the successes and failures that were experienced. Debriefs are one of the first things to be eliminated when a team is pressed for time. This is unfortunate, because without intentional reflection informed by stakeholder feedback, there is no way for a team to improve. Individuals, often fearful of criticism or of drawing negative attention after a failed project, can find reasons to put it to bed and move on to the next project. Reframing these often stressful meetings into a positive chance for personal growth and encouraging participation can have lasting benefits for everybody involved. Debriefs are an integral part of the project life cycle and are absolutely essential to a well-run analytics team.

The structuring of a typical analytics project debrief has the following steps:

Solicit Feedback   As a service function, analytics needs to ensure that stakeholders are getting what they need in terms of deliverables and communication. All processes need to be grounded in business outcomes, and those need to be informed by the stakeholders. Prior to a debrief, leaders should connect with the executive sponsor, department leads, and all individuals who worked with the team to understand their overall perspective and evaluate it alongside feedback received during steering committee meetings and sprint retrospectives. Stakeholders should not be invited to the debrief session. Often, if the individuals work closely, the stakeholders will be hesitant to be critical in front of their colleagues, and opportunities for improvement can be glossed over to spare feelings or be polite. Here are some beneficial questions for the project sponsors:

- Apart from the project objective, what was your personal desired outcome?
- Was this achieved? If not, what was missing?
- Were you confident in the success of the project at the beginning? Throughout the process?
- Was the level of communication adequate? Why or why not?
- Can you offer any advice for personal improvement for the people on the project team?
- Can you provide comments on the quality and timeliness of the deliverables?
- Is there anything you wish had been done differently?

Aggregate Uncover issues and themes from the feedback sessions, and consider the perspectives of those involved. If a stakeholder did not receive the outcome they wanted, highlight that as a communication and stakeholder management gap, not a technical fault. Ensure that feedback is kept anonymous and not read directly, as it can devolve the session into a guessing game.

Prepare Questions Even after participating in dozens of debrief sessions, individuals will still enter the meeting with a sense of apprehension. Preparing open-ended and leading questions in advance can help to stimulate conversation. For more taciturn team members, it can be helpful to have specific questions prepared on their parts of the project. The following general questions can guide the discussion:

- Were there any risks or dependencies that came up through the course of the project that we did not originally identify? If so, how could we have foreseen them?

- How were the sponsors to work with? What can we learn for future projects with them? What did we learn about their communication preferences? What did we learn about their priorities?

- How were the individual contributors within the sponsors team? Did we identify any people who are passionate about analytics in the business?

- Did we identify any other potential projects?

- How did the team work together internally? Externally?

- Were there any scope changes that we should have foreseen?

- Were the instructions always clear?

- Were there any organizational or political barriers? Did we identify any active analytical detractors?

- Was our toolkit effective?

- Do we expect adoption challenges? How can we support this going forward?

- Did you feel included in the project? Did you feel ownership? This should be included in personal conversations as well.

- Was the business project team responsive? Were decision makers available?

- Were you able to allocate the required time to the project? Were there external factors or ad hoc requests that took your attention away?

- Did you take advantage of opportunities for relationship building?

- Were the presentations and deliverables well received?

- Was this a personally gratifying project?

Opening   Sessions should begin positively, as a fraternal gathering to celebrate and reflect on a completed project. Participants should be reminded that the purpose of the meeting is to become stronger, and that all statements should begin with "we" to avoid the assignment of blame. Following, review the original purpose of the project, and provide a brief summary of the timeline with dates and major milestones or scope changes. Every success should be highlighted, with individual recognition given to prevent defensive posturing.

Round Table   There are three primary questions that need to be answered in a debrief session. What went well? What went poorly?

And what would we have done differently? For each of the major themes, ask each participant individually for their perspective. Leaders should be prepared to lead the conversation and to redirect if the tone becomes negative, but do not avoid drama. Leaders need to actively mine conflict to get the team interested and to see the threats as personal (Lencioni, 2004). Do not accept superficial responses, and seek to find the underlying causes to issues. After the three primary questions have been answered, and the project-specific questions have been addressed, share the stakeholder feedback with the team. Ask if this changes their perspective of the project performance and give individuals a chance to refute any criticisms while encouraging the team to respect different perspectives.

Closing   Properly run debrief sessions should end with a feeling of catharsis. Remind the team of the successes in spite of the challenges, and resolve together to meet the next project better prepared and informed. Call out the individuals who participated the most, and recognize that while it is an uncomfortable session, it is one that's necessary for personal growth and for the improvement of the team. For larger projects, this can be a good opportunity to treat the team to lunch.

Communicate   The larger team should be informed on the outcome and learnings from every debrief. Brief bullet points on each of the three key questions as well as the goal of the project should be shared.

One of the most powerful questions that can be asked in a debriefing session is, If you had to redo the project, knowing what you know now, how long would it have taken you? This question stimulates conversation about what led to delays in the project and will uncover misses by the team. By their nature, analytical projects are iterative and will have a meandering path toward completion. In retrospect, the path will appear much more straightforward than it actually was. No project will ever achieve this perfect path, but reflecting on how it could have been achieved in retrospect highlights what can be done in the future to get closer to that path.

There are several psychological benefits to debriefs. As these sessions become second nature, team members will be more likely to evaluate their decisions and justifications in real time. People tend to choose the nearer good over the more valuable one. Knowing that their approaches and decisions will be discussed and challenged can help individuals to become more mindful as they try to determine the root cause of project issues in the moment. This can create a more responsive and emotionally intelligent team that is able to empathize with the stakeholder. Additionally, having the formal opportunity to discuss challenges they faced on a project prevents the buildup of negativity and gives an outlet for frustration.

The key tangible outcome to strive for, however, is actionable insights. As the narrative of the project unfolds through the comments of the stakeholders and the experiences of the team and with the oversight of the leader, opportunities for changes in process should become clear. This opportunity may be as small as a preference for face-to-face communication from a certain sponsor or as large as the need for specific training. Gleaning these insights needs to be a goal for the session.

Done well, debriefs have a transformative effect on analytics teams and on their relationships with stakeholders. It stimulates positivity and creates a mindset of continuous improvement.

Summary

The clearest evidence of the benefits of standardized processes can be seen in data science and analytics teams that lack this standardization. Practitioners flounder, reacting to requests for information, while deadlines slip, scope changes, and deliverables are inconsistent. Stakeholders eventually get what they wanted, but the path is long and arduous. Both parties leave the exchange feeling stressed. Future initiatives are derailed by support requests and ad hoc changes, the cascading impact of which leads to a huge burden of maintenance duties. Engagement drops, and future hires are tasked with maintaining a shoddy patchwork of models and routinized activities, which hinders any success they may have otherwise had.

In the alternative scenario, practitioners and stakeholders alike know at each stage what to expect, what is expected, and how to manage their interactions. Rather than responding to requests for impromptu status updates, the team can focus on their primary analytical activities. The removal of ambiguity improves cognitive fluency, and the team is more productive and engaged. Stakeholders are similarly confident that interactions are following a predefined and agreed upon delivery model and leave the engagement satisfied with the result.

Strategy defines the *what* of the analytics team—a goal and a set of guiding principles on how to achieve that goal. Process defines the *how*—the behaviors and activities of the team in the execution and delivery of projects. The most important component of data science and analytics teams, however, is the *who*. Strategy and process support and enable the team, but the team comprises individuals, and the ultimate success of the team is determined by the people.

References

Cotton, D. (2016). *The smart solution book: 68 tools for brainstorming, problem solving, and decision making.* FT Press.

Davenport, T., & Kim, J. (2013). *Keeping up with the quants: Your guide to understanding and using analytics.* Harvard Business School.

Defense.gov. (2003, Nov. 6). *News transcript: DoD news briefing—Secretary Rumsfeld and Gen. Myers, United States Department of Defense.* Retrieved from www.globalsecurity.org/military/library/news/2003/11/mil-031106-dod01.htm

Denning, S. (2018). *The age of Agile: How smart companies are transforming the way work gets done.* AMACOM.

Equal Credit Opportunity Act (Regulation B of the Code of Federal Regulations), Title 12, Chapter X, Part 1002, §1002.9.

EU GDPR. (n.d.). *Article 22 Automated individual decision-making, including profiling.* Retrieved from www.privacy-regulation.eu/en/22.htm

Lencioni, P. (2004). *Death by meeting: A leadership fable.* Jossey-Bass.

Manifesto for Agile Software Development. (2001). Retrieved from https://agilemanifesto.org

McAfee, A., & Brynjolfsson, E. (2017). *Machine, platform, crowd: Harnessing our digital future.* W. W. Norton.

McQueen, R. (1985). *Risky business: Inside Canada's $86-billion insurance industry.* Macmillan.

Project Management Institute. (2006). *The standard for portfolio management.* Author.

Project Management Institute. (2008). *A guide to the project management body of knowledge* (4th ed.). Author.

Schumpeter, J. A. (1983). *Theory of economic development.* Transaction.

Schwaber, K., & Sutherland, J. (2017). *The scrum guide.* Retrieved from www.scrumguides.org/docs/scrumguide/v2017/2017-Scrum-Guide-US.pdf

Taylor, F. W. (2006). *The Principles of scientific management.* New York: Cosimo.

Vollenweider, M. (2016). *Mind+machine: A decision model for optimizing and implementing analytics.* Wiley.

Zajonc, R. B. (1980). Feeling and thinking: Preferences need no inferences. *American Psychologist, 35,* 151–175.

People

How to structure and engage a team, establish productive and parsimonious conventions, and lead a distinct practice with unique requirements.

Strategies and processes, no matter how expertly devised and deployed, live or die on the strength and abilities of the people on the team. This fact may not be immediately evident to those more technically minded individuals who, through education or predisposition, favor and focus on the solution rather than the problem. It is human ingenuity and collaboration that creates value—never tools and data. The latest deep learning approach running on the most powerful GPU cluster means nothing if it is not directed toward a productive end. Colin Powell (2006) said, "Organization doesn't really accomplish anything. Plans don't accomplish anything, either. Theories of management don't much matter. Endeavors succeed or fail because of the people involved. Only by attracting the best people will you accomplish great deeds." All other considerations are constructs designed to support and enable the work that people are doing for other people.

In analytics groups tuned for performance above all else, unrelenting mechanistic production only serves to alienate the practitioner from their work, exploiting them as a resource, eliminating any sense of fulfillment, and causing them to lose any authentic ambition and creativity they once had. Regardless of salary, benefits, environment, or other enticements, any productivity gained through optimization at the expense of people will be short lived. Curious, adaptable, and passionate people, given the proper tools and supported by a genuinely caring manager who provides oversight and guidance in terms of process and strategy, can have resounding success. Conversely, strict legalistic adherence to process and a domineering strategy of talent extraction over a group of depersonalized automatons is bound for failure. While strategy and process are important enablers, it is the people that make or break an analytics team.

Analytics teams that have evolved naturally without a formal strategy can still add value to the organization. Though they may be reactive and lack vision, they can still execute on moderately sized medium-term projects. Similarly, without consistent processes, they can still deliver on projects, though inconsistently and with much pain. However, without the right people in place, no analytics team can be successful. The establishment of an analytics culture, intentional relationship building, and the hiring of qualified and passionate people is essential to an analytics function and needs to be the primary consideration of any leader. Everything the team does starts and ends with the people.

This chapter is organized across two primary topics: building teams and leading teams. These represent the outward considerations of a leader, such as hiring and succession planning, and the inward considerations, such as team conventions and managing conflict.

Building the Team

In most cases, the hiring of people for certain roles is a matter of confirming technical proficiency, assessing their work ethic, evaluating whether their personality is a fit with the culture of the team and organization, and ranking them against a pool of those who happened to apply. As long as the individual has demonstrable skills, this line of thinking goes, they will be able to perform the job. Carpenters can build, accountants can account, and engineers can design. For less analytically mature organizations, this reasoning is usually extended to the data science space, and job descriptions and success criteria are crafted that seek out the most gifted academics, broadly experienced in natural language processing, neural networks, computer vision, GANs, reinforcement learning, big data, TensorFlow, NoSQL, and so on. The inevitable outcome of staffing analytics teams within a traditional organization entirely with deep academic data science skills is clear—disengaged practitioners and an unfulfilled mandate.

Having a true understanding of the daily activities and responsibilities of a data scientist, and the underlying characteristics of a successful practitioner, is necessary to developing job descriptions and success profiles that ensure that the best possible talent is onboarded. Deciding who to bring onto the analytics team is one of the more impactful decisions a leader will make. Every person represents the team—all of their successes and failures are shared by their peers and their leader. Every individual that joins the team also influences it by diluting or reinforcing key characteristics of the group. Extraverted sociable people can bring that characteristic out of their peers, while thoughtful and skeptical people can make the group more inquisitive and mature. Dour and pessimistic people can make every success feel like a failure, while optimistic and passionate people can inspire others to be as well. Secure and confident leaders can be a boon for the team and the organization, ensuring the long-term development of analytics. Conversely, functionary itinerants and sleepy statisticians, regardless of credentials or technical skill, paint the practice as transactional and technical rather than business enabling and value generating.

Data scientists and analytics professionals are unique. It can be tempting to search for parallels into better understood fields of practice and describe them as a blend of their composite accountabilities, but in truth they are a distinct group, and individually each has their own unique motivations and priorities. Leading these teams can be highly challenging, dramatic, and frustrating but supremely rewarding. The value creation potential of a high-functioning analytics team is massive, and with support and guidance from an effective leader who has strong relationships with the business, leaders can enable great change in the organization and personally rewarding development for their team members.

Success Factors

Technical abilities, and especially an intrinsic technical intuition, are table stakes for an analytics practitioner. The work of an analytics team is done when the fingers are on the keyboard, and each team member from the most junior analyst to the leader of the function need to be conversant in the practice, the tools, the languages, and ultimately to the application of data science theory to business problems. This theoretical and technical side needs to be balanced with an instinctive drive toward value creation, however, and not simply as technology for technology's sake. Along the other axis of development, team members need to be balanced between individuals striving for higher levels of management responsibility and those who find deep satisfaction in the work itself. Choosing individuals who are passionate about the field and their personal development while still committed to remaining in the role for at least two to three years is important for the stability of the team and the successful delivery of longer-term projects. Success, generally, is a matter of an appropriate balance between these poles of technology versus business and high drivers versus core contributors.

The characteristics of a successful data scientist can vary significantly between organizations. Consultative, broadly educated, and mature practitioners can be successful in legacy environments such as financial services and the public sector. Energetic coders with deep knowledge of particular fields of practice can be equally successful in a startup or technical organization. General success in the field, however, tends to be for those who are somewhere in the middle of the two extremes, adjusting for specific corporate culture and industry norms.

In *Building Analytics Teams*, John Thompson (2020) uses the following fitting descriptors, among others, to describe the characteristics of analytics practitioners:

- Optimistic yet skeptical
- Intensely curious
- Mostly introverted
- Logically left and right brained
- Intelligence
- Self-critical and prone to perfection
- Social, but reserved

These descriptors define the natural characteristics of most analytics practitioners. While it is difficult (and often counterproductive) to attempt to distill a person into a series of adjectives and attributes, there are several other features that are important for a successful team. It should be noted that no one individual will have all of these characteristics. Teams are a blend of individuals, often with different traits, which results in frictions that spawn creativity and progress. There are eight soft traits for analytics practitioners that are critical to success:

Curious Every strong data scientist and analytics professional will, without exception, exhibit a strong natural curiosity about their work and the world around them. They will become animated at discussions of exogenous data sets and speculate enthusiastically about the drivers of consumer behavior. They will notice things that others do not, and they will see connections that others do not. In most cases, it is this deep and instinctive curiosity that has driven them toward a career in data science. Data scientists without curiosity are like ageusiac chefs or dyscalculic actuaries—technically capable, but grossly disadvantaged.

Adaptable Every strong practitioner will also, again without exception, be exceedingly adaptable in how they approach problems. They will find ways to make things work regardless of obstacles and find great personal satisfaction in doing so. They will not wait for detailed instructions or condemn a project as impossible. They will be stimulated by challenge and happily adjust their approach to deliver.

Consultative They can build relationships with key people and naturally see that as part of their role. Their previous successes will leverage relationships as much as technology. They will enjoy teamwork and collaborative projects.

Skeptical They do not take things at their face value and will instinctively distrust heuristics and traditional ways of approaching problems. They will try to disprove assumptions and trust data over instincts. At the same time, they will adjust their own positions without reservation in the face of compelling evidence.

Creative They will prefer open-ended problems around which they can craft their own solution. They will be personally gratified by original problems and often will have creative personal hobbies or side projects. They are not motivated by money but rather by their passion.

Business Focused They tend to be motivated toward solving applied business problems. They do not need to fully know the business, but they need to develop an interest in the problems of the business and learn to speak the language of the business.

Egalitarian They will see analytics as a team endeavor and work with rather than for their direct supervisor. They never personally wield title as a proxy for authority, nor do they view hierarchy as an indicator of intelligence. They seek the best solution, and artfully challenge people to defend their approach and premises regardless of their position.

Competitive   Though collegial with their in-group and personally caring toward their peers, they will be competitive outwardly. Driven by a need to achieve and deliver value, they will be personally motivated to find ways to execute on projects regardless of issues with dependency or formal authority.

Of these characteristics, the primary are curiosity and adaptability. Without these, all others will fail to foster success, and all others will naturally emerge if these two are present.

There is a deep divide between the business and the analytics function due to a lack of mutual intelligibility. Problems and projects are misinterpreted, and often groups have divergent interests and priorities, which leads to non-operationalizable deliverables. For example, the marketing department may request a segmentation model, the unspoken subtext being that they ultimately wish to understand their customer. The analytics function, not understanding the subtext, responds by providing a table of results that maximize behavioral differences through agglomerative clustering, which is technically appropriate but wholly insufficient for the underlying need of the stakeholder. The absence of a common knowledge base can quickly derail a project. These fundamental differences can balloon into conflict without mutual understanding and without the presence of translators who can serve as intermediaries between these two camps. Certainly, well-rounded teams need specialists with deep knowledge in relevant areas, but blended personalities should be the norm. More-established geeks can often decry this perspective, pointing to celebrated eccentrics in the field, and while it is true that every Jobs needs a Wozniak, it is equally true that every Wozniak needs a Jobs.

The archetypal surly guru, their bitterness tolerated because of their indispensable skills, is gone. In the past this was considered a sign of credibility—that the truly technically gifted needed to be a little bit eccentric, and it was the cost of doing business with these enigmatic sages. Modern data and analytics practitioners need to be professionals and to enable the business through a consultative and mature approach rather than the raw application of technology. The gurus have traded their hoodies for oxfords.

For the past several years, analytics professionals were primarily career transitioners from fields such as mathematics, physics, and other sciences.

This was out of necessity, given the relative newness of the field. These people are well-regarded as practitioners because they often have cultivated their soft skills and have a collaborative disposition. They are able to bring a broader skillset to bear on problems. This default is changing recently, however. With universities and colleges offering data science programs, it has become a valid and established career path, and people for whom it is a job rather than a vocation are coming onto the market. For some, analytics integrates work into their life and becomes part of a unified whole—offering them deep personal gratification and in exchange provides their employers with a productive and valuable member. For others, unfortunately, it is just a job they have trained for that comes with a very respectable paycheck. Young adults, looking for a career path, nudged by a guidance counselor who read a career brief recently, pick the path as they would a menu item. Every leader has been in the situation of choosing between a passionate and enthusiastic yet provincial applicant and the sleepy soul who is perfect on paper. Often, the safe bet is made, and the vibrancy and vitality of the team suffers as a result. If ability, creativity, and adaptability are there, passion trumps PhDs every time.

People perform at their best when they are working in the service of others and when they are working alongside those who share their passion and focus on the end user. When these teams are working on compelling and impactful projects, when they can see the results of and feel ownership over their output, and when communication is open and egalitarian, they can accomplish great things. Fiercely independent all-stars who are forever seeking the limelight and who are self-assured in their brilliance are often hugely productive. The fabled 10x developer can be a great help if they are able to work effectively with stakeholders, but often that productivity comes with a 10x ego as well. Leaders should always seek plainness and parsimony, so that the team is preserved from the dangers that attend those who are always aiming for outward greatness and technical ease. The short-term benefits of employing all-stars is often outweighed by the long-term relationship damage and lack of continuity. Analytics is a team sport, and organizations are best served when individuals are selected with that understanding.

Self-directed personalities and a strong sense of agency and autonomy are important for individuals working independently on projects. Those particularly conscientious practitioners have the natural tendency to act as order takers and to find comfort in delivering to established processes and plans rather than to build the plan themselves. They seek stability and psychological safety by abdicating their agency but unfortunately also surrender their job satisfaction and personal growth. Individuals, for their personal development and the health of the team, should always be encouraged to be self-sufficient and to offer up their own views and input. The team should be encouraged to view their employment as the company purchasing their skills and effort, not their outputs. Organizations do not hire data scientists to tell them what to do but to receive their input and to add value to the business.

Finally, successful data scientists need to be parsimonious in how they approach problems. Every project needs to be prioritized on the basis of its value to the organization, but within each project the time spent honing and perfecting models must be evaluated as well. The first 3 days of model tuning is much more impactful than the last 10, and the marginal benefit of each additional day of effort should be evaluated against the backlog of projects. This paradigm does not sit well with a large proportion of data scientists, especially those more junior team members who want to produce the best possible work. By establishing the success factors and team conventions that support this behavior, the team will organically gravitate toward this outcome and encourage each other to maximize business value.

Team Composition

Within the larger sphere of data and analytics practitioners there are several classifications that have unique success criteria. While the individuals should still maintain the qualities mentioned above, placements that account for these focuses can set a person up for greater achievement.

Product Owner People who have worked on projects with a long-lived output can often move into a quasi-product ownership role, supporting the long-term development of the tool. These individuals need to be highly confident and able to balance the competing needs of stakeholders. They need to be cooperative, yet able to say "no" when necessary. They need to be structured and to have a higher-level view of the functions they are working with.

Project Manager / Delivery Manager Practitioners who lead workstreams or projects need to be structured, procedural, highly confident, and able to push respectfully. They need to be risk averse, and to instinctively think ahead to identify potential issues. They are affable and have strong personal relationships with people throughout the organization yet are respected for their discipline and ability to control projects. They are able to circumvent bureaucracy and are able to secure access for contractors and to negotiate with IT. Ideally, these people also have specific training in delivery methodologies such as Agile. They need to naturally be driven to deliver to timelines and find satisfaction in managing the activities of their peers with equal parts humility and eagerness.

Business Analyst These people are detail oriented and are very organized communicators. They are adept at discovering underlying problems and ask probing questions. They can elicit trust in their stakeholders and balance well between structure and progress. The business analysts need to be able to enter a project and help to support integration with disparate teams. They are naturally highly collaborative, personable, and communicative. They typically have strong relationships throughout the organization and deep industry knowledge from the perspective of multiple functions. This gives them a strong foundation for framing problems and defining functional requirements.

Data Engineer These people need to be structured and highly technical. Despite being primarily a back-room function, they need to be able to communicate to stakeholders having different levels of understanding and to advise confidently on technical matters. They need to be detail oriented and enjoy optimizing processes and algorithms.

Data Scientist As the role most responsible for developing the solution, it is most important that they be creative and balanced between the technical and business aspects of a project. They need to be technically conversant but to focus on the final deliverable and be naturally parsimonious. It is necessary that they understand the technology and mathematics but see them solely as tools for a functional end.

Front-End Developer These more creative data professionals tend to focus on the interaction between end users and the analytical product. They are artistic and derive great satisfaction in building dashboards, presentation decks, and compelling visuals. They focus on usability and clarity and are able to remove unnecessary chaff to make visualizations more compelling.

This team composition, exhibiting the above success factors and contextualized to the individual organizational culture and team dynamic, must also inform how hiring is undertaken for the function.

Hiring and Onboarding

The hiring and onboarding of data scientists and analytics professionals is typically constrained by the policies of the organization, but wherever flexibility exists, the process should be modified or extended within a few key areas.

Most practitioners have experienced the typical formulaic hiring process that has been established at large organizations. After submitting a résumé, and reentering details into the recruitment CRM, a non-technical recruiter compares it against a list of desired traits and experiences. After an introductory call with a recruiter, a technical exercise, and a final interview with the hiring manager, the candidate joins the organization. This process has the tendency to select for those who are academically and procedurally inclined but who lack the creativity and adaptability that is so important to the practice. Recruiters, lacking analytical experience and vernacular, struggle to assess intangible characteristics, instead proposing candidates who have the requisite number of years' experience and who mentioned the correct keywords on their CV. Technical exercises are clinical, with a clean data set and an objective measurement of success, the direct opposite of a real-world project. The final check for personality fit with the hiring manager leads to the selection of the best of those that were presented.

There are a few key areas where leaders should intervene to break out of this cycle. Firstly, leaders should request that all applications be sent, unfiltered, to the hiring manager for preliminary assessment rather than being prescreened by human resources. For larger organizations where this may be impractical, it is important to establish with the recruiter what nontechnical traits are valued and how they may be exhibited. Hiring managers are in a much better position to assess the skills of the applicants. In addition, hiring managers should be directly involved in the first screening interview with the candidates and evaluate the person based on personal fit and the success criteria described earlier, with technical ability evaluated afterward. While technical abilities can be learned on the job, creativity and adaptability are innate and should be the first selection criteria.

The subsequent technical interviews, usually carried out by their would-be peers, should be as undefined as a typical project that they would face. Their performance should be assessed in how they assess the situation, how they present their rationalization and results, and how they perform in the face of ambiguity rather than coding conventions and confusion matrices. The use of case studies at this stage is a great way to evaluate their aptitude for problem solving.

The final decision to hire or return to market should be a discussion between the hiring manager and the candidate's future peers and based on the totality of the experience, not just on technical metrics and a formulaic grading rubric. Given the importance of teamwork and an egalitarian outcome-first culture, hiring should be largely a team decision.

The above presupposes that the hiring manager does not have a warm candidate from another organization, which should be the typical case. At any given time, there should be several potential new hires who are ready to join the team under the personal guarantee of other team members. Analytics professionals who are within the appropriate industry and location should be known if they are at all involved in the local analytics community.

Talent Development

When people first enter the workforce, they often have a misunderstanding of the requirements for professional advancement. Often people in their life will have given career advice that was entirely appropriate in the corporations of the past but is outdated in today's business environment. It used to be that people could expect after enough years, once they had proven their loyalty to the company, a managerial position as well as training in how to be successful in that new role. Baby boomers, and to a lesser degree Gen X, worked in a business environment where tenure and loyalty were rewarded with advancement and opportunity, and they tend to offer advice from that perspective.

Employment, for better or worse, is now more of a temporary relationship between an employer and an employee. At any point in that relationship, either party can, with minimal consequence, decide to terminate the arrangement. The implication for the employer is that they are more free to seek talent that aligns to their needs, and for the employee it means they can seek opportunities that match their personal ambitions. If they can hold positions for at least 12 to 18 months, it will not impact their future employability. This fluidity leads to, with several caveats, a greater potential for alignment between the parties.

This is particularly the case for data science and analytics, which has become an extremely high-turnover profession. There is a deficit of practitioners, competitive wages, and a cycle of large transformational projects separated by less-interesting incrementalist projects. For these reasons, it is unrealistic to expect practitioners to be long tenured. They should be respected and encouraged as individuals with the expectation that they will leave one day and the hope that they will come back. The constant flow of talent brings energy and fresh perspectives that help to stimulate an environment of innovation and should be encouraged. Professional development, with this understanding, should be done with the intention of supporting the technical and personal formation of the individual for their own sake rather than in strict alignment with the long-term technical roadmap for the organization.

Regardless, many practitioners still work under the misapprehension that they will advance in their career if they have tenure and improve their technical abilities such that they have a body of knowledge that can support the technical guidance of a team. Most believe that once they achieve a certain number of years of experience as an individual contributor, they are entitled to a managerial position, regardless of their skillset or personal propensities.

Professional development occurs along two complementary paths—the hard skills and the soft. Maintaining technical relevance and an awareness of new technologies and methodologies is important, but only in as much as it enables and supports the mandate and deliverables of the team. Different levels of technical proficiency will be required depending on the industry and the analytical maturity of the organization, and different levels of training are needed to support and maintain those skills. Advancing beyond that limit is in most cases a misuse of resources and can even lead to dissatisfaction if the newly acquired skillset cannot be used. In most cases, technical training should be secondary to soft skills. For analytics practitioners, the key differentiator is in the soft skills or business knowledge that allows for truly valuable insights and for their effective communication. The purposeful development of these skills can act as a multiplier for team productivity and set up the individual for a more successful career.

Professional development can take the form of formal study, such as entering an MBA program; on-the-job training, such as leading a workstream in a larger project; or technical development, such as attaining professional accreditation in a particular technology. It may be a matter of improving personal-relationship-building skills by setting goals to meet people in different parts of the organization or through improvement of public speaking through Toastmasters. Professional development takes many forms. The most important part is that the process is intentionally directed toward an end that is motivating and important to the practitioner. Professional and personal development can only be achieved through the practitioners' own diligence and effort, not through time on post or a checklist of proficiencies and tasks. Leaders or organizations creating a landscape of hurdles and targets that the individual must achieve is a misguided attempt to shift people into a particular path. This devalues creativity and diversity of thought and reduces the long-term effectiveness of the team. Professional and personal development needs to come from the individual and be based on their professional and personal goals.

Though it is important that it be built into the leadership model, the ultimate desire for professional development needs to come from within. Individuals need to continually self-assess themselves in light of their continued development and changes in the organization and the practice of analytics (Drucker, 2008). Committing an intentional evaluation of oneself in terms of strengths, weaknesses, values, and sense of belonging can lead to a more clear view of a person's own path. Ignoring these important sessions of introspection can give over control of one's career to the preferences of others. Leaders should encourage this self-evaluation regularly through the sharing of their own goals and through more subtle Socratic questioning to lead the individual to key areas of reflection.

Leaders can best serve their team members by helping them unlock what it is they genuinely want out of their career. Many work under the belief that they can only be successful if they reach ever higher managerial positions. Data scientists, generally, have entered the field because they have a natural predisposition toward technical analysis and deep thoughtful reflection on a problem. This tendency toward a detail-oriented highly technical career path is usually in contrast to the extroversion and big picture thinking that management requires. The most technically successful individuals on the team, if promoted into a managerial position, find themselves in a role that they have no passion for or are not equipped for and have limited success as a result. The team as a whole suffers for the weakness of the new manager and suffers again for the loss of what often was the best technical resource.

Fortunately, most big tech organizations have realized that this traditional career path is not appropriate anymore. They have created alternate paths of professional advancement, which exist in parallel to the managerial stream, often up to the second or third level of management. For highly exceptional technical practitioners, this means that they can achieve the level of director or VP without the expectation of functional management or people leadership. This sets the expectation from the start of their career that they will have opportunities for development regardless of their passions and disposition. Unfortunately, this is a rarity in traditional corporate culture that uses existing organizational design policies in creating roles for analytics teams. Leaders are well served by seeking to influence these role definitions and in influencing decision makers to introduce similar parallel development opportunities for technical practitioners. Without these opportunities, retention of mid-career practitioners will be a particular challenge.

Analytics is a rapidly changing and broad profession. In the face of uncertainty around technologies, the natural intuition for practitioners can be to pursue technical accreditation and to achieve mastery over as diverse a toolkit as possible. They seek to collect achievements with distinct medals or shareable certificates. If this is guided by genuine curiosity and sincere desire for proficiency, it is certainly a worthwhile pursuit, but when it is being done in the hope of professional advancement, leaders should intervene and work toward building a personal development plan.

Similarly, some practitioners seek formal education at the exclusion of all else in the hope of advancing in their careers. They may collect degrees to showcase their competence. Again, if this is driven by a true love of learning and is done for its own sake, it is a healthy hobby. If, however, it is considered a precursor to a promotion, leaders need to work with the individual to build a personal development plan.

Like developing a strategy for the function more generally, a personal development plan has three discrete steps.

- First, a current state assessment, a candid assessment of the capabilities of the individual across the technical, personal, and professional categories. This can rarely be done passively—it requires a deep and thoughtful introspection combined with fully transparent feedback from past leaders and peers.

- Second, defining the target state. The individual needs to understand where they could go, and more importantly where they want to go. Deciding to pursue management should be by exception, never the default path. Again, this is not a casual exercise and requires in many cases years of deep self-reflection combined with brutally honest assessments.

- Finally, a plan for closing the gap and realizing their ambitions.

One of the kindest things a leader can do for people on their team is to support them through the process of collaboratively developing these plans. Almost all organizations have some sort of professional development template with capabilities split across certain categories, and even checklists for self-assessment; however, these are always broad-brush approaches and offer little value when viewed in isolation. Leaders, after becoming familiar with the person and their work, are often in a better position to offer a genuine assessment than the individual regarding current performance and the range of potential futures.

Without providing guidance surrounding professional development, individuals can invest time and energy in nonproductive pursuits, and actively reduce the effectiveness of the team while simultaneously expecting to be rewarded. Conversely, promoting capability development toward a productive end that aligns with both the desires and predilections of the individual and the future vision for the team can be a mutually rewarding pursuit and help to strengthen the relationship between the leader and the practitioner.

Highly technical practitioners can often consider formal course-based education the sole path to learning a new skill. Leaders should encourage people to view learning and development as a mosaic and find opportunities to develop both hard and soft skills through each avenue, including both formal and informal activities such as these:

- Self-directed learning
- Learn by doing or on-the-job training
- Shadowing
- Hackathons
- Open learning
- Distance learning
- Toastmasters
- Boot camps
- University degrees or diplomas
- Vendor presentations
- Public seminars
- Volunteering
- Boards, agencies, and commissions
- Secondments

Every high-performing individual will, whether verbalized or not, have the internal need to advance and develop in order to feel fully engaged in their work. This internal need is usually proportionate to their potential and performance. Leaders should work with members of their team to identify opportunities for improvement, make suggestions on how to address those gaps, make time available for the practitioner's development, and solicit resources to dedicate to learning and development. Teams need the continuous influx of new ideas and new modes of expression so that they may maintain creativity and passion in their work. Leaders, individuals, and the team as a whole all benefit from an intentional focus on personal growth.

Retention

The factors that influence job satisfaction and ultimately impact retention are different for everyone. Typically, data science practitioners are very vocal about technical considerations but are not particularly forthcoming in their personal situations or ambitions. They will vehemently decry esoteric aspects of a project but may be reticent to ask for a raise or a promotion. They will often struggle with the introspection needed to uncover their underlying motivations, driven by an uninspected id. Without this ability to effectively self-interrogate, their needs are inarticulate and primal. Because of this, by the time a team member asks for something, it has likely been emerging on their radar for some time, turned from instinct to artifact, artifact to issue, and increased in significance until it has reached a point that they are willing to endure the discomfort of raising it with their leader. These issues, usually raised in passing or as a "by the way" at the end of a conversation, should be taken seriously. If a person says they are wondering if the company is right for them, it likely means they are actively interviewing.

The number of job opportunities available to high-performing data scientists means they have a reduced tolerance to everyday corporate frustrations. Most have entered the field with real passion and are not simply looking for compensation and peaceable work. Quarterly reporting, repetitive tasks, budget constraints, and projects that do not challenge their abilities or add value can all lead to drops in productivity and engagement. Without a feeling of ownership or tribal loyalty, there is little that can keep a practitioner in an unfulfilling role besides complacency or avoiding the inconvenience of finding a new job. Those in highly specialized roles in the narrow intersection of industry and function may endure years without salary increases or recognition or development opportunities, but analytics professionals, being so in demand, are not so inclined or constrained.

Compensation should be competitive within the region and industry and commensurate with experience so that it does not become a factor for disengagement. Though it is rarely a major motivating factor for high-performance practitioners, it must be in line with the practice, which is often higher than that of other knowledge workers. Often, performance-based compensation or a heavier weighting to at-risk pay can be an appropriate compromise that balances earning potential with internal policies around pay equity. The opportunity for professional advancement, especially among individual contributors, is likewise essential to retention. An important consideration for any professional, but for data scientists especially, is that they are given the opportunity to pursue passion projects. The amount of time allocated should not be so much as to allow them to lapse into complacency, however. Individuals need a creative outlet, especially if their other projects are not challenging or fulfilling. This is a frequently unexplored need, and one that practitioners can find themselves experiencing without understanding the source of their frustration. Often leaders need to support their team in identifying projects that they are passionate about, which energizes and vitalizes them, even if they do not independently seek them out. Some progressive organizations, such as 3M and Google, formally allow and encourage employees to allocate a percentage of their time to passion projects.

Retention is a challenge for any team, but this is not altogether a negative. With the rapid developments in the field, it is important to have a healthy crossflow of talent and an influx of new ideas and methodologies. Without the dynamism that comes from change, teams can become quickly outdated without being aware. It should not be assumed that with proper care a leader can expect to keep practitioners for several years, but rather the goal should be to manage the flow of talent to ensure continuity and a positive transition when the time comes. Practitioners who leave on good terms, having strong and lasting relationships, may return in the future bringing new ideas and a renewed passion.

Departures

Despite best efforts by leaders and team members, there are always situations where the relationship is not salvageable. It could be that the individual wants to develop their career in a different direction, that the leader is seeking practitioners with different skillsets, or simply that there are performance issues and the work ethic is not present. Unless there are clear outward signs of nonperformance or disengagement by the individual, termination can impact the morale of the team and decrease trust in the leader. One of the clearest outward signs that a practitioner is not fully engaged is a lack of enthusiasm for the work and reverting to an order-taking mentality. If the leader has established a strong enough relationship that they are comfortable sharing the underlying issue, it may be discovered that there are externalities that are affecting performance. Certainly, in these situations a compassionate leader should make all efforts to support their team members through their personal issues, including a leave of absence or schedule flexibility; wherever possible, all efforts should be made to help the person find success in the organization. However, when it is not so clear, when performance has been declining without apparent cause, or a new hire is not meeting expectations, it is important to intervene before the overall performance of the team declines and overall morale suffers.

High-functioning teams require high-functioning practitioners who are collaborative and self-motivated to deliver quality results and to add value for their stakeholders. This is a wonderful self-reinforcing situation, where the strength and passion of team members inspire their colleagues, who in turn inspire others. Meetings are energetic, challenges are celebrated, and a spirit of optimism permeates everything. It only takes one shirker, or one person who is simply punching a timecard, for the self-perception of the team to change from a tribe to casual coworkers.

If a struggling team member does not have compelling personal reasons for their poor performance, a visible final chance for redemption should be given. Success breeds success, and it could be that the individual simply needs a win before they can regain their confidence. The other common desire that can go uncommunicated is that the individual has become functionary and does not feel agency. If the person has never had the opportunity to lead a large project or workstream, and there is still hope for them to become a good performer, then they should be given that chance to deliver.

In the end, if the performance is not there the individual needs to be exited to find their happiness elsewhere. Policy changes between organizations, but given the size of the community, the steady crossflow of talent, and the importance of reputation, as much respect and compassion should be shown as possible, providing positive yet candid references, attributing positive personal intentions, and as much as possible offering feedback for their development. Often it takes a failure to help a person realize what they need to do to change, and an honest discussion with that person can be truly valuable for them. Steve Jobs, Thomas Edison, JK Rowling, Michael Bloomberg, and Lee Iacocca were all fired from different jobs before finding their place, and many of them attribute that termination with their eventual successes. Misaligned expectations are not an evaluation on the worth of a person, and this should be communicated with empathy and respect.

Conventions vary between organizations on whether individuals are given notice prior to termination or are exited immediately and given payment in lieu of time served. On the surface it would appear the more compassionate route would be to offer them the time to transition their projects and to have the opportunity to say goodbye to their colleagues; unfortunately, in practice it almost always damages the engagement of the team. Unless the termination is the result of a layoff or reduction in work, it is typically preferable to immediately walk the person out. It is certainly the more difficult of the two approaches but necessary to maintain positivity within the team. Performance-based terminations are seldom a surprise, either to the individual or the team. If all efforts were made to support the outgoing individual prior to the final decision, then there is little benefit gained for anybody involved by having them continue to be in the office.

Departures, whether voluntary or involuntary, are one of the more difficult responsibilities of a leader. The sting of a termination can never be completely removed, but if a leader can handle the situation with respect and compassion, it can be at least mitigated. Acknowledging the human cost and the impact to the individual's life, as well as offering whatever personal support possible, can help the person to move forward and learn from the experience.

The Data Scientist Hierarchy of Needs

Owing to the frothy market for data science and analytics practitioners, most people have several opportunities available to them at any time. Leaders and organizations cannot maintain a high-caliber team if they cannot meet the needs of high-caliber individuals. The best talent will be poached, and only those without other opportunities will remain.

As with Maslow's hierarchy of needs, practitioners, depending on where they are in their career and the resources available in their current role, will have different needs and different motivating factors (Maslow, 2013). Once each of the base needs are met, they will have the tendency to focus on the next item in the pyramid (Figure 4.1). For example, without access to quality data with which they can develop their predictive algorithm, they will not be as concerned with team-building activities.

Physiological Practitioners need reasonable compensation, vacation time, and benefits that are comparable to the current local market. Alignment of interests to corporate performance through at-risk pay, employee share purchase plans, or profit sharing can also assist in meeting this need while at the same time reducing the fixed compensation costs of the organization.

Tools and Data Professionals need the proper tools to be able to perform their jobs well. Like a carpenter making do without their hammer, data scientists need their employer to provide the necessary infrastructure for them to be successful. Issues with data governance, data availability, or stinginess with applications can lead to dissatisfaction.

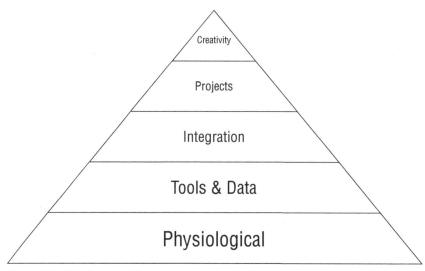

Figure 4.1: Needs pyramid

Integration   People need to feel accepted and integrated into the team and the larger organization. Opportunities for fellowship and a sense of shared purpose make a person happy to come to work and to contribute beyond what they otherwise would.

Projects   Practitioners need to feel that they are making a difference with their work. High-value and impactful projects and opportunities to develop the self-esteem of the individual and to earn them the respect of their colleagues are immeasurably more compelling than transactional tasks.

Creativity   People need to feel that they are free to be creative and able to try new approaches and methodologies—that they can add value in their own way.

Ensuring that the needs of the individuals are being met and understanding what their motivations are is essential to maintaining a high-performing team. Through recurring one-on-one conversations, leaders need to establish where the individual is on the hierarchy of needs and act quickly to keep their engagement high. Data scientists are in high demand, and dissatisfied practitioners can quickly find new opportunities that meet their needs.

Culture

The culture of a group has a huge impact on the success it will have. As Peter Drucker said, "Culture eats strategy for breakfast." That is not to say that strategy is unimportant, but without the culture to support a strategy, it will fall flat. Every enterprise has an overarching culture that permeates each function or division to some degree. Each function in turn has its unique subculture.

Data science culture, if it can be generalized (and caricaturized), is that of scrappy and intelligent outsiders battling against a sclerotic bureaucratic legacy of vestigial processes long past their use-by date. Wielding truth in the form of mathematics, they flow gracefully through an organization bringing enlightenment and illumination. Caring little for materialism, these hoodie-wearing warrior monks hop between tasks and groups, their laptops covered in arcane stickers, helping their sweetly ignorant colleagues come into the twenty-first century. This hyperbolic and idealistic self-perception is rarely mutual, as for the most part analytics teams are considered a branch of IT—socially awkward techies who do not have a grasp on the needs of the business but can be helpful in certain situations. The truth is somewhere in the middle.

Culture must be purposefully developed and promoted and the ideal character traits praised such that it is guided toward a productive end. Culture will influence the team regardless of intentionality, so analytics leaders are well advised to exercise control over this important contributor to their success. As described earlier, distinct cultures exist for the in-group (how the analytics practitioners interact and how they perceive themselves and their role in the organization) as well as for the out-group (how the analytics function represents themselves and is perceived by the rest of the organization).

The default culture of an organization is mutually reinforcing through extant processes, influential individuals, self-perception, and corporate legends. Regardless of the progress that is made toward true data-driven decision making, this default culture can reemerge and push back. It is important that culture be a consistent element and subtle direction given in tone and framing to encourage the desired behaviors.

Ironically, well-integrated analytics teams who consider their stakeholders as colleagues are rarely successful. Rather than considering them as customers, and their problems being the responsibility of the analytics team to solve, they tend to empathize on a personal level and support incrementalism over disruptive change in order to reduce stress for their friends. Strategic advisors, to truly add value, need to operate from an objective position. In all interactions, stakeholder groups need to be treated as clients. The human impacts of change need to be accounted for at all stages of the project life cycle, but psychologically the team must consider the sponsoring business unit as their clients.

The Hofstede cultural dimension theory is a widely used quantitative assessment for international business. The dimensions of this theory provide an excellent jumping-off point for a discussion of the different ideal in-group and out-group cultural orientations for an analytics team.

Ideal in-group data and analytics teams have the following cultural characteristics:

Power Distance   Concerns the attitude of the team toward power inequalities and the relationship between leaders and subordinate practitioners. Healthy data science teams need to be egalitarian and technocratic and to make data-driven decisions. Leaders should provide input and advise their team and have established their credibility such that the advice is accepted based on respect rather than position. Position should be a sign of increased responsibility, not of power and authority. This can be cemented by discouraging the mentioning of title during introductions and by giving project-level leadership to junior members.

Individualism   The amount of interdependence between team members. Conformity of opinion or approach or speech or personal style stifles creativity and kills team engagement. Every individual should be comfortable within the team and be empowered and encouraged to bring their full self to work each day. Promotions and recognition should be based on merit, and leaders should seek opportunities to recognize team members individually.

Uncertainty Avoidance   How the team deals with an unknowable future. Most data scientists are relatively *laissez-faire*, comfortable with their niche sphere of control and content to let larger external forces guide the company. Leaders should instill a sense of control and responsibility in the team for the direction of analytics within the organization and include even junior team members in strategic discussions. Comfort with uncertainty is natural for those who work with probabilities, but this attitude can be destructive if not modified. Leaders should set the expectation that all practitioners anticipate potential nontechnical events, understand the impact to their projects and the function, and have a personal action plan for mitigation.

Long-Term Orientation   The priority that the team places on tradition over disruption. The team should be absolute iconoclasts and never accept the status quo. The value that the team offers is that they are capable of changing business processes to improve decision making. Relying on traditional techniques, even as a starting point, can limit the alternatives available to the team and be the seed of destructive incrementalism. As with the Toyota Way, analytics leaders need to set the expectation of *Genchi Genbutsu*—go and see for yourself.

Masculinity or Competition   The desire of the team to be the best, balanced against cooperation. The romantic notion of the team being in overt competition against forces that are bent on stagnation provides an emotional push toward excellence that cannot be achieved with process control and well-crafted strategy. People have a desire to be part of something bigger than themselves, and leaders should construct a narrative that supports that. Building dashboards can seem meaningless, but within the team they should be framed in a way that it is part of a larger battle against inadequate business practices, and imperative to the success of the organization. Healthy competition should be encouraged between members, as long as it does not lead to disunity. Competition to analytics teams from different companies should be encouraged as well. The team should have the sense that they exist in a state of grace, favored by the organization and an important part of its future.

These characteristics are modified somewhat in their relation and presentation to the rest of the organization. These adjustments are not at the expense of authenticity or personal integrity but rather the behaviors and orientation of a healthy and competitive team when they are engaged in their work. These changes are as follows:

Power Distance   Stakeholders should not have uncertainty about who is making decisions or who they should approach with questions on a project. While egalitarian inwardly, the team should have a single project leader for each engagement and a single point of escalation. The team should be perfectly aligned at each interaction with the client and defer to the project lead unless that decision making has been clearly delegated. The analytics leadership team should be equally prepared to discuss the function itself.

Individualism   The team should be perceived as strongly united for the course of a project. Any overt disagreement around approach or technical aspects should take place privately. Similarly, deliverables and processes should be consistent regardless of the person leading the project or workstream. Stakeholders should be able to expect an identical level of service for each engagement.

Uncertainty Avoidance   In discussions surrounding the future of analytics in the organization, each member of the team and particularly the leader should be able to passionately articulate a clear vision. For individual projects, the team needs to show deference to the business and seek their perspective on potential events and risks that could threaten the success of the initiative.

Long-Term Orientation   Though the team should be inwardly skeptical of all existing processes, proper respect to established conventions is important for healthy relationships with stakeholders. The team should seek to understand the perspective of the business and the events that led to the current state. While a healthy analytics team should be perceived as a disruptive force in the enterprise, this needs to be data driven and from a place of humility rather than hubris.

Masculinity or Competition   Similarly, the team needs to be sensitive to the difficulties that their involvement can create for stakeholders and operate empathetically and compassionately. The team should balance their healthy desire to implement analytical solutions with the longer-term needs for positive relationships with the organization.

Most people are defensive. Framing the situation as an intentional culture change has an implication that the current culture is deficient and needs to be altered. In particular for a leader new to the organization or team, associations must be as positive as possible. Rather than calling it out as a culture change, identify specific characteristics in the culture (heuristics, hierarchy, order taking, etc.) that need to be changed and focus on the positive impacts of altering that behavior. Reward and celebrate those who agree and exhibit those behaviors.

For a culture change to be successful, it is necessary to first identify the need for the change. Once people understand and agree with the need for change, there needs to be a compelling vision for the future. Once people understand the need and the vision, they need to see and understand the plan. Identify those who are excited by the plan and take them on the journey.

It is difficult to change the culture of an organization, in particular with long-tenured employees. Each person is influenced by their lived experience, the culture of their division, the company as a whole, and whatever subcultures they associate with. Culture changes cannot be accomplished by decree but rather by the careful application of team conventions that encourage desired behaviors and discourage destructive behaviors. New leaders should not insert themselves into a new team and begin addressing symptoms of the underlying cultural issues because they risk putting the team into a defensive mode.

Once the appropriate culture has been established for the analytics team, it is important to maintain pressure that discourages a return to habits. The "bad old days" need to be present as a narrative device and the dangers of its return ever present. Strategy and process is imperative to the success of an analytics team, but without the motivating force of a positive culture, the team can become mechanistic. Having an appropriate culture gets the best out of everyone, acting as a multiplier to each capability, and supports the success of the function.

Innovation

Analytics projects that are ideated and developed solely by the accountable business unit can only build out that project from the same basis and knowledge framework responsible for the existing, and presumably insufficient, process. Innovation does not happen without some conflict and the introduction of new ways of thinking. As Henry Ford said, "If I had asked what people wanted, they would have said faster horses." Analytics practitioners add value when they can apply lessons from other functions or industries or are able to see connections between different functions. To do this, practitioners need to have a naturally innovative mindset and be guided by their leadership to view projects and deliverables not as a set of instructions but as guidelines.

In *Innovation: The Classic Traps*, Rosabeth Kanter highlights three main issues with innovation in an enterprise (Kanter, 2006):

Strategy   Lack of project balance between incrementalism and transformation.

Process   Strangling projects with bureaucracy.

Structure   Separating innovation from the business.

The spirit of creativity and innovation within a team needs to be cultivated and controlled to sustain an imaginative energy that dreams big but at the same time does not disregard their customers and business constraints. Finding that balance between quick-win incremental quality-of-life improvements and big inspirational transformative initiatives is important for both the organization and the individual practitioners.

Few data scientists entered the field to enable incremental improvements or to build operational dashboards. Whether they were specifically educated in data science or pivoted on their passion, a career spent adding standard deviation metrics to existing reports does not inspire. But at the same time, mature practitioners cannot ignore the fact that theirs is a service function. Basic tasks that are not particularly challenging are an opportunity to build skills, establish rapport with the business, and provide the group more runway for future large projects. While always putting business needs first, a truly innovative analytics team should aspire to do what is best for the business, not just strictly what is requested. In *The Lean Startup*, the author recounts the typical process for a startup or intrapreneurial team within an enterprise: after landing on an idea, many instinctively seek confirming evidence, or even work without data, letting the assumptions of the business stand in. Without feedback or accountability, the project eventually fails. The team celebrate it as a learning opportunity and move on without any true improvements in effectiveness and ultimately no closer to the mental shift required for rapid adaptation in project ideation (Ries, 2011). Data scientists should look for disconfirming evidence at every step of a project.

From the perspective of the business, investing in a large team of highly skilled analytics professionals who focus solely on moonshot projects with a low probability of success is a large risk. Similarly, marginal improvements to existing processes with guaranteed success can only produce a group of order takers with limited value to the enterprise. An innovative analytics practice needs to have a balance in project effort and size. They cannot reject opportunities that are too small out of pride or simply add incremental changes and features to their products that confuse their end users. Project pipelines, and the individual practitioners within the team, need to have a balance between moonshots, midrange ideas, and incrementalism so that the team can be sustainably innovative.

Every innovative team is a parsimonious team. Introducing onerous budgeting requirements or red-yellow-green progress reporting to an absentee project management office for divisional aggregation can quickly kill the spirit of a team and conflate procedural milestone progress with actual outcomes. Measuring is not controlling, and most control is illusory. There must be flexibility in controls and an appreciation of analytics as a creative team rather than a technical one.

Finally, innovation cannot be contained and constrained to a single function. Some organizations, with the best intentions, create separate innovation teams that serve as advisors in cross-enterprise projects. Creativity is ephemeral; if an organization attempts to capture and control it, assigning it as one would any other mechanical task, it quickly evaporates. The best enablers of innovation are authentic and collaborative relationships. Analytics practitioners focused on value creation interfacing directly with people from the business, within a framework that rewards risk taking and creativity, can deliver amazing things.

Innovation needs to be an animating energy within the team and not simply a supporting criterion for individual projects. Each practitioner portfolio should have some element of innovation and create positive personal satisfaction within the individual. Regardless of the effort involved or likelihood of success, these projects need to be present and shared broadly at both the personal and team level. Innovative projects, once completed, are quickly forgotten by both stakeholders and the practitioners responsible. Regardless of the impact made by a project, there is a tendency for people to quickly return to a level of normalcy, something known as the hedonic treadmill (Brickman & Campbell, 1971). As St. Augustine said, "Desire hath no rest," and analytics practitioners by their nature want to be involved with creative and transformative projects. Best-in-class analytics functions cultivate creativity and see huge rewards in terms of retention, engagement, and quality of work.

Communication

The formal definition of communication is the act of transferring information between two parties. This simple definition, however, belies the depth and power that communication has. The method and style of that simple transfer of information can make the difference between an exchange that is productive and strengthening or one that offends and weakens relationships. Project updates can be delivered in a terse email, in bullets or prose. Bad news can be provided by a timid voicemail on a Friday evening. Dissatisfaction can be communicated with folded arms and unresponsiveness. Complex data science concepts can be shared by visualizing on a whiteboard. Complex moral or political issues can be addressed by depersonalizing through a parable or through generalization using allegory. Being strategic in how information is transferred, contextualizing it to the individual, and being conscious of the preferred outcome can make the difference between a team that is savvy and one that struggles to sell their ideas.

Communication is critical not just for analytical leaders but for all stakeholder-facing people on the team. In poorly performing teams, communication can be considered a means to an end, a necessary tool for understanding the problem and relaying the solution, and completely detached from the individuals being impacted. Rational people, guided and motivated by logic and data, can find comfort in the certainty of an R^2 and share that metric expecting the same edification in their stakeholders. This approach invariably falls flat. Practitioners need to frame their work, at all stages of the project life cycle, in a way that aligns with their client. Highly successful analytics teams need to focus on communication as much as they would any other professional skill.

Communication starts with listening. It is vital to achieve the full potential of the team, to understand the individual, the environment, the problem being faced, the risks and the limitations. It is equally important to enter into communications with stakeholders from a place of sincere empathy, understanding as much as possible the perspective and priorities of the individuals on the team.

In the film *Pi*, Max becomes obsessed with a 216-digit number, in the end seeing it in every part of his life. In a dramatic scene, his close friend Sol eventually tells him, "You want to find the number 216 in the world, you will be able to find it everywhere. 216 steps from a mere street corner to your front door. 216 seconds you spend riding on the elevator. When your mind becomes obsessed with anything, you will filter everything else out and find that thing everywhere." While Max was seeing this number, life went on as normal for everyone else in the world. Every trade and every profession suffers from this tunnel vision to some degree. Carpenters cannot visit a friend without at least subconsciously evaluating the integrity of their house. Dentists cannot see a smile without noticing misaligned teeth. Without the occasional realignment from a friend like Sol, worldviews can get very narrow.

Data scientists need to understand that most people in the world give little thought to their field of practice. For most, artificial intelligence is something from the movies, and there is a general unease about automation. In marketing, finance, human relations, operations, and every other part of the organization most individuals are performing their jobs almost completely unaware of what data science is and how much it impacts their life. They may be aware that there is an analytics team in the company but not know exactly what they do. From this place of relative mutual ignorance, individuals are asked to participate in a project with a team they are told will change their processes.

Communication between the analytics function and the stakeholder team alone is often not enough. Every project should have sponsorship from function or division leadership to provide assurance to the stakeholder team. Line managers should likewise be involved, as should the leaders of other impacted teams such as IT or BI with whom the business is more comfortable with. These mutual acquaintances can grease the wheels and make collaboration more effective and from a place of familiarity and trust.

The amount of technical detail should always be adjusted to match the level of sophistication of the individuals on the team. Well-presented insights that are visually appealing and follow principles of information design are much more impactful than exhaustive tables and graphs. Frontline operational workers may only need to know outcomes and changes, while finance teams will want to understand the model from base principles. High-esteem professionals such as engineers and actuaries in particular may want all methodologies described in excruciating detail so they have a deep understanding of the changes and can properly assess the risk to their team. Analytics practitioners need to be able to adjust their style and level of communication on the fly so they can accommodate the differing needs of stakeholders.

Sometimes, members of the team may feel the need to be intellectual bullies and provide unnecessary detail so that they can showcase their intelligence. Leaders need to discourage this behavior in the strongest possible way and privately discuss the motivations for this with the offender. Often, low self-esteem or a misguided perception of what professionalism sounds like is the culprit. Leaders are well advised to encourage simple speech in the team, following Einstein's advice that "if you can't explain it simply, you don't understand it well enough."

The best technical abilities will be useless if a project cannot get traction due to poor communication. Practitioners should be guided toward developing their communication abilities as they would a new technology and always be looking for opportunities to improve upon it. Courses such as Dale Carnegie or membership in Toastmasters need to be given the same weight as would be given to technology certifications for an individual to find true success in the field.

Succession Planning

The goal of succession planning is to ensure the continuity of the business or function such that there will never be an opening for which another employee is not prepared. Understood in theory to be important, it is in practice often an afterthought, and many enterprises struggle with sudden departures, temporarily assigning an unprepared candidate in an "acting" capacity while posting publicly for the vacant role. Assuming no damage was done in the interim, the new leader lands in the position cold, without adequate foreknowledge, and spends months familiarizing themselves with the organization, the individuals on the team, and the mandate. The individual who had been "acting," often resentful that their posting was only temporary, sees their opportunity for promotion pushed further into the future and becomes disengaged. The succession alternatives decrease, and the new leader stacks the team with people from their own network. This is an unfortunate but common exercise and is costly in terms of lost productivity, embedded knowledge, and engagement of those who are left behind from previous leadership.

Every leader who seeks to advance in an organization should not consider leaving their role until they have trained one or more individuals who are prepared to lead the team. For those individuals who have been focusing on developing their leadership abilities and show an interest in organization and bigger-picture strategic thinking, a succession plan should be developed and maintained in consultation with the individual and the executive sponsor for the analytics team. This helps to prevent the previously described scenario. If deliberate and transparent, succession planning is a key factor in retaining top talent.

Those individuals who show a particular strength in bigger-picture thinking and stakeholder engagement should be encouraged to develop in their leadership abilities. These people need to be enticed to remain with the organization for continuity and for the planning and execution of more complex multiyear analytics projects. They need to know and be reminded that their conduct is noticed by other people and that they are under greater obligation to conduct themselves appropriately at all times. Individual contributors on the team with managerial ambitions will regard the personal characteristics of the recently promoted as implicit success factors and mimic them in hopes of the same outcome.

There are several characteristics that mark an individual for leadership potential, such as self-awareness, motivation, and self-regulation (Goleman, 2014). When identifying potential for leadership, there are three key success factors:

Empathy   Having an intuitive understanding of the drivers of stakeholders, including their fears and motivations, is an unteachable but valuable skill. Solutions need to always be designed for the individual and should solve the underlying need, not the specific request. Understanding the interplay between teams and individuals and predicting requests in advance is the mark of a great leader in an analytics role.

Social Skills   There remains a fundamental distrust of analytics, especially among low-maturity organizations. Leaders who are able to establish rapport with stakeholders and engender confidence will have fewer change requests and experience less resistance.

Motivation   Leaders need to be motivated by the desire to add business value and to support others. Individuals who are motivated by the practice itself are better suited to roles in academia or as an individual contributor.

Potential leaders who have the baseline technical competence combined with these success factors are much better able to support a team than those who have a high degree of technical expertise. William Penn wrote in *Fruits of Solitude*, "He that has more Knowledge than Judgment, is made for another Man's use more than his own." (Penn, 1682/2001). Selecting and grooming for these skills ensures a stack with longevity, and without key person risk.

In building out a succession plan it can be tempting for a leader to hedge their bets and spread the effort across a number of people so that if opportunities arise there are many people to choose from. In practice, given the amount of time that needs to be invested in preparing people for leadership, and the amount of transparency required for true understanding of the nontechnical aspects surrounding the function, having a group of potential successors only leads to dissatisfaction and a loss of focus.

The ideal state is to focus on a single person who shows the aptitude and has the desire to fill a leader's role after their departure. This should be clear to both them and the team, and in any absence around vacations they should be able to stand in. The expectations for this candidate should be shared with the executive sponsor of the analytics function and all efforts made to ensure their continued development and involvement in larger functional strategy and decision making.

The continued engagement and retention of the individual is important for the leader personally as well as for the organization. Full transparency with the candidate and their explicit acceptance of the understudy role and personal commitment that they will be candid around their ambitions is essential. Also, essentially, their performance needs to be evaluated as a candidate for the leader's own role, and not for the role that they currently hold.

Potential Pitfalls

As discussed, most practitioners have great qualities that enable the important work they do. There are two potential pitfalls, however. Both the Dunning-Kruger effect and the Diderot effect are the other side of the coin for the curiosity that motivates most analytics professionals.

When curiosity is disordered, practitioners can lose sight of the ultimate business aims of their work. Understanding these effects can help to identify and eliminate them before they become problematic.

Dunning-Kruger Effect

Analytics practitioners need to maintain a healthy interest in their technical proficiency and to keep abreast of developments in the field of data science. Working in isolation, unaware of best practices, people can often fall behind their industry peers without realizing it. Worse still, as their modest and outdated skills are still beyond those of others in the organization, they can consider themselves experts in their field and see no need to improve.

The Dunning-Kruger effect is a cognitive bias whereby people with a limited understanding of a subject do not have the knowledge to accurately assess their own skills and as a result overestimate their abilities. The original interest in the subject was sparked in the 1990s when McArthur Wheeler, an amateur bank robber, put lemon juice on his face in the belief that it would make him invisible to security cameras. In discussion with Wheeler afterward, it was revealed that he made this determination because he understood that lemon juice was used for invisible ink. Wheeler did not have the base knowledge necessary to understand how ridiculous this connection was. In a similar way, pleasantly ignorant data scientists can assume positions that are objectively false because they do not have an adequate body of knowledge to draw upon.

This cognitive bias is endemic in the analytics field, where practitioners need to have proficiencies across several capabilities. The less experienced individuals, especially in those capabilities they are least exposed to, assume their abilities are intermediate. On the other end of the spectrum, those individuals who have a strong understanding of a capability yet have been exposed to people much more advanced than themselves know that their knowledge is limited and likewise assess themselves as intermediate.

As people continue to learn and grow within the field of data science and analytics, they quickly realize that each bit of knowledge they acquire over their career enables them to see many more concepts that they did not consider. This leads to every practitioner, except the most oblivious, considering themselves intermediate or average. Intermediate SQL abilities, for example, can be as simple as joins or aggregate functions or as sophisticated as architecture and distributed transactions, depending on the exposure the individual has had.

This bias is not solely with technical capabilities. Citizen data scientists, who have worked in an environment where they were free to set procedural standards, will often believe they have much more mature project management skills than they probably do.

The consequence of this widespread issue is that analytics talent needs to be comprehensively assessed during the onboarding process and throughout their time with the organization. Self-assessed capabilities need to be challenged and a thoughtful interviewing system put in place.

Diderot Effect

The Diderot effect (Diderot, 1875) is a phenomenon where a person, having no previous knowledge of a product or class of products, acquires one and begins to spiral into a period of rapid consumption. Once the person has an item within that class, it is incorporated as part of their identity, and their infatuation leads them to seek out complementary products. For example, a newly graduated lawyer may, as is tradition, receive a fountain pen as a graduation present. Their colleagues politely comment on the quality and gravitas that the pen imbues the new graduate with. The graduate quickly discovers that they also need a blotter, an assortment of inks, cleaning solution, and new stationery. They find previously unimaginably expensive writing instruments now justifiable and seek opportunities to treat themselves. After their fanaticism runs its course, they rediscover the convenience of a disposable ballpoint and relegate their expensive collection to a drawer.

This situation happens very frequently in data and analytics groups, where individuals learn of a new technology or approach and seek out ways to apply it, products that support it, and complementary products that support those products. This passion for the field is positive and should be celebrated, but where a natural curiosity gives way to an intemperate zealousness and Diderot effect, it should be controlled and identified by others in the group. Animal spirits can lead teams down expensive and time-consuming paths unless teams are judicious and value-focused.

Data lakes were advertised as the future of databases, and there was a widespread belief that once all the data of the enterprise was staged and available for consumption, remarkable insights would effortlessly emerge. New data lake solutions and tertiary products were being released seemingly every week, and fear of missing out encouraged rapid and premature migrations. Expensive new infrastructure was stood up that would allow all unstructured data to be stored alongside traditional relational databases. Data scientists became anxious that without data lake experience, they would not be competitive in the future and pushed their leaders to adopt this new technology, exaggerating its usefulness. The complexity of analysis increased and necessitated new tools such as Spark. Tools came out that could interface with Spark and reduce the complexity, such as Databricks. Eventually, without a compelling use case for these tools and infrastructure, as many as 60 to 85 percent of data lake migrations failed (Lukianoff, 2020). Though definitely an important and powerful development in the practice of analytics, the fact is that most companies did not need to adopt this platform.

Failures such as these stem from a fundamental misunderstanding as to the purpose of the analytics function. Data scientists provide analyses to the business that create value for the end customer and a competitive advantage to the business. The irrational exuberance toward data lakes was, in almost all cases, vanity projects by teams who lost sight of their core mandate.

The Diderot effect needs to be protected against, and each new fad and technology needs to be rationally and objectively assessed against the capabilities and needs of the organization. Maintaining the philosophy of parsimony can help to guard against these situations—if an analysis can be quickly and reasonably completed in something as simple as a spreadsheet, then that should be the approach. Likewise, if a particular business problem legitimately requires Kafka and Spark, then that should be the approach.

Leading the Team

One of the most intangible of personal qualities, yet paradoxically the most immediately identifiable, is leadership ability. Several resources exist that attempt to define it concisely, but arguably none have exhaustively and definitively captured what it truly means to be a leader. What can be named, however, are their characteristics.

Good leaders are respectful and genuinely care about the people on their team and the people within the organization. Being emotionally intelligent, they listen to people from a place of sincere empathy. They are authentic and openly share their strengths and weaknesses. They realize that their conduct is noticed by others and understand that they are under greater obligation to look carefully to themselves.

Good leaders demonstrate superior personal integrity and instill trust in their teams. They openly admit when they are wrong and are always seeking to improve. They are honest and straightforward, simultaneously caring deeply about their team members and being willing to offer and receive difficult feedback (Scott, 2017) . They say things that are not nice sometimes, but they are never intentionally hurtful. They praise and elevate their team publicly and offer their criticisms privately.

Good leaders are enablers; they remove roadblocks and help their team to find answers. They do not have all the answers, but they have the relationships to quickly find them.

Leaders are not bossy or managerial. They do not earn their authority by title or declaration. They are not personally attached to their ideas and do not feel the need to be the smartest person in the room (Thorp, 2017).

Experienced analytics leaders are exceedingly difficult to find. The natural predispositions that make them strong in terms of analytics tend to make leadership and soft skills challenging. For those who combine a deep technical understanding of data with the ability to translate it into a business context and to lead a project, people leadership can be developed like any other skill—as long as the natural inclination toward value creation is present and the individual authentically cares for the people on the team.

People have different motivations for seeking leadership, and for most functions it could be argued that so long as the neophyte exhibits the characteristics of a good leader it does not matter whether the source is genuine. For most functions, that may be true, and the outward expression of leadership is all that is important, but for analytics it is more nuanced. It is important, though, that people are pursuing leadership because they have an authentic desire to lead teams and to do so for its own sake. For those pressed into leadership, or for those who pursue it simply because they feel like they are supposed to, there is a double loss in that the productive output of the individual is lost and they are not likely to be successful in the new environment and with new expectations.

Traditional organizations tend to create only two or three levels for individual contributors, which provides ambitious people no other avenue for promotion other than through leadership. This normalizes a transition between two quite different professional paths. Whenever possible, analytics leaders should seek to create additional specialist or advisory role classifications, creating a parallel career stream for the individual contributors who seek technical depth rather than becoming a people-leader. Leaders should also coach people down that path as a default, only promoting leadership positions for those particularly well suited or who independently voiced a desire. Any who would be leaders within an analytics team should passionately pursue opportunities to lead and not fall into the role accidentally or because they feel it to be the normal course of a career. Leadership should be from a service mindset, technically collegial, and from a place of genuine interest in leading projects, making a difference, and supporting the team. Kingdom-builders and Napoleons exchange short-term project-level success for long-term relationship damage, and though that can be employed tactically, it is rarely worthwhile.

Often analytics practitioners will have arrived at their field from different avenues. Previously engineers, actuaries, consultants, or scientists, people will have a different view of what leadership looks like. It is important to determine this perspective through regular conversations. The ideal collaborative yet service-oriented mindset of an analytics team can appear overly deferential for those coming from a professional background where their opinions are final. For those coming from a consulting background, for example, adaptability can be confused with vacillation. It is important to discuss openly the decision-making process with the team so that conventions can be established and trust maintained. Understanding the priorities and motivations for project sponsors, and how to adapt project deliverables in response, can be difficult for those who perceive a singular technical path to success. Transparent walkthroughs of the decision process, including all intangible considerations, can assist in helping the team to develop these leadership abilities and see more than the models and data.

Integrity and knowledge alone are not enough for a new leader to navigate the implicit rules of an organization. If an individual knows what is right and wrong in a professional setting, that person should theoretically be able to always select the right path with the information they have. However, in reality, as soon as a person sets their mind to overcoming one fault, they will be surprised by failure in another area. Personal disposition and inclination are always stronger than reason and training, and without a continual conscious effort to the contrary, indolence will draw a practitioner into improper habits. Achieving mastery of a field through time and experience, hitting Gladwell's 10,000 hours (Gladwell, 2011) works well for technical and procedural efforts, but for areas such as communication where there are personal characteristics influencing the activities, an individual will always experience a pull toward what may be weaker in their nature. The counteracting force to this needs to come from without, and through the positive guidance of a leader who understands the individual and their personal proclivities.

Ultimately, what a data science and analytics leader must aspire to be is what McKinsey calls a translator (Henke et al., 2018). This role is far

removed from frontline delivery or coding. Translators do not need deep data engineering and architecture experience, or an expansive software development CV. Their primarily role is in bridging the gap between the business-facing part of the team and the data scientists. To do this, these translators need to be able to establish credibility with both sides. They need to know at a high level how modeling and scripting work so that they are able to ask the right questions and help the team navigate toward an effective solution. They also need to know at a high level what the business actually needs so they can frame the solution appropriately. What these individuals need is domain knowledge, general technical fluency, project management experience, and an entrepreneurial spirit.

Leadership is a nebulous concept, difficult to describe yet immediately identifiable. Other business functions can abide a fairly broad range of characteristics in leadership from the dictatorial to the saintly to the innocently incompetent. Analytics, being at once highly technical, advisory, a shared service, project management, change management, and all while interfacing with several complex and incompatible divisions within the enterprise, has a very demanding set of specific capabilities. Finding a person naturally well suited to the role is a challenge, as what compels one to be a leader rarely pulls them toward analytics, and what drives a person into data science is rarely what makes them aspire to leadership. It is only through a careful cultivation of certain skills and through intentional career guidance that an analytics leader can be developed.

Data Scientists as Craftspeople

Those unfamiliar with data science and analytics can be forgiven for thinking that the process of deconstructing business problems to systematically and programmatically optimize or automate can itself be considered a systematic and mechanical process. This view, however, significantly undervalues the role that creativity plays in the process and the passion that has enticed most analytics professionals to pursue a career in analytics.

To be at their best, a data scientist needs to not only understand the problem being addressed but to contextualize it within the tapestry of internal data pipelines, stakeholder relationships and capabilities, external factors, the competitive environment, regulatory frameworks, behavioral drivers, and operational requirements. The breadth of knowledge and creativity required to see the connections between the elements is so complex that it is impossible to generalize into a systematic approach that will work in every instance.

In the well-known parable of the stonecutters by the business guru Peter Drucker (1954):

While walking, a traveler came across three stonecutters and asked each of them what they were doing. The first replied, "I am making a living." The second kept on hammering and replied, "I am doing the best job of stone cutting in the entire country." The third stopped, looked up at the traveler with a visionary gleam in his eye, and said, "I am building a cathedral."

Applying the parable to data and analytics professionals, the parallels are clear. As with the first cutter, for some people it is simply a job, and there is a great deal of work to be done in cleaning data, setting up pipelines, and other procedural tasks. As with the second cutter, for those with passion for their field certainly there are new models, new algorithms, and ways to improve performance and accuracy. The truly exceptional craftspeople and leaders, however, can put their work into perspective and understand that it is a contribution to a larger goal.

As Joseph Schumpeter (1936) said, "It is not the owners of stage-coaches who build railways." Stakeholders have an interest in the status quo and are often less innovative. The mindset, and associated cognitive biases, that created a problem has a much harder time resolving it than a person with a different perspective. Practitioners need to maintain these characteristics of creativity and contextualization and to be able to apply their body of knowledge, intuition, and past experiences to a project from ideation to sustainment. In this way, they are far more like craftspeople than automata. This is a view shared by Alteryx, who coined the term *data artisans* to describe them.

Once it has been understood to be an artisanal practice, there are several natural takeaways in terms of the management of a high-performing data science team.

End to End   Being involved in a project from the original discussions with a stakeholder to the final handover and closeout meeting gives an individual a feeling of ownership and connectivity to the project and the organization. It builds relationships, supports professional development, and greatly impacts job satisfaction. Alternatively, deconstructing a project into an assembly line of individual tasks can be alienating, reduce engagement, and introduce key person risks.

New Products   Being involved in the creation of a new product or process is much more psychologically gratifying than incrementalism. It is rare that a practitioner can share their workday in an exciting way at the dinner table, making the ability to point to a press release for a new product they had involvement in hugely satisfying.

Cost Cutting   Despite being appealing to the business, an overemphasis on analytics as a tool for cost cutting reduces engagement within the function and reduces trust with other business units. While almost all practitioners appreciate efficiency, they are also aware of the human cost.

Respect   Without discounting the importance of healthy conflict within a team, all opinions and ideas should be respected and heard. Craftspeople have a wealth of knowledge, and often seemingly unrelated episodes can be applied to current problems if the idea is given space to crystalize without criticism or dismissiveness.

Egalitarianism   Hierarchical and top-down approaches to management for a team of craftspeople does not work. Leaders should play a supporting role and be an equal to the other members of the team, not a boss that issues decrees. Decisions should be made based on data, not on salary band.

Idiosyncrasies   Whether a firmly held position on variable naming conventions or a fondness for loud mechanical keyboards, practitioners should have the ability to express themselves fully inasmuch as it does not disrupt the team or their deliverables. Project delivery needs to be consistent, but all other aspects of how that is achieved should be under the control of the individual. Creative solutions will never emerge from a team built on compliance and uniformity. Supportive and positive environments foster creativity and greatly improve engagement.

For a leader of a team of craftspeople, there are certain requirements to success. Credibility needs to be established and a relationship built on mutual respect. The leader does not need to understand a language or technique at the level of the specialists on the team but needs to be conversant to the point that they can ask the right questions and appreciate a clever solution as a peer. Without that credibility and the respect of the individuals on the team, it will be difficult to maintain control over processes or provide the support they need to develop.

Leaders also need to be willing to remove administrative roadblocks. Timesheets, expense reports, arrangements for training and hotels, and all other irrelevant distractions should be minimized as much as possible to allow the team to focus on their work. Leaders should shield their team from the inherent partisanship and horse trading of the corporate world.

In the 2011 documentary *Jiro Dreams of Sushi*, the titular Jiro describes himself as a *Shokunin*, a person who passionately dedicates himself completely to bettering his craft. He feels obligated on an almost spiritual level to improve. This level of passion is not uncommon among data scientists, and it is essential that they have a leader who is able to challenge them, understand them, and offer an environment where they can grow.

Team Conventions

For a data and analytics team to be at their best, they cannot be a simple mechanistic executor of analytics projects or robotic managers of arcane processes. Teams are groups of people, and people need a gripping narrative and sense of identity and purpose. Teams need to have a patina; they cannot be clean and distant from core elemental senses.

Team conventions are those intra-group principles and rules that a team operates under. Some of these are explicit, such as the agenda for recurring meetings, and some are implicit, such as how decisions are made or how the team perceives itself.

Gabriel Marcel, a French philosopher, promoted the idea of creative fidelity. Marcel believed that for an individual to reach their fullest personal expression, they needed to be a thinking, emotive, creative being. There is nothing human in simply doing or reacting. He said that "a really alive person is not merely someone who has a taste for life, but somebody who spreads that taste, showering it, as it were, around him; and a person who is really alive in this way has, quite apart from any tangible achievements of his, something essentially creative about him" (Marcel, 2017). The primary goal of team conventions is in support of this idea of creative fidelity. Every individual on the team needs to consider themselves as participating in the strategizing, planning, execution, ownership, and delivery of the team. Leadership must be exercised, but practitioners need to have a creative outlet and agency over their professional lives in order to be at their best.

The outcome of this, if accepted as desirable, is that titles are a meaningless appellation. Managers, analysts, specialists, engineers, and scientists may have different roles and responsibilities, but it cannot be within a formal hierarchy based on dominance and subservience. Egalitarian teams, founded on mutual respect, where the goal is the success of the project and the development and support of one's peers, are the most successful teams. Analytics teams should not perceive themselves as employees or colleagues of their stakeholders, engaged in a mutual struggle, celebrating "hump day," and looking forward to the weekend.

Teams should bring a consultative mindset, driven by purpose and creative fidelity to bring value and results to those who are their clients.

In the daily flow of work for most professions, there is an oscillation of high- and low-stress periods. Engineers may have high-stress client meetings in the morning and carve out the afternoon for technical work with understood approaches. Lawyers may spend their morning doing due diligence and their afternoon in a high-stress courtroom setting. Like mowing the lawn or doing the dishes, a task with less cognitive demand can have a pacifying effect and reduce stress. For a properly run analytics team, though, there are few such occasions to let their guard down. From design thinking sessions to data discovery to exploratory analysis to modeling to validation to stakeholder handover to sustainment, every phase requires creativity and novel approaches.

It needs to be that there is a degree of comfort and fraternity within the team to establish a sanctuary from a very demanding profession. Without this sense of refuge, it is easy for individuals to get burned out or see themselves as isolated and unsupported. The way to frame the team as this place of peace is through the careful and intentional development of team conventions.

These conventions need to be authentic and sensitive to the preferences and limitations of the team. There may be a blend of religious constraints, family situations, and dietary restrictions that should influence the team activities. Happy hour can leave out those who choose not to drink, and evening activities can exclude those with children. Team builders, often criticized as synthetic and forced, should be discarded, reframed instead as casual activities and communicated as a genuine attempt to get to know each other outside of work. These need to reflect the group and be an opportunity for individuals to share parts of their life they otherwise struggle with.

Another often overlooked team convention is the establishment of group rituals. One ritual in particular that provides a sense of comfort and stability to a team is the informal institution of a team restaurant that is attended solely for celebrations (such as recognition, onboarding, etc.) and only for the inner team. The creation of group-defining rituals can help to improve the bonds within the team and to boost performance (McGinn, 2017). These rituals can take other forms, including ringing bells, taking selfies, a group cheer, a phrase to close out meetings, or a mascot.

Individuals need to feel that they can bring their whole selves to work. Adjusting their language or censoring themselves so that they can more easily blend in creates an environment of inauthenticity and has material impacts in terms of productivity and emotional well-being (Robbins, 2018). Every member of the team should strive to be authentic, show humility, and view each other as people rather than resources. Leaders need commitment and intention to create this type of environment and to lead by example, openly discussing their aspirations, being vulnerable, and sharing their humanity.

Formal Meetings

The overarching philosophy of parsimony has it that as much time as possible should be dedicated to value-generating activities by eliminating all superfluous activities. Modern professionals spend approximately half of their time in meetings, and for the most part these meetings are nonproductive replacements for email or a chance to confirm a decision that has already been made or to provide an opportunity for participants to ask questions.

The alternative, a group of individuals acting with complete autonomy, communicating only as required, paints an equally dismal picture of misalignment and rework.

Recurring meetings should be purpose-driven and serve to enable the work, not to be a distraction. Done properly, these meetings form part of the self-identity of the team and are an opportunity to set the tone and the theme of the practice. As with family meals, the purpose goes beyond consumption into bonding, where small rituals are established, and people find comfort. While not exhaustive, the typical recurring meetings for an analytics team include the elements discussed in the following sections.

Daily—Optional Check-in/Huddle/Standup

The daily standup is a cornerstone of Agile, meant to energize the team, share immediate priorities and roadblocks, and prepare the practitioners for the day. For smaller and tightly integrated teams working on a few projects, this is an essential meeting to maintain cohesion and alignment and to catch issues as quickly as possible. Without these meetings, it can be a week until roadblocks are identified.

These meetings are typically 15 minutes or less, happen three to five times weekly, and are meant to prepare each person for their next task and clear up any uncertainties. They are rapid and face to face.

For larger analytics teams or those with several smaller, individual in-flight projects, a daily huddle can sap energy rather than introduce it.

Only sub-teams under a first-level manager or project-level teams should participate.

Weekly—Mandatory Kickoffs/Tactical

The weekly kickoff is a chance for the entire team to gather and share the status of their projects as well as their overall priority for the week, to solicit any help needed, and to share any new developments.

These meetings are also an opportunity for the leader to share any news or developments from the previous week. Wherever possible, leaders should be completely transparent with their teams. It is a sign of respect and helps them to put into perspective any changes in priorities and the rationale behind certain decisions.

For a leader, this meeting is one of the most important ways to reinforce which behaviors are positive and negative for the team. For those who find innovative solutions, those who identify potential projects, or potential data science champions in the organization, immediate and enthusiastic recognition in front of their peers is a powerful incentive. Similarly, those who need to report weekly that their tasks remain incomplete will feel naturally compelled to solicit help rather than hide their inability to deliver.

Structurally, these meetings comprised announcements by the leader, followed by a round table two- to three-minute summary of the status of each in-flight project and any other news from each practitioner on the team. Leaders and other team members can and should ask clarifying questions as appropriate, and the facilitator should feel confident to defer larger questions for strategic review sessions.

These meetings are essential to the individuals seeing themselves as a team, and the idea that the team succeeds or fails together needs to be set. Practitioners should be encouraged to offer help to each other during these sessions and to offer advice for resolving problems.

Quarterly—Strategic

Without an effort made to the contrary, individual contributors on the team will naturally view their role as solely project delivery and execution, and will become order takers. The strategic vision for the team will be a memory or, worse, a mascot and be an Edenic but unachievable state. The purpose of the quarterly strategic review is to assess the performance of the team over the prior three months against the strategy for the team as well as to address any bigger questions that have come up.

The following topics are among those that should be discussed:

- Relationships within the team
- Relationships with other stakeholders
- Eminence-building opportunities
- Pending or completed organizational changes and their impact to the team
- Competitive threats
- The state of analytics within the enterprise
- Team, stakeholder, and organizational morale
- Changes or developments in the data science field
- Summary of debriefs for the quarter

These meetings should be an uncomfortable and critical self-assessment rather than a quarterly ratification of a nominal strategy. Healthy conflict should be encouraged and expected, and practitioners who dissent from the popular opinion should be celebrated. Leaders should lead by example and offer and request candid feedback, accepting any criticism with grace and humility. The team, and each individual, needs to commit to relentless self-questioning and self-investigation and to pursue absolute excellence in the work they do. These meetings provide an opportunity for team members to share that commitment in the presence of their colleagues.

These meetings, if carefully planned and facilitated, should have the participants leaving feeling a sense of catharsis. Ending with a team lunch is a great way to bookend the potentially difficult and awkward conversations with a small celebration and to reward the team for their candid participation.

Coffee Chats

Almost every organization encourages managers and employees to have a regularly scheduled coffee chat, one-on-one, touchpoint, or other such short meeting. The benefits are clear—done well, these meetings improve productivity, increase employee engagement, and build solid relationships. Unfortunately, the full range of benefits are seldom realized. Overwhelmed managers delay or cancel the conversations or use them to run through task lists that pragmatic analysts quietly accept. Employees, hesitant to openly share their perspective and concerns with distant managers, assure them that everything is fine. Bottled frustrations, interpersonal misalignments, and generally poor communication lead to wasted time and solidify a hierarchical and transactional relationship.

Data scientists, as craftspeople with a high level of autonomy, have particular needs that must be met to get the most out of these meetings. These one-on-ones include a number of best practices:

Prioritize   Leaders should make these discussions a priority and let their team know they are a priority. Canceling these meetings sets a tone that they are a low-level concern and are the first thing to be cut when time is constrained. While it is understandable and necessary to need to move the meetings around stakeholder meetings, they should never be canceled. Leaders should apologize whenever they are moved and reiterate that the meetings and the individual are a priority for the leader both as a manager and as a person.

Building Trust through Feedback   For a practitioner to offer feedback to a leader is difficult and leaves them open to retribution. To do so is an act of trust and shows that the relationship is strengthening. Leaders should never get defensive and never reject the comments. Doing so will set the tone that the practitioner is not to offer any feedback. Leaders should always give sincere appreciation for feedback and accept it as being completely valid from the perspective of the practitioner. It is wise to take time to consider the feedback before responding and to bring it up at the next scheduled meeting.

Focus   Make the discussion about the employee. Catch problems when they are small. Leaders should realize that while they may have a dozen or more such touchpoints in a week, individual contributors on their team will only have one. It is important that leaders take notes and follow up on any commitments that they make. Though it is easy to become overwhelmed with larger teams, it needs to be a priority to prevent resentfulness and the sense from the perspective of the practitioner that it is just a checklist for their manager.

Tasks   Leaders can often make the mistake of starting these conversations with a brief summary of work in progress, hurdles, and all the project-related questions that they may not have had a chance to ask during project meetings or daily scrums. This implies that the priority is the work and that the personal concerns and hopes of the practitioner are secondary, topics addressed only at the end of the call and only if time permits. Regardless of in-flight projects or priorities, task-level discussions should be had only at the end of the meeting, and only if there is complete mutual certainty that all outstanding personal questions and concerns have been addressed.

Surprises   Occasionally, if there is a mutual respect, practitioners may raise red flags. This will often be top of mind for them but relayed in passing in the last few minutes of the conversation because of nervousness on their part. Seemingly off-the-cuff remarks implying that they are thinking more about their future or having some issues with colleagues are almost always a sign of a much larger problem and one that should be given full attention. In these cases, it is important to immediately set a time to discuss in more detail and to investigate thoroughly.

Authenticity   Unless a leader is genuine in their relationships with the practitioners on the team, they cannot expect the same in return. It is important for a leader to share, with some discretion, their personal situation and motivations. Leaders who put up a façade of professionalism are not approachable, and it creates an implication that the team should follow in this fakery.

Gossip   It can be tempting for leaders to consider members of the team as friends and share personal details about other people on the team, or express grievances. Often leaders defend this as being candid and setting an atmosphere of trust. In practice, this almost always leads to distrust. Gossip is viscerally appealing but people will be less open as a result for fear of being gossiped about in turn.

Assumptions   Leaders can project their personal motivations onto their team members and instinctively coach them in a direction that they themselves would like to go. Leaders need to understand the individual and their own personal goals before they begin to offer personal advice. For some team members, technical proficiency and depth of understanding are a priority, while for others, the priority is career advancement and face time with leaders. Making assumptions about what is important to the individual can set the relationship on the wrong footing early on. From the beginning, leaders should explicitly ask what the personal goals of the practitioner are so that they can adjust their feedback and coaching appropriately.

The benefits of these conversations go far beyond tangible improvements in quality and engagement. People spend most of their waking hours at work, and for many it is the source and summit of their personal lives. For almost all working people, their self-actualization and self-worth comes at least in part from their performance at work and their feelings of being respected and appreciated. These conversations are a way to truly make a difference in that person's life and to change a transactional employee/employer relationship built on mutual exchange into a source of meaning. Practitioners who find meaning in their work and feel respected vastly outperform those who are simply earning a paycheck.

For leaders as well, these conversations are the sole opportunity to assess the general sentiment of the team. In weekly startups, project updates, team builders, and mandated performance reviews, symptoms of underlying discontent arise only once they have become problems. Mature leaders need to have a holistic knowledge of their team, indi-vidually and collectively, and be aware of burgeoning issues before they become a more visible problem.

Managing Conflict

One convention for the team that needs to be consciously set by the leader is the attitude around conflict. Practitioners tend to fall into two camps, either expressly avoidant or logically direct yet impersonal. Those who are avoidant can feel unheard, disrespected, and eventually withdraw and become disengaged from the team. They can view conflict as uncomfortable, unproductive, and personal. Those who are more direct can see things in black and white, with a single logical solution. If they are overruled yet remain inwardly unconvinced, they too can withdraw and become disengaged from the team. They can view conflict as an illogical and emotional reaction to the truth. Without a leader who can address the conflict and facilitate these difficult conversations, the person with the louder voice will prevail to the detriment of everybody.

Conflict should not be avoided. It is inevitable in a productive and healthy team, and it results in new solutions and perspectives. The key is to allow conflict to arise in the right climate and use proper constructive communication (Runde & Flanagan, 2008). For conflict to be healthy, it needs to be heard and implicitly understood within an environment of safety and mutual trust. When members of the team know each other as people, not employees, they will normally attribute positive intentions to their comments. When they have worked together on teams and respect each other's abilities and experience, they will view it as a fraternal correction rather than an attack. Creating this environment is a proactive way to protect against conflict devolving into toxicity.

Once conflict arises, the team needs to be explicitly aware of the expectations around communication. Each participant needs to be fully free to express their emotions and perspectives so long as it is relevant to the project being discussed. People should always be free to critique an idea but never a person. Each participant also needs to seek to understand the other person's viewpoint rather than seeing it as a battle to be won. Leaders can facilitate and encourage this by asking clarifying questions around assumptions and rationale. Leaders can also reduce the pressure during a meeting by calmly restating the last claim, ostensibly for their own understanding. Offer encouragement openly and acknowledge that there is a healthy difference of opinion that is coming from a mutual desire for an ideal outcome.

Conflict is particularly challenging for virtual teams. When your colleague is challenging your premises in person, you can see their body language, hear the timbre of their voice, see the wandering of their eyes. If they are facing you and becoming animated or sullen, it can become clear to you that they are thinking through other solutions. All these nuances, however, are lost during video chats. Seeing only the face of your antagonist while the rest of your team observes silently feels confrontational and pushes people toward defensive posturing. Small lags in Internet connections exacerbate this by causing people to talk over one another and to remove the little polite deferrals that are a part of face-to-face communication. In cases where team members have never met face-to-face, without a personal relationship and base understanding of mutual affectations, there is no familiarity or trust. In these cases, it is important for the leader to act as a facilitator and mediator in the conversation. Repeat a grounding statement, that all participants are there to improve the project and outcome. Interject when personal attacks or attempts to bring up past grievances happen. If necessary, parking lot the item and book a follow-up meeting when participants have had a chance to pause and reflect.

External conflicts are different in that they provide an opportunity for a team to rally around what they perceive as a personal threat and to cement feelings of fraternity. Without villainizing individual stakeholders, leaders need to actively mine for conflicts and drama (Lencioni, 2004). The presence of danger can help to solidify social bonds and create a more integrated team.

As a leader, it is important to lead by example. Visibly seek feedback, and warmly welcome critiques. Offer genuine thanks for any opposing views that are offered, especially when less vocal team members partic-ipate. Leaders should try to always be a role model for the ideal person-ality combination of somebody with strong beliefs that are weakly held.

Relationship Management

The heart of data science and analytics is in finding connections between elements of a business problem that others have not identified and using technology to integrate them into a more productive process. Without a broad understanding of the practice, the industry, the players, the spoken and unspoken rules, the politics, the roadmap, the function, and the technology, the best that can be aspired to is incrementalism. That broad understanding cannot come from self-directed study or intuition, it can only come from relationships with others. For this reason, it is impor-tant that relationship development and management is a primary goal for any analytics leader and made a priority for each individual within the analytics function.

The essential characteristic of successful relationship building is inten-tionality. Leaders cannot passively await introductions to stakeholders and depend on years of accidental collaboration to bring them to a collegial friendship. Leaders who want to be successful within an organization need to intentionally seek out relationships in every sphere. Leaders need also to set relationship building as a quantifiable expectation for every member of the team, regardless of level. In every project, a parallel within the business should be explicitly assigned to one of the analytics or data scientists involved. The development of that relationship should be a key personal takeaway from the project, and that individual should be evaluated at least partially on their ability to create those relationships.

Those relationships need to be genuine. It should not be simply a means to an end, even if the end is a more fruitful interplay between the teams. Authentic personal relationships, for the genuine benefit of the other, are both more productive and more personally rewarding.

Most people find it challenging to develop a network within an organization. Introverted individuals might depend on introductions and land on a small but close group of supporters. People with more moderate dispositions may in their first few months arrange coffee chats and recurring touchpoints that are eventually abandoned. For those who are tasked with actively building and maintaining relationships with individuals outside of their function, it can be difficult to do so authentically and successfully. The typical reaction by practitioners, struggling to meet expectations in this new accountability, is with introductory emails and offers of service. While this is a great step for an initial introduction if there is otherwise no overlap or opportunity for a more natural opening of dialogue, in isolation it is rarely successful. Leaders need to offer concrete advice to their teams in how to achieve networking goals.

In *The Autobiography of Benjamin Franklin*, Franklin relays a lesson he had learned, "He that has once done you a kindness will be more ready to do you another, than he whom you yourself have obliged" (Franklin, 2012). He recounts how a man whom he finds it difficult to establish a connection with joins his club. After learning that the man has a rare book, Franklin sends a polite note asking if he may borrow it and afterward returns it with a thanks. He finds then that the man is eager to support him after this event and addresses him more respectfully. Similarly, the best way to establish a bond with an internal stakeholder is through a small reciprocal favor. Rather than a self-contained unconditional offer of support, which the leader likely receives daily from vendors and consultants, request advice on in-flight work as part of the initial networking effort. Follow up within a few weeks expressing gratitude and share how the advice helped with the project. An alternative is to solicit advice from individuals on topics they may have familiarity with. Even something as simple as asking for directions or restaurant recommendations is sufficient to establish a connection.

Another important consideration is that every individual has a personal preference around communication style. More introverted people might prefer an email or instant message. More outgoing people might prefer a drive-by and face-to-face conversation. Some traditionalists favor a phone call, while for some in Gen Y, an unannounced phone call is considered a rude demand on their time. Analytics practitioners, with relationship management as a defined accountability, need to be aware of the communication preferences of their stakeholders and be willing to adapt their own style to suit. Leaders should coach newer practitioners to be able to observe the communication style of their customers and to adapt accordingly. Flowery emails should be responded to in kind, and those stakeholders who use video in their Zoom calls should be accommodated with the same respect. Generally, data scientists lean toward the introverted side of the spectrum and send long emails that are equal parts stream of consciousness and technical exposition. It is incumbent on the leaders of these teams to highlight the importance of crisp communication at the level and in the preferred style of the recipient. Practitioners must showcase adaptability, not expect the stakeholder to adjust for their own convenience.

Relationships are the exception to the general rule of parsimony. The building of connections should never be tactical and minimized to preserve time for productive endeavors. Relationships should be eagerly sought out and cultivated and be thought of as beneficial independent of immediate work concerns. These relationships should not just be within the organization, or the team, but across all the spheres the individual works within. Some of the different personas of focus are as follows:

Team   Understanding of the aspirations, motivations, and situations of each of the individuals on the team is important for overall camaraderie and ensuring that leaders are in a position to advocate for their team in a way that aligns with their desires.

Business Unit or Peers   Knowing the accountabilities, weaknesses, pain points, and politics of those within the business unit or one's peers can help an individual to avoid landmines and find opportunities to add value as well as maintain visibility into the political space.

Leaders   As a leader should be close to their team, they should also seek to understand their own leader and their motivations and ambitions.

Skip Level   The leader's leader is often the person who will make the decisions that impact the leader and their team. Having a good relationship with one's own leader can help encourage positive advocacy, but people should not let the successful growth of their function and career depend on a single manager who is incented to keep resources to themselves.

Diagonal Skip Level   The peers of a leader's leader are often contributing votes on any decisions that affect the analytics practice. Depending entirely on any one individual for advocacy introduces unnecessary risk. Establishing rapport with others within that group ensures more support is available for resourcing.

Vendors   Sales representatives and relationship managers for software are typically very well connected within a community. They are a prime resource for scouting talent and knowing what is happening at other organizations in the community.

Academia   Universities depend on industry contacts to provide real-world experience to their students through co-op terms as well as to source capstone projects and give practical seminars. In return, they provide raw horsepower, a unique perspective on problems, and a pool of talent to draw on.

Practice   Having a strong network of colleagues within the practice of analytics helps an individual to keep current with developments in the field as well as to be aware of the movement of talent. This is particularly the case for analytics leaders within a specific region or city. They can offer unofficial assessments of applicants, share news and best practices, and keep each other aware of upcoming career opportunities.

Industry   Successful practitioners need to have an understanding of industry trends so that they can speak intelligently to the needs of the business. Though care must be taken to avoid the potential perception of collusion, knowing others within the industry allows the sharing of best practices and challenges from competitors.

It is an uncomfortable truth that each project and interaction is within an environment influenced by politics. Each stakeholder has their personal ambitions and drivers and their own relationships and challenges with the other individuals in the company. More junior practitioners can attempt to recuse themselves from this fact and expect that their work will speak for itself. Though this is an admirable ideal to reach for, in practice it rarely plays out as expected. Projects can be killed seemingly without reason, and previously committed resources pulled just as they are needed. Politics is the troll guarding the bridge (Rasiel, 1999). Every practitioner must consider the incentives and drivers for those they are working with. Maintaining a situational awareness, without directly intervening or participating in destructive politics and derisive polemics, is a necessary skill for practitioners, and in particular the leaders of these teams. Willful ignorance of the politics involved in decision making can have a large effect on the impact an analytics team is able to make in the organization.

It is also important that leaders consider the environment within which they are placing decision makers. Having a strong relationship with stakeholders can inform decisions around communication style, what time of day they are most amenable, and how to structure and facilitate meetings. Professions with high self-esteem will evaluate scenarios differently depending on their mood (Kahneman et al., 2016). These subtle changes to approach can make the difference between a productive exchange and one that is based on emotionality. Project leaders should explicitly ask at the beginning of projects what stakeholder preferences are surrounding communication and recurring meeting but also be observant to the conditions that can make individuals less amenable.

Politics can also unfortunately lead to personal attacks against analytics leaders, or against the team as a whole regardless of the successes of the team. This can appear capricious or personal but is in many cases simply coming from a power struggle elsewhere in the organization. Prudent leaders should seek to be aware of these struggles but not get involved personally or try to pick winners. Respond to threats as they are happening and understand the motivations of the people involved (Heifetz & Linsky, 2002). The priority should remain the success of the team.

Practitioners need to consider the emotional posture and organizing frame of the individuals from the business with whom they are working. It can be challenging to consider the perspective of others, in particular given the differences the individuals may have in priorities, responsibilities, and vocabulary. Poorly performing analytics teams can often place the burden of understanding on the business, expecting that once they educate themselves they will see the benefits of the proposed solution. Stakeholders should be communicated with respectfully, with the burden of understanding and adaptation to BU norms placed on the project lead. Practitioners need to empathize with the individuals they are working with and understand their driving forces:

Anxiety   The imposition of the analytics function in their work, whether they are inwardly optimistic or pessimistic, is an anxiety-inducing experience. The project means additional work for them and will likely require them to change their processes in the end. Practitioners need to understand that their involvement introduces personal stress into the lives of the stakeholders and individual contributors on their teams and to be respectful and kind.

Loss of Expertise   Processes that the individuals have possibly themselves created are going to be changed or removed, and the expertise they have in some cases spent years developing will be immediately devalued. They can perceive this as a loss of station and as a personal attack. They can be defensive and actively seek to sabotage the project. They may also be gracious and eager to learn the new technique and develop their abilities in new areas. It is incumbent on the project leader to make this assessment.

Loss of Continuity   The training plans, succession plans, and organizational design of the stakeholder group will potentially need to be modified. Individuals who were hired for a certain skillset may need to pivot to maintain relevance. Automation may introduce redundancies and lead to dismissals. When the analytics team has moved on to their next project, the work has just begun for the stakeholder. This should be appreciated by practitioners and all effort made to mitigate the negative impact for the client.

Lack of Mutual Understanding   Often the language used between the analytics function and the business are completely different. Each business unit has its particular *patois* and defines metrics slightly differently. Analytics practitioners should not impose their vernacular on stakeholders but rather seek to understand and define the terms and processes of the team. Rushing to solution a problem, or making assumptions, can lead to visible failures and relationship damage. Stakeholders should be respected as clients in an engagement, not as fortunate recipients of unassailable wisdom.

Priorities   The individuals on the team are typically evaluated against metrics that are much different than those that are important to the analytics team. While practitioners are motivated by efficiency, productivity, performant models, and new technology, the stakeholders are often looking toward different qualitative measures of business performance. Resentment can build if the analytics team openly distills their effort into quantifiable metrics that are not relevant to the stakeholder.

Motivations   The individual contributors, project sponsor, executive sponsor, and all involved parties are independent human beings who have their own personal goals and motivations. Some might be seeking promotion, some actively seeking a new job, and some putting in time to retirement. Some may have new babies at home, while others are taking care of ill family members. What could appear as passive acceptance of recommendations could vary significantly depending on the organizing frame of the individual. Practitioners should seek to understand where the individuals are personally and adjust communication and delivery to accommodate.

Personal Fears   Despite all the benefits of data science and analytics, the mainstream media is usually unkind toward the practice. There are misperceptions that automation will lead to widespread unemployment, that it is primarily responsible for increases in global wealth inequality, and even that it is necessitating policies around universal basic income. Individuals will have heard that the computers are getting smarter, that they are recognizing their faces, and that the large technology companies are influencing their lives in invisible ways. Whether it is conscious or unconscious, many of these people can attribute this at least partially to data and analytics teams and have a fundamental personal distrust. Practitioners should seek always to make a personal connection with individuals to reduce this distrust.

Without a seat at the table, the focus and future of an analytics team will be decided by other people. Analytics leaders need to make every effort to involve themselves in discussions at every level.

Owning the Narrative

It would be inconceivable for an organization to maintain parallel human resources functions. Individuals may have a background in HR, or a natural predisposition that entices others throughout the organization to seek advice from them regarding their benefits or vacation allotments. However, when a decision needed to be made, it would be the HR function that would have the final word. The same could be said for several other functions, such as operations, finance, and IT. In analytics, however, many organizations are decentralized either by design or by a lack of vision and have decentralized analytics practitioners, larger divisional teams, or in a worst-case scenario, function-specific teams running independently of a centralized analytics team.

When analytics begins in an organization, it typically evolves naturally from pockets of technical sophistication before organically gathering into a Center of Excellence or centralized function. This initial accretion is followed by rationalization and paying off technical debt, followed by a stable period of growth and value creation for the organization or division within which the team exists.

Without strategic oversight, however, other functions seeing the successes of the team will often seek to onboard their own data science resources to ensure committed support and to control the planning and execution of projects. This arises regardless of the quality of service provided by the existing analytics function and is a natural desire of other teams that is often not controlled or understood by leadership.

This secondary decentralization is more dangerous than the initial one and has the potential to introduce a level of technical debt that can never be fully unwound. Competing priorities and cross-communication between upstream dependencies in business intelligence and IT can lead to confusion regarding direction and tools. The proliferation of data sets and analytical sandboxes create future reconciliation issues as new metrics are developed. Depending on relationships with the leadership of the parallel function, other functions in the organization may pick and choose to get priority service.

For these reasons it is imperative that leaders within the centralized function control the narrative around analytics within the organization and establish themselves as the authority regardless of hierarchy. The processes, strategy, and technology stack that is in use must be promulgated as the default analytics approach and all stakeholders educated in the value offering of the team. Colin Powell (2006) once said, "Experts possess more data than judgement." If no analytics leader appears to exercise control over the practice of analytics within an organization, individual leaders will make those decisions using whatever understanding they may have.

Without explicit authority over the new individuals, it can be challenging to exercise this control. In practice, resources are often dispersed and an analytics leader must lead by influence rather than direct control. The Community of Practice is a powerful tool for setting one's team as the analytical leads in the organization and providing an avenue for recurring touchpoints with the incoming practitioners and an opportunity for collaboration and eventual assimilation. Leaders should also seek to establish their team as the thought leaders in analytics through the organization by ensuring consistent yet nonintrusive communication among leaders. This can be accomplished by sharing conference notes, blog postings, and invitations to presentations by the analytics team. Attendance or knowledge transfer does not need to be the goal with these communications—rather, they should be a subtle reminder that the team exists, is on top of the industry trends, and is actively seeking to involve others in the organization in their practice. Intentional relationship building and management is essential to owning the narrative around analytics in an organization.

Leaders who have properly built relationships should be aware in advance of any moves toward onboarding new citizen data scientists and be involved in the creation of job descriptions and the establishment of an analytics strategy for that team. If leaders are aware of these initiatives, they are well situated to encourage the functional leader toward hiring somebody from their own personal network. Placing individuals that the leader is comfortable with and has an existing relationship with ensures that communication will be strong and that they will have the technical bent that works well with the established processes.

These admonishments can have a Machiavellian air but serve a pragmatic purpose in advancing the analytical maturity for the enterprise. Without conscious effort to counteract, visibly successful analytics teams will encourage others to stand up that capability, leading to future failures, confusion, and devaluing of analytics as a practice. In the best interests of the organization and the team, it is important to establish control to regulate this destructive exuberance.

Performance Metrics

Establishing the appropriate performance metrics for an analytics function serves to promote the behaviors that are best able to support the successful execution of the mandate of the team. In modern meritocratic workplaces, where industry constitutes honor, personal cultural adaptation can mean leaning more heavily into statistical metrics as an indicator of success (Markovits, 2020). Ironically, in a practice based on data and statistical modeling, these statistical metrics can lead to a false sense of security and incentivize incorrect behaviors. Analytics is a creative practice and cannot be effectively evaluated with this approach. It is important that analytics teams are assessed based on the value that is created or on the customer benefit they provide and not on the dry statistical metrics of model performance. Establishing these as normal criteria within the team is essential to steering practitioners away from these damaging metrics.

Some organizations, with relative immature data and analytics practices, set targets around how many projects to complete in a year. The function, logically, pursues low-value quick-turn POC projects and will rarely focus on operationalization or value creation. Similarly, some organizations set targets around collaboration, incenting the analytics function to spread themselves thin to achieve well-intended targets. The ideal overarching metric for an analytics team is value creation. This is often hard to measure but is critical to reinforcing with the team. Deliberate measures must be taken to capture, quantify, and communicate the value delivered. Every project that the team completes should improve efficiency, improve revenue, or reduce cost. Teams and individuals should be evaluated primarily based on their contribution to that metric.

Taking a cue from the consulting world, some organizations assess their individual practitioners on the revenue associated with their work. This incentivizes individuals to seek out the projects with the highest-value metric and supports the organic formation of smaller self-governing teams. While better than the previous examples, this approach does run the risk of concentrating personal development of the team in a few key individuals. This focus on value creation must be balanced with a conscious effort to ensure the ongoing development of more junior members of the team and balance it with break fixes, enablement projects, and executive decrees.

Other important performance metrics, both qualitative and quantitative, for an analytics team are as follows:

Productionalized Models   Assessing practitioners based on their total output can encourage a machine gun approach to analytics. Leaders should call out the productionalized models that the individual has developed or contributed to and assess them based on the final quality and resilience of the model. POC projects, while important in the long term, must be understood by the team to be of no value until productionalized.

Model Performance   Practitioners need to be reviewed based on their holistic vision of a model. Potential issues such as overfitting, complex and non-parsimonious algorithms, poor performance, and lack of resilience all need to be considered.

Defects and Errors   All practitioners, regardless of experience, will create processes, models, and scripts that contain errors. In fact, an absence of errors may indicate that they are not pushing themselves or developing. When enthusiasm leads to carelessness, and in particular when operationalized models have errors, it reflects poorly on the team and the individual. No practitioner should make the same error twice.

Planning Compliance   The up-front project planning involves intake, scoping, requirements gathering, and stakeholder communication, which are all necessary skills for a practitioner to develop and should be highlighted as equally important to technical proficiency.

Delivery Compliance   Similarly, the project execution, closeout, documentation, operationalization, and final handoff are all essential components of a successful project. Practitioners should support the stakeholder from ideation to delivery and assume a service-oriented mindset.

Managed Value   Without a compelling reason to do otherwise, practitioners will naturally gravitate toward whichever projects are the most interesting or have the most vocal proponent. The managed value is the total value-add, in cost savings or revenue generated, that can be attributed to the team and to an individual. This can be further divided into the total value that the practitioner was responsible for leading or as an individual contributor.

Strategic Alignment   Projects need to build on each other, interoperate, and be part of a larger strategic initiative if they are to provide the most value. Practitioners should be recognized for framing and planning projects in such a way as to enable or promote the long-term vision of the analytics function.

Enablement   Practitioners should seek to advance analytics within the organization and not simply take orders and deliver on projects. Intangible contributions to the mandate of the team such as through training, delivering lunch and learn sessions, or participating in Art of the Possible sessions are all important to the promotion of a vision with the organization and to build the self-confidence of the individual.

360 Feedback   Being such an interpersonal profession, it is important that individuals are well regarded and that their peers and reports enjoy working with them. Traditional linear reporting structures with twice-annual performance reviews neglect the important nuance of the complete mapping of relationships the individual maintains. Leaders should be constantly aware of how the team member is working with others within the team and with stakeholders.

These metrics are, again, subordinate to value generation.

One of the undervalued indicators of success for individual contributors is the ability to confidently advocate for their ideas, especially in the face of opposition by others. It has been shown in studies that people would rather fit in with their peers than be correct. In an experiment where people were asked to select the longer of three lines, people if asked independently were correct 100 percent of the time. When the experiment was repeated in a group and the other participants (who are actors and part of the study) choose a shorter line, 40 percent of the time the participants will choose the shorter line as well in order to fit in (Asch, 1951). This stunning finding shows how deeply ingrained the pull toward groupthink is. If an individual can be wrong about something as obvious as the length of a line, their willingness to accept something as nebulous as business models can only be imagined. For this reason, it is important to instill a spirit of courage in people and to always acknowledge and reward people for dissenting. Leaders should not ask whether or not the team agrees with an approach but rather ask in what ways that approach could be wrong.

Evaluating the performance of other leaders within the function introduces additional complexity. Managers certainly need to be able to support the technical activities of the team, but their primary measure of success is how well they are able to engage, develop, and motivate the individuals on their team. There are two fundamental and opposing views around motivation and how people view their relationship with work (McGregor, 2006) . Theory X, the dominant philosophy up to the middle of the twentieth century, had it that people need external motivations if they are going to put in their best effort. People were inherently lazy, as a rule disliked work, and would work as little as possible to fly under the radar. If paid a piece rate, they would work until they had enough to eat for the day and spend the remainder of their time in leisure activities. The implications of this theory are that managers need to supervise their employees, punish those that do not pull their weight, check timecards, and generally centralize decision making and authority. In the 1950s, organizations tended to move toward Theory Y, which had it that people are internally motivated and have a natural desire to be productive and engaged employees. They see work as a rewarding enterprise and feel personally rewarded when their work is meaningful. The role of a manager in this case is to remove roadblocks, delegate decision making authority, and craft an environment where the individuals can be successful.

Good leaders are those who know how to have a fully open and candid relationship with their employees and are able to offer direct feedback grounded in a mutual understanding that the leader cares personally about the individual. Good leaders care personally but challenge directly (Scott, 2017).

Most practitioners and managers dislike the performance management process yet at the same time wish they were receiving more feedback. During year-end evaluations, both people shed their humanity for a moment, furtively go through the motions in a choreographed dance, then quietly return to their work with the understanding that what occurred was a painful necessity, endured at the behest of their employer. More forward-thinking companies no longer go through the annual performance evaluation process. Rather, they have biweekly sessions or encourage managers to provide immediate feedback. The traditional method rewards and punishes for events that often happened six months ago or more and does not help to incentivize the desired behaviors. These exchanges have the opportunity to be a hugely beneficial and cathartic experience where both individuals have the chance to be completely candid with each other, but unfortunately this is usually not the case.

Though analytics leaders need to abide by the policies of the organization, great leaders will navigate it so as to provide what was ostensibly intended during the drafting of these policies. Genuine leaders, caring for the development of their team, will thoughtfully reflect on the performance of the individual across all facets of their role, adjust their feedback to account for the future ambitions of the individual and frame it using the language and level of familiarity appropriate to that practitioner, and bring real examples. This exercise should not be a bullet list of activities completed in the previous few weeks but a script created with care and built over time.

Reviews and assessments are an awkward experience for leaders and their reports—in particular for egalitarian teams where authority is earned through experience and respect, not title. Leaders should push through that awkwardness and personally commit to providing the most comprehensive review that they are able. It is an opportunity to show great kindness to the team and show both a genuine caring for their development and an affirmation that people are noticing the work they do. Performance reviews have a bad reputation, but analytics leaders and teams, working within the constraints of the organization, can and should change that mindset to one of positive anticipation.

Summary

The easily recognizable output of an analytics team is usually a script, model, or analysis of a problem. The final deliverable, physically, is usually a small file or a few coefficients. However, the true value delivered is a business outcome, and it is easy to disregard everything that had gone into the creation of those few coefficients—the stress of missing data, disappointment with operational constraints, the difficulties setting up computing environments, the friendly debates with colleagues about approach, the late nights, and the presentation dry runs. For the weeks or months leading up to the creation of that final deliverable, analytics practitioners were working with each other, with stakeholders, and with the project sponsor understanding the problem, the limitations, the timelines, the environment, the players, the technical aspects, the human aspects, and the outcome. It was not the processes, the strategy, or the application of the newest technology, it was people working together using the best of each other to accomplish a goal.

Without understanding data science and analytics as a team sport, and practitioners as being craftspeople, leaders can consider talent as being a combination of capabilities. Hiring and retention becomes based on the acquisition of more technical capabilities, building toward a team of individuals working in isolation, distant from the business, seeking instruction, and avoiding responsibility and ownership.

Analytics teams are most successful when they hire and develop people who are intrinsically motivated and passionate about their field. People who are excited to work on large projects, to talk about their work, and to help others to understand and appreciate it. Data science and analytics teams have an absolute need for a coherent strategy, parsimonious yet supportive processes, and productive and engaged people. As with the legs of a stool, gaps in any of these will ultimately end in the failure of the team. Nothing, however, will lead to failure quicker than not having the right people.

Without effective processes, a team will be slow, stakeholders will be frustrated, and the end result may not be as good as it could have been. However, work will get done. Without a strategy, teams will probably never influence the organization or deliver on truly transformative initiatives. Again, however, work will get done. Without the right people, though, failure will be immediate, visible, and painful (Figure 4.2).

It is clichéd to say that people are the most important asset in a company. Intuitively and by experience we know that after most individuals leave, a new person is hired, and after some time for them to ramp up, they are about as productive as their departed colleague. For data scientists, as

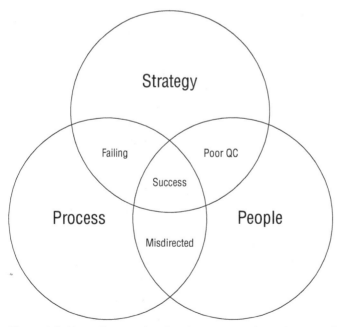

Figure 4.2: Venn diagram showing strategy, people, and process for analytics teams

a creative profession, this commodification of labor has not happened. The difference in productivity and ability can be staggering. Similar to software development, there are key 10x individuals, who are as productive as 10 of their colleagues. Those individuals are simply better able to interface with others, to deconstruct a problem, and to develop a solution. In contrast, an ill-equipped, disengaged practitioner who cannot explain concepts, who idles behind their keyboard, and who derails conversations to build their self-confidence and flex their mathematical muscle is ultimately is worse than having a vacancy.

There is nothing more important for a leader than to attract, develop, and mind the talent on their team. We return again to Colin Powell's great quote, "Organization doesn't really accomplish anything. Plans don't accomplish anything, either. Theories of management don't much matter. Endeavors succeed or fail because of the people involved. Only by attracting the best people will you accomplish great deeds."

References

Asch, S. E. (1951). Effects of group pressure upon the modification and distortion of judgments. In H. Guetzkow (Ed.), *Groups, leadership and men; research in human relations* (pp. 177–190). Carnegie Press.

Brickman, P., & Campbell, D. T. (1971). Hedonic relativism and planning the good society. In M. H. Appley (Ed.), *Adaptation-level theory* (pp. 287–305). Academic Press.

Diderot, D. (1875). Regrets on parting with my old dressing gown. *Oeuvres Complètes* (Vol. IV). Garnier Fréres. www.marxists.org/reference/archive/diderot/1769/regrets.htm

Drucker, P. F. (1954). *Practice of management*. Harper & Row.

Drucker, P. F. (2008). *Managing oneself*. Harvard Business School Publishing.

Franklin, B. (2012). *The autobiography of Benjamin Franklin*, Norton critical edition. W. W. Norton.

Gladwell, M. (2011). *Outliers: The story of success*. Back Bay Books.

Goleman, D. (2014). *What makes a leader: Why emotional intelligence matters*. More Than Sound LLC.

Heifetz, R., & Linsky, M. (2002, June). A survival guide for leaders. *Harvard Business Review.* https://hbr.org/2002/06/a-survival-guide-for-leaders

Henke, N., Levine, J., & McInerney, P. (2018, Feb. 1). Analytics translator: The new must-have role. *Harvard Business Review.* www.mckinsey.com/business-functions/mckinsey-analytics/our-insights/analytics-translator

Kahneman, D., Rosenfield, A. M., Gandhi, L., & Blaser, T. (2016, Oct.). Noise: How to overcome the high hidden cost of inconsistent decision making. *Harvard Business Review.* https://hbr.org/2016/10/noise

Kanter, R. M. (2006, Nov.). Innovation: the classic traps. *Harvard Business Review.* https://hbr.org/2006/11/innovation-the-classic-traps

Lencioni, P. (2004). *Death by meeting: A leadership fable.* Jossey-Bass.

Lukianoff, M. (2020, Feb. 4). The success and resounding failure of "big data": A retrospective view from the top of the Hype Cycle. Towards Data Science. https://towardsdatascience.com/the-success-resounding-failure-of-big-data-50b3f17756f1

Marcel, G. (2017). *The mystery of being.* Andesite Press.

Markovits, D. (2020). *The meritocracy trap: How America's foundational myth feeds inequality, dismantles the middle class, and devours the elite.* Penguin Books.

Maslow, A. H. (2013). A theory of human motivation. Rough Draft.

McGinn, D. (2017). *Psyched up: How the science of mental preparation can help you succeed.* Portfolio.

McGregor, D. (2006). *The human side of enterprise, annotated edition.* McGraw-Hill Education.

Penn, W. (1682/2001). *Fruits of solitude.* The Harvard Classics (Vol. 1, Part 3). P. F. Collier & Son. www.bartleby.com/1/3

Powell, C. (2006). *Leadership primer.* United States Department of the Army. Retrieved from www.hsdl.org/?abstract&did=467329

Rasiel, E. M. (1999). *The McKinsey way: Using the techniques of the world's top strategic consultants to help you and your business.* McGraw-Hill.

Ries, E. (2011). *The lean startup: How today's entrepreneurs use continuous innovation to create radically successful business*. Currency.

Robbins, M. (2018). *Bring your whole self to work: How vulnerability unlocks creativity, connection, and performance*. Hay House Business.

Runde, C. E., & Flanagan, T. A. (2008). *Building conflict competent teams*. Jossey-Bass.

Schumpeter, J. A. (1936). *The theory of economic development: An inquiry into profits, capital, credit, interest, and the business cycle*. Harvard Economic Studies.

Scott, K. (2017). *Radical candor*. Macmillan.

Thompson, J. K. (2020). *Building analytics teams*. Packt.

Thorp, E. (2017). Inside out empathy: Explore the underestimated superpower essential for building, developing, and inspiring a rock-solid team. ELF Solutions.

5

Future of Business Analytics

This book has referenced and quoted a broad range of great thinkers and leaders including Frederick Taylor, William Penn, Bertrand Russell, Peter Drucker, Ben Franklin, Yogi Berra, and Colin Powell. These individuals have, through either deep study or a semi-accidental remark, shared an insight that has maintained significance and relevance. People often consider these people (at least some of them) as heroic in their sagaciousness, choosing to intentionally disregard the full picture of their person. Many had decidedly nonheroic notions around what we would now consider basic human rights or maintained habits that would be bizarre to contemporary readers. We can assume, with perhaps a little hubris, that if these great thinkers had reflected deeply and considered their presuppositions, they would come to the same place we are. The ideas that we consider offensive or clearly false seem obvious to us, but given their lived experience and the accepted knowledge of their time, they were simply taken as axiomatic. It is safe to assume that in the future our conventional wisdom around data science and analytics will be similarly considered anachronistic and inexplicable. What will future business leaders think of this time, when data science and analytics was in its infancy? What will we be embarrassed that we missed in 20 years? How will our strategies and processes hold up over time?

What technologies will rise, and which will fade? What might the job market look like for practitioners?

It may be that what is now the field of data science will be ingrained in the thinking and processes of all business units in the future and will not exist as a distinct function. Because of advances in AutoML and machine learning as a service (MLaaS) offerings, little programmatic or mathematical understanding will be needed, and while considered a dead profession, it exists in spirit throughout all enterprises and functions. Supervised and unsupervised classification will be included in the high school curricula, and though few will know which algorithm is being used or the foundational mathematics, all educated people will know when one technique should be used over another. Alternatively, it may evolve into such an integral and concentrated field that specialization and division of labor wins out over the current move toward breadth.

Data science and analytics is presently seen as the most recent incarnation and aggregation of several antecedent fields such as systems engineering, operations research, and statistics and enabled by advances in computer science. In the fullness of time, it may be just one of many titles that practitioners will have had. The statisticians who became decision support personnel who then became advanced analytics practitioners before becoming data scientists and artificial intelligence researchers may receive a new job title but retain their underlying mandate for supporting the business with deep analysis.

Regardless of the larger changes that the practice may experience in the future, it is safe to assume given current trends in the industry that in the short to medium term, the practice will see overall change occurring in a few key areas:

Process   Citizen data scientists will need to develop skills as business analysts and in project management. Stakeholders will grow to expect project delivery maturity from practitioners. Individual practitioners working in isolation will be unable to deliver on the large transformative projects, and once the low-hanging fruit has been addressed, teams will not be able to progress without rethinking their processes.

Explainability   Models that cannot be understood by the business, or provide observation-level justification for decisions, will lose ground to more transparent and comprehensible models. Approaches that support ML interpretability such as SHAP or LIME will grow in usage.

Management and Leadership   Failures in the reporting line of analytics teams at the nontechnical juncture, combined with the ever-increasing criticality of the function, will lead to the development and recognition of a managerial class to provide more effective oversight. University programs will evolve that are more focused on the business aspects of analytics than the technical.

Integration   The development of this managerial class of analytics professionals will in turn lead to more parsimonious teams who will not promote or accept complex approaches when a simple one will suffice. Technical specialists and aristocrats will lose status within organizations to business-focused analysts. The analytics function will continue to work toward better incorporation with the business, and there will be an ever-greater value placed on business understanding. It will not be acceptable for data scientists to provide analysis without context.

Technical Divergence   The large and growing differences in sophistication and infrastructure between the data science and analytics function in digital native and technology companies compared with those in traditional legacy companies will lead to a difference in skillsets that is such that practitioners in either type of organization will have difficulty moving between them. This may lead to a less fluid job market for mid-career professionals.

This chapter discusses specific trends and forces that will drive change in the practice in the future.

AutoML and the No-Code Movement

Though most traditional organizations may have little use for cutting-edge technologies today, there are some that are advanced in certain functions to the point that they can find significant incremental value in pursuing these more advanced projects. It is, however, difficult to secure the talent required for these roles outside of contract positions. At this level of technical depth, these organizations are competing with Google, Amazon, and the other digital native companies. In a report by McKinsey & Company, the authors describe a multinational retail conglomerate that needed to create a very compelling package including education perks and salaries up to 20 percent higher than market rates so that it may attract the more than 30 data scientists that were needed to address priority analytics use cases (Hürthen et al., 2020). When organizations opt for abrupt investments in data science teams, those teams need to add value quickly to offset the high associated costs. Unfortunately, the projects capable of generating the profits to pay for the new function are likely multiyear initiatives. Offering the required salary premium can also lead to dissatisfaction with current employees once they become aware of the disparity in compensation.

AutoML represents a new approach to the typical data science and analytics workflow by automating as much of the process as possible. Rather than having a team of expensive specialists, organizations purchase tools that are capable of performing rote tasks such as model selection and tuning through a user-friendly interface, allowing the data scientist to focus on the more sensitive areas of the project. Solutions also exist to perform simple data tasks. Practitioners spend most of their time in acquiring, cleaning, and transforming data. Products that reduce the amount of time spent in this area can greatly improve the efficiency of even a smaller analytics team.

The no-code and low-code movement is similar, with its proponents advocating for a practice where most of the work is performed using tools rather than scripts. The use of these tools benefits the profession by removing idiosyncrasies in development and imposing consistency. Given the high turnover of analytics practitioners, onboarding new talent can be greatly expedited when processes are visual workflows rather than complex scripts. Vendors have seen this demand, and many tools are available that are reducing the amount of work involved in a typical data science project. Gartner (2019) estimates that within the next five years, low-code applications will represent 65 percent of all new applications. In another study by Forrester (Rymer et al., 2019), they suggested a market value for low-code applications at over $21 billion by 2022. In the future, familiarity with these tools will be important for practitioners.

Detractors of the no-code and low-code movements claim that the proliferation of these approaches will reduce customizability and devalue the skills that programmers have spent years honing. Further, without the advanced skills that allow them to understand the model fully, they are challenged to optimize performance or remove bias. There is no doubt that there is truth to these concerns, but the improvements in terms of time to value and the reduced dependencies on expensive talent make this a worthwhile trade for most organizations.

It needs to be restated that for most organizations, the product is not the code. The code executes a transformation, tunes a model, generates a report, or resets pricing and availability of products and services.

If done properly, the process is invisible to the end customer. Whether this coding was done in a high-prestige coding language or through a batch file is irrelevant in the end; what matters is the functionality of the final product and the amount of time invested in creating that product. The no-code movement has microeconomics on its side, and it is likely that this and AutoML will continue to grow into the future.

In the short to medium term, it is very unlikely that AutoML and low-code solutions will replace the traditional data science development stack, but over the long term, improvements in the quality and robustness of these tools will enable domain experts to perform a lot of the traditional data science activities. Data scientists with deep statistical knowledge will still be required to reduce the risk of black box models and validate model performance, but the value of having broad programming experience will continue to depreciate. Similarly, except for digital native organizations where properly tuned processes are essential, it is likely that the availability of these tools will reduce the importance of advanced SQL abilities.

There will always be a role for pure data scientists and statistical experts who are able to understand analytical solutions from base principles and to develop custom applications or optimize accuracy beyond what these AutoML solutions are capable of. The most robust MLaaS solution cannot fully integrate domain knowledge or the human understanding of data origins into the model. These solutions also cannot account for potential ethical implications or regulatory requirements. For those industries that need to report to a governing body, such as financial institutions, the claim that a model was selected solely on the recommendation of a drag-and-drop data science suite will not be accepted. The practice in general needs to maintain a deep understanding of the algorithms to reduce risk.

The other consequence of the proliferation of AutoML and no-code alternatives is that rather than training data scientists to become conversant in an industry and function, they can work toward upskilling domain experts who are better situated to find high-value use cases for analytics.

To prepare for this a practitioner within a traditional business domain should seek to differentiate themselves based on ingenuity and cross-functional skills rather than on deep technical prowess. In the future, recruiters will not seek those who can use scikit-learn but those who understand machine learning. Practitioners should become familiar with low-code ETL tools in this space such as Alteryx and KNIME as well as low-code data science tools such as DataRobot and Dataiku.

Data Science Is Dead

In the mid-2010s, data science and analytics engagements followed a strict "collect, analyze, report" structure. Stakeholders from the business would provide a team of data scientists with a data set and a question and in most cases a hypothesis based on their professional intuition. This mindset was often associated with proof-of-concept projects, intended to be a first step into analytics and to show the potential of the practice, a stage that many organizations have struggled to move beyond. The data science team would clean the data set, interpolate or extrapolate as needed, opine over distributions, detect and deal with outliers, and eventually run a predictive model or classification algorithm. The summary statistics would be presented along with some light exposition in a presentation that would seldom be fully understood but would typically confirm the intuition of the project sponsor.

Thankfully, this approach is all but dead in most mature organizations. With the premium commanded by data scientists, analytics groups are being pushed to prove their value and to justify their growth. Without being able to point to a direct contribution to increased revenue or reduced cost, these teams will be disbanded or experience frequent leadership shuffles and reorganizations.

The role of data science managers has transformed since the beginnings of the practice from one of a technical specialist, tasked with guiding more junior staff, to that of a line manager with full profit and loss accountabilities. New software and data infrastructure is being continually evaluated against the project backlog, and teams need to prove out a return on investment before funding is released. There is no longer implicit trust in the word of the function; everything needs to be documented and proven.

Despite the stress that this introduces, the additional pressure of ensuring value creation has caused the practice to rapidly advance in the organizations that are using them successfully and allowed the function to earn a seat at the table. Data science is influencing business decisions, and new product development is being informed by the work of the function. Rather than being thought of as a backroom function, analytics is finally enjoying its debut as a core function within most successful enterprises.

What this means for a new entrant into the field, or a practitioner seeking to advance, is that they cannot rely on old heuristics and exceptional technical depth to be their sole path to promotion. The only thing that matters for a data scientist is their ability to create value in an organization. If they can produce that value by acting as an intermediary between different divisions, or by hands-on development in TensorFlow, or by the development of a complete data pipeline, or even a quick spreadsheet, a practitioner needs to be business-first and to identify those opportunities for the most parsimonious application of their abilities to enabling the success of the business. Anything else is misguided and self-indulgent.

Data scientists are no longer able to idle while awaiting a project that aligns to their technical skillset and ambitions. It is not appropriate for a practitioner to expect that their narrow toolkit should sustain them for their career. Every practitioner needs to adopt a growth mindset in order to be successful and to find the most expedient approach for delivering on their engagements.

Data scientists had commanded a significant compensation premium given the high demand for their abilities, and for specialized areas of practice in particular. They would exist at the intersection of a region, industry, function, and technical skillset and be able to set their own salary. This intersectionality has decreased in importance over the last several years and will likely continue to do so into the future.

The region in which a person operates is no longer important for most organizations. There is a trend toward remote work, and the COVID-19 pandemic has accelerated this. While it has opened data scientists to more opportunities to work at different companies, it has also increased the competition for desirable roles. Employers of choice such as digital natives have gained in bargaining power as a result.

In a similar way, the industry or function in which a data scientist operates has become less important. As the role of the practitioner has changed from one of providing a technical service to one of acting as an enabler for others, the importance of industry-specific knowledge has decreased. In many cases, it is advantageous for a practitioner to have cross-industry and cross-functional experience so that they can introduce new ways of thinking. As with the move toward remote work, this has led to an increase in competition for jobs and the move in bargaining power toward the employer for high-prestige organizations.

These changes have also led to a huge increase in the amount of outsourcing that the practice is seeing. As data science has become a known quantity, and as familiarity has increased, the need to have a personal relationship and the establishment of trust has decreased in importance. For almost all hands-on-keyboard analytical technical services, there is no need to have local talent available. Consulting firms tend to hire regional project leads, who oversee the work of a largely offshore data science workforce. For activities such as data labeling and classification, the lower labor cost has been extremely attractive.

This move toward commodification has been exacerbated thanks to organizations seeking to standardize and de-risk. In a study by Deloitte, it was found that organizations who are making a concerted effort toward adopting AI technologies are tending to purchase more applications than developing custom solutions (Ammanath et al., 2020). This option had not existed until recently, and organizations who wanted to develop their AI capabilities had to hire talent and depend on them to develop scripts and models that interfaced with their existing data. New products such as GUI-driven ETL applications allow SQL novices to build out data pipelines with comparable performance to what a team of database administrators would have been able to achieve in a fault-tolerant environment. Without the need for face-to-face communication or a well-integrated analytics team, much of the implementation of these systems can be carried out by offshore contractors.

For the practitioner, this means that it is essential to focus on the nontechnical aspects of the practice and to develop adaptability and cultivate personal creativity. Collecting technical accreditations is no longer enough to maintain relevance, as there are tens of thousands of individuals worldwide who have those accreditations and are willing to work for less. If a practitioner wants to differentiate themselves and ensure their future success, they need to focus on project management, strategy, communication, and establishing productive relationships with others in their organization and in the practice. One of the major themes of *Minding the Machines* has been the importance of parsimony to a high-functioning analytics function. That push toward simplicity needs to exist as well at the personal level for an individual to be successful in the future. Practitioners cannot continue to conflate sophistication with success and deliver plodding and complex solutions to simple problems. The most successful data scientists in the future will be those who are the most parsimonious, establish effective processes, and execute quickly and decisively on projects. As William Penn said,

---

Elegancy is a good Meen and Address given to Matter, be it by proper or figurative Speech: Where the Words are apt, and allusions very natural, Certainly it has a moving Grace: But it is too artificial for Simplicity, and oftentimes for Truth. The Danger is, lest it delude the Weak, who in such Cases may mistake the Handmaid for the Mistress, if not Error for Truth. (1682/2001)

This is not a novel philosophy, but one that it seems each culture and individual needs to discover for themselves.

Data science, as it was originally, is dead. The data scientist of the future is a businessperson who leverages technology to enable others, not a person who develops algorithms in isolation.

The Data Warehouse

The original promise of the data warehouse was that eventually all of the data in the organization would exist within a well-designed and maintained central repository and serve as a single source of truth from which the different stakeholders could perform analyses, generate reports, and monitor the performance of the business. Very few organizations have seen this promise fulfilled despite significant investments in architecture and data integration. Different groups build transformations on transformations and create their own definitions for key metrics, and the end result is that facts and figures are often unreconcilable between functions.

It was the hope that formalized data governance, as well as massive efforts and investments in master data management, would fix this through the establishment of processes and the exercise of authority over access and usage, but this too has had many visible failures and introduced bureaucracy rather than benefit and did not address the issues of data integrity and trust.

The source of these two failures ultimately is pride and a lack of continuity. As an example, performance measurement for one business unit may be based largely on revenue for which they have no ability to influence, so they devise and report on a calculated metric for their revenue, eliminating non-core sources. Other related metrics, such as cost of sales, ROI, and so on, multiply in response. Adjacent cost centers perform similar numerical gymnastics by creating multiple definitions of cost, which add an exponent to the number of extant measures. Discrete choices, which make sense in isolation and given the incentives to the decision makers, explode into a confusing mess of data and a lack of consistency across the organization. Each introduction of a new metric leads to restatements of previous reports. Each recurring report looking at year-over-year changes needs to be duplicated to match historic definitions to provide continuity. This proliferation in reports leads to many being unused, and because it is often easier to maintain them than eliminate them, few are ever removed from service.

Every so often, however, despite all this, organizations will clean house. They migrate to a new database, or to the cloud, and they start fresh. In doing so, they face a choice between logical rationalization and re-creating their miseries in another location, and given the price tag associated will often hold their breath and start over. Despite all the anxiety and trepidation, organizations are invariably relieved and unburdened from the archaic processes they had maintained for years.

Unless new EDW software gets much better at migrating in situ data, these decisions, driven by advances in technology, will lead to a world of better and more trusted data, with fewer reconciliations and fewer legacy processes. Each time organizations make these shifts and shrug off old processes, the quality of data improves and the amount of time required to understand, deconstruct, and document the upstream workflows will decrease as well.

There will always be a natural split between the data engineering and the analytics part of analytics. In the future, however, the dependence on data engineering abilities within the data science practice should decrease. Data scientists have long needed to have advanced SQL abilities to be able to interface with the data at source and to have the ability to deconstruct the cascading transformations that shaped it. While SQL will likely always have a place in the toolbox of a practitioner, the level of familiarity required will decrease over time along with the business-imposed requirements of reconciliation.

True Operationalization

For most traditional organizations with low analytical maturity, there is an implicit distrust in decision support models and a sense that without human intervention or involvement, the process will not work. This distrust in the practice is compounded by a distrust in the underlying data. Models that have been implemented tend to pass through three sequential stages of operationalization based on the level of trust:

Parallelism   Conceptually, processes have been developed and discrete subtasks are available for productionalization. For a period of weeks to months, these subtasks are run alongside the traditional approaches to establish trust and ensure parity.

Human Gatekeeper   All aspects of the process have been developed and properly implemented, but for confidence in the successful completion of the process, a human gatekeeper manually kicks off one or more of the subtasks and confirms successful completion of the process.

Confirmation   The process has been developed and implemented and is automatically completed at some determined schedule. On completion, an analyst may spot-check the results and inform other stakeholders that it has been successfully completed.

Even in some more analytically mature organizations, processes that could be fully automated may not advance beyond one of these stages. In financial services, for example, the consequences of an error can be so significant that decision makers may never be fully confident in letting the process become completely automated. This is particularly the case when an organization struggles to move beyond the parallelism stage, leading to an indefinite duplication of effort.

The operational consequence of this is that for each process that has been only partially productionalized, some time must be dedicated from the analytics function to maintain, operate, run, report on, and adjust. The process becomes a quasi-product and consumes some part of the capacity of that practitioner. As the portfolio of a team grows, the management of these quasi-products increases in complexity, and the time available for value-added activities decreases. Few entered the field to babysit processes, and engagement drops as this misuse of their time increases.

The other consequence of this is that the cadence of the process is limited as a result of the human involvement. For example, if a dynamic pricing algorithm were to be used to assign a price to a product based on current trends in consumer behavior, it would be beneficial to have as close to real-time model tuning as possible. Sudden swings in behavior due to exogenous factors should be incorporated into the model immediately, otherwise less of that potential value will be captured. Unfortunately, if the product is not fully productionalized, it would require humans during business hours to initiate each step and report up that it had been successfully completed. At best, the team may tune this model a few times a week. Conversely, if the process were fully automated, the only limiting factor is technical through data availability and processing power.

As Gen Xers and millennials rise in leadership positions, this inherent distrust is beginning to dissipate. Having been raised with technological ubiquity, this new cohort of leaders is more open to fully automated processes and more likely to recognize the risks of human error. This is also supported by organizations that have had these processes running in some cases for years without issue or have robust error-handling capabilities. Daily reporting that a process has been completed is gradually being replaced by occasional exception reports when a process has failed.

What this means for current practitioners is that in the future it will become more important to build these fault-tolerant processes and to anticipate ways in which failure could occur. It will not be enough to create a process consisting of a linear serialization of scripts. The second impact is that practitioners will need to develop breadth in their capabilities and a focus on the last mile. It will not be appropriate for an individual to focus on modeling at the expense of operationalization. The future practitioner will need to be able to deliver a product that works from data acquisition to modeling to execution, integrates with business process and workflows, and can withstand missing or incorrect data.

Exogenous Data

The data science function within traditional organizations has, to date, relied mostly on internally generated data to craft their models and insights. This is mainly because the outputs the team has been seeking to optimize have been an internal metric such as sales or conversion or revenue. The secondary reason is one of control and access. The same databases and systems that provide the performance metrics also have customer information, behavioral information, or other independent variables that could be included in a model, often available through an existing view or transformation. This adjacency has meant that a model could be quickly developed using the data on hand.

Practitioners have been realizing over time that behavioral models cannot rely solely on internally generated data to paint a complete picture. Customers have a rich life outside of the few touchpoints that they have with an organization and are influenced by several factors. The employment rate in their region, their social media activity, the humidity, their sense of well-being, the price of canola, the HDI, religious services attendance, the GNP, trends in local rent prices, and the Gini coefficient may all influence their decision making in some way. Organizations who are equipped to quantify these exogenous drivers of behavior and identify leading indicators of impactful changes to their business are at an advantage over those who are relying on retrospective reporting, and the implicit assumption that the organization can drive behavior, to make changes.

One example of this is in the use of data science for predicting safety incidents. It is often known what directly contributed to an event, but the ability to leverage exogenous data provides a more complete understanding of the leading indicators and indirect factors that contributed.

Models based on this more fulsome picture can provide insights that lead to more impactful changes.

In the future, the dependence on exogenous data, including the gathering and modeling and interpretation of the results, will become more important. Governments will make more data available to benefit industry and society through initiatives such as the Canadian Open Data 500 and Data.gov in the United States. Contributory data companies will increase in number and relevance, and membership in these directories will be all but mandatory for certain industries. Data collection companies will provide aggregate information in the form of real-time indices and competitive information. Companies that exist solely to collect, aggregate, and distribute exogenous data as a business model will continue to grow in relevance.

Practitioners will need to be familiar with these data sets, to know which are appropriate in different cases, how to acquire the data effectively, and how to create a parsimonious model that best integrates the internal corporate data and the exogenous data sets.

Edge AI

One of the limitations of consumer AI technologies is that it depends on remote processing of input. For example, when a person uses a voice recognition tool, their recording is sent to the cloud for transcription. These transcription services have benefitted greatly from the massive amount of audio data available with which to train the dictation engines. Comparisons between modern dictation software and first-generation software show a vast improvement. Originally the approach was to use local temporal pattern recognition and force the user to enunciate every word individually. While it was much quicker than current approaches, this yielded tepid results, and any accent would render the software useless. With machine learning and the explosion in available data, the potential accuracy of the tools has exploded as well. Unfortunately, to realize the maximum potential of the newer algorithms, users need to send their transcription to the cloud where it is processed. This creates latency, increases costs for the provider, and adds a security risk if the user is sending anything private.

The promise of Edge AI is that processing of data will occur closer to the user, or at the edge of the system. This reduces bandwidth requirements, improves latency, and improves privacy. For some applications, such as facial recognition and autonomous vehicles, Edge AI will be a requirement.

Current practitioners, especially those working in a consumer-facing environment, need to understand the implications of Edge AI and how it may impact future approaches.

Analytics for Good

For most of the time that it has been a distinct field, data science and analytics has been the purview of academia and the corporate world. Though there are several technologies in development that have the potential to do a lot of good in the world, they have been developed for primarily commercial purposes. Over time, as the value of the practice becomes clear, and as use cases develop, government and nonprofit groups will begin to move into the space, and job opportunities will become more widespread.

In a related study by McKinsey, 160 noncommercial use cases for AI were found that hit on all 17 of the United Nation's sustainable development goals (Chui et al., 2018). The study found that small tests were being conducted in approximately a third of these use cases, suggesting that as they continue to scale, more opportunities will become available.

Data science and analytics practitioners, like most, have a personal desire to see a positive impact from their work. While it is gratifying to help a corporation improve its top line revenue growth, or to support the development of a novel product, over the course of a career it can lead to moral questions of value and motivate people to seek other opportunities. As with lawyers taking lower-paid positions in environmental or poverty reduction areas, the analytics field will likely see a migration of new graduates and experienced professionals to these nonprofit and governmental enterprises. This will lead to more competition for entry-level and experienced talent in the commercial sphere and provide upward support to salaries in these settings.

To attract and retain talent, organizations with a developed analytics practice may begin to leverage their teams for social good. Universities may also allocate their research capacity to more socially beneficial purposes or be encouraged through government support through grants and bursaries. Religious leaders are also beginning to see the potential for good that analytics has and are promoting research into the ethical application of the practice toward solving the world's problems. In a recent address, Pope Francis reflected that artificial devices that simulate human capacities, are in fact, lacking in human qualities. These machines cannot take into consideration the phenomena of experience or that of conscience. [. . .] This must be taken into account, when imposing the regulations for the use of these machines, and in researching them. In order to work towards a constructive interaction between humans and the most recent versions of these machines, which are radically transforming the scenario of our existence. [. . .] if we are able to make use of these references in practice, the extraordinary potential of new discoveries can radiate their benefits on every person and on humanity as a whole. (Merlo, 2019)

The Vatican later went on to sign a document developed to support an ethical approach to AI and co-signed by IBM, Microsoft, FAO, and the Italian government.

For individuals with long-term ambitions to enter these fields, it would be advisable to develop a broader portfolio of use cases and an understanding of global issues and potential analytical applications. Though marketing and financial analytics will have use cases in even NGOs, the novel application of AI has the highest potential for transformation within nonprofits and government fields.

Analytics for Evil

What would McCarthyism have looked like if there was as much data available then as there is now? If Senator McCarthy had requested access to personal emails and social media data in the national interest, it seems likely that it would have been made available. It is not far-fetched to believe that the United States could have put in place something like the Chinese social credit system to identify potential political enemies.

Like scientific management in the 1920s, the emotionless application of data science to human productivity has the potential to alienate and reduce individuals into a row in a data set. People become less human, a series of multipliers, their life boiled down to a set of features with different coefficients determining what schools they get into, what careers are open to them, their mortgage rate, and their insurability. This leaves them dehumanized and alienated, removing all agency from their lives. Without responsibility for their own success, the drive for achievement dies out.

Applicants to a certain organization may be automatically screened against the entire hiring history of that enterprise. Based on the tenure and performance of others whose education, zip code, and employment history place them into the segment that was determined by a black box classification algorithm, an individual may be excluded from consideration before being reviewed by a hiring manager. Universities may compete based on their average coefficient in hiring regressions, and people may look up their Environics score for a particular area before selecting a house out of concern that it will impact their future employment prospects or the educational prospects for their children. The positive feedback loop of these human-selection models could lead to massive disruption to how decisions are made.

For those institutions not aspiring to outward appearances of rationalism, the potential abuses for data science are even more disturbing. In *The Dictator's Learning Curve*, William Dobson (2012) speaks of dictators who,

> faced with growing pressures, the smartest among them neither hardened their regimes into police states nor closed themselves off from the world; instead, they learned and adapted. For dozens of authoritarian regimes, the challenge posed by democracy's advance led to experimentation, creativity, and cunning. Modern authoritarians have successfully honed new techniques, methods, and formulas for preserving power, refashioning dictatorship for the modern age.

Despotic totalitarian governments, with access to the personal information of their citizens and having no qualms about using it for surveillance and the exercise of control in the interest of public security, would have many use cases for analytics. In *The Minority Report* (Dick, 1956), criminals are arrested before committing their crimes, after being identified by a group known as "precogs" who base their judgments on probabilities. Although he wrote it in 1956, the author came stunningly close to modern ML-based judicial decisions on parole hearings. Without competing voices and a moral framework that values individual choice and freedoms, it would be intoxicating for decision makers to continue down this path and base policing on probabilities.

Opportunities in this space will likely become more widespread in the future as political polarization continues. Though likely very few aspire to be involved in this type of work, individuals with backgrounds in the social sciences and criminology are well suited to guiding the development of these areas of practice into a responsible and ethically defensible process. The described dystopian state is likely to appear in small steps that are individually justifiable, and the involvement of well-meaning analytics practitioners can serve to steer it into a productive and beneficial place.

Ethics and Bias

The ethical application of machine learning is one of the most discussed trends, and this will likely continue into the future. Some organizations, in particular digital natives, have moved quickly to realize value from their massive data sets without considering the source of the data or the implications of using it to train their models. Beyond the purposeful use of analytics to intimidate and subjugate, well-meaning decision support models can have significant negative impacts if they are not assessed for bias.

There have been several examples recently of these decision support models having bias that led to embarrassment for their owners. Amazon, for example, was found to have been using AI to evaluate applicants. That AI was trained using historical data that had results for mostly men, and as a result it would select primarily male applicants for progression through the recruitment process. Though this project has been canceled and the team has been disbanded, research continues in this area (Dastin, 2018). In another case, it was found that Google Translate, when a language did not have specific genders, was making assumptions based on the adjectives. For example, if a subject was hardworking, it would be made male, and if it was lazy, Google would make it female (Sonnad, 2017). Beyond being embarrassing, these events can have an impact on people's lives and mar the practice.

The presence of bias in these models is in most cases a result of embedded bias in the data. "Artificial intelligence" is not intelligent; it can only mimic human behavior and optimize key metrics it is provided. If a model is trained on data that has deep bias, then the resulting model will retain and in some cases increase that bias. For example, loan risk models may suggest higher risk for poorer areas, restricting their access to capital and increasing their default rates as a result.

These cases have led to government intervention in many cases, including the European Union forbidding automated decision making when it has a significant impact on the user's life through their sweeping GDPR regulation.

In the future, all practitioners will need to understand the ways in which bias can enter models and demonstrate that they have taken steps to avoid it. Data acquisition will need to consider the original collection methodology, and again demonstrate that no bias is present. Operationalized models will be assessed and adjusted not just on their accuracy but on their bias across certain groups. For future leaders in the practice, familiarity with the field of AI ethics will be essential.

Continued privacy breaches and the growing distrust and potential breakup of large technology companies will lead to more privacy regulations and limitations on what features can be included in models. All modeling will need to be checked for bias, and standards will evolve that guide this. Practitioners will be expected to know the limitations for each scenario and have processes in place for identifying potential violations.

Analytics Talent Shortages

One of the defining features of the profession has been its shortage of practitioners. This has led to high turnover, high compensation, and a power imbalance between employee and employer. This paradigm has come about even when the number of use cases for business analytics has been relatively small, largely within the marketing and commercial functions. As businesses have seen success in this area, they have slowly begun experimenting with other business units, but this remains a small part of the practice.

The natural curiosity and experimental nature of the practice will continue to push the boundaries of where analytics lives in an organization. One of the fathers of modern statistics, Karl Pearson (1892), wrote, "The scope of science is to ascertain truth in every possible branch of knowledge. There is no sphere of inquiry which lies outside the legitimate field of science. To draw a distinction between the scientific and philosophical fields is obfuscation." Practitioners, business leaders, and researchers are all continually seeking new use cases for data science, and this will in the future certainly lead to increases in demand for talent.

Despite the presently limited application, the demand has continued to surge beyond the number of new practitioners. In a 2020 LinkedIn jobs report, the role of the data scientist has an annual growth rate of 37 percent and has been a top job since 2017.

There are four contributing factors that will support this trend into the future:

Increasing Corporate Penetration   Having found success with marketing and commercial divisions, organizations are beginning to set the analytics function loose on other parts of the company such as finance, human resources, and operations. In addition, intra-industry competition is leading to the adoption of more sophisticated processes and necessitating reductions in model latency, which is supporting the move toward real-time machine learning.

Increasing Labor Costs Forward-thinking traditional organizations have begun to experiment with automation and have begun to see successes that have increased confidence in the approach. Continued increases in labor costs for Western countries are pushing organizations to deploy sophisticated robotic process automation and modeling solutions, which are replacing entry-level analysts with algorithmic processes. Analytics professionals who develop and support these processes will continue to be in demand.

Practice Bifurcation The practice of analytics is dividing between those who support traditional organizations and those more technical practitioners who work with digital native companies. The amount of overlap between these two groups has been reducing over time. This has led to less talent being available for each role. As digital natives continue to outpace traditional organizations in terms of sophistication, this trend will likely continue.

NGO Opportunities The use cases for analytics in noncorporate settings is increasing rapidly, in particular for entry-level and senior-level talent. Despite lower compensation, the social good associated with many of these roles is very compelling and will over time lead to more people leaving the commercial space. This trend is also supported by government investments and research grants.

Despite the opposing forces coming from the broadening of the field through remote work, and a preference for cross-industry and cross-functional skillsets, it is likely that demand for the practice will continue to outpace the supply of talent.

This is certainly beneficial for the current practitioners, who will continue to see high demand in their field and resulting high compensation, but the analytics talent shortages will ultimately slow the progress of the field and reduce adoption. Without more practitioners to fill the roles, nongovernmental organizations will struggle to attract talent, and traditional companies will not be as willing to experiment with expensive resources, keeping them engaged in tried-and-true applications instead.

Predicting analytics to be an economic driver in the future, governments are investing in education and supporting startups to be well situated in this space. Canada, for example, has invested in the practice through the establishment of several regional institutes such as the Alberta Machine Intelligence Institute, the Vector Institute, and Scale AI, the Canadian AI supercluster. These investments have contributed to job growth of

500 percent over the previous four years (Deloitte, n.d.). In the United States, a resolution has been signed in the House of Representatives proposing a unified approach for building AI leadership (Jasper, 2020); while this awaits Senate approval, it shows the importance of a clearly articulated national strategy. In 2019, President Trump signed Executive Order 13859, directing the federal government to pursue a number of initiatives supporting American AI innovation and responsible use (The White House, n.d.). In fact, as of February 2020, there are 50 countries that have developed an AI strategy to ensure they are not left behind (HolonIQ, n.d.).

Governments will need to continue to invest in data science and analytics to remain competitive and establish themselves as leaders. This is critical because data science and AI is not just a product but a General Purpose Technology (GPT). Similar to how the combustion engine led to advances across a broad set of fields such as military technology, air travel, and manufacturing, data science has a multiplicative impact on the areas it touches. Investments in these GPTs gives the host country a competitive advantage and raises the standard of living (Lipsey et al., 2005). McKinsey proposes similar expansion of supports for analytics professions in the United States, suggesting AI residencies and boot camps for academics and mid-career professionals who would be able to become more involved in the field without the time burden of a PhD (Chui et al., 2018).

The current and future shortage of skilled business analytics professionals will give more bargaining power to present practitioners but will also slow the growth of the field. Should governments intervene to establish dominance, the whipsaw effect could lead to a boom in corporate investment without commensurate returns. Ideally, market forces will continue to drive the growth of the field to ensure sustainable growth while simultaneously supporting a favorable career for current and future practitioners.

Death of the Career Transitioner

The most senior and successful data science and analytics practitioners currently are career transitioners coming from areas such as engineering, the sciences, and finance. This is necessary because of the fact that until recently, specialized programs in data science did not exist. Those pioneers, with a wealth of experiences and learnings from their multidisciplinary background, paved the way and established best practices in addition to informing the academic programs that are in place today and beginning to gain traction.

Those academic programs, which had begun as highly technical specialist diplomas and degrees, have been gradually homing in on the best combination of business fundamentals, technical proficiency, and mathematical foundations. Though there are certainly still challenges for graduates of these programs to adopt to the more nebulous working environment, they are rapidly improving.

At the same time, job descriptions that had previously stipulated individual technical proficiencies *a la carte* are more and more beginning to request that entry-level applicants have official academic credentials specific to the practice of data science. Even though there is still the opportunity for those who have transitioned to enter as experienced hires, newer cohorts are almost entirely specifically educated in analytics and are evaluated based on their credentials.

This can only lead to the death of the transitioner, with the eventual outcome being data science groups consisting solely of those who are bachelors of analytics or diploma-holders.

This homogenization of the practice will lead to a reduction in creativity as the breadth of experience and spirit of innovation that got the practice to where it is today is replaced by curricula designed to make graduates more uniform in their abilities.

In the future this presents an opportunity for differentiation among graduates as the outgoing generation of data scientists seek people with their vision and outlook to replace them. The individuals who have been part of a practice that has been built on artisanal qualities of passion, service, and excellence will want those same qualities. Successful data scientists of the future are well advised to differentiate themselves by seeking to improve in those areas.

Lawyers who have a background in accounting are especially well equipped to be successful as tax attorneys. Writers with a colorful background who have experienced real hardship are especially able to express that hardship in prose. Ability without inspiration is like an excellent writer with nothing to say. Similarly, data scientists who have a unique background will always be successful and have a unique value proposition to employers and outperform their more functionary peers.

References

Ammanath, B., Jarvis, D., & Hupfer, S. (2020, July 14). *Thriving in the era of pervasive AI.* Deloitte. www2.deloitte.com/us/en/insights/focus/cognitive-technologies/state-of-ai-and-intelligent-automation-in-business-survey.html

Chui, M., Harrysson, M., Manyika, J., Roberts, R., Chung, R., Nel, P., & van Heteren, A. (2018, Nov. 28). *Notes from the AI Frontier: Applying AI for social good.* McKinsey & Company. www.mckinsey.com/featured-insights/artificial-intelligence/applying-artificial-intelligence-for-social-good

Dastin, J. (2018, Oct. 10). *Amazon scraps secret AI recruiting tool that showed bias against women.* Reuters. www.reuters.com/article/us-amazon-com-jobs-automation-insight/amazon-scraps-secret-ai-recruiting-tool-that-showed-bias-against-women-idUSKCN1MK08G

Deloitte. (n.d.). *Canada's AI imperative: From predictions to prosperity.* www2.deloitte.com/content/dam/Deloitte/ca/Documents/ca-175/prediction-to-prosperity/ca175-EN-prediction-to-prosperity-AODA.pdf

Dick, P. K. (1956). The minority report. *Fantastic Universe.* (January).

Dobson, W. J. (2012). *The dictator's learning curve: Inside the global battle for democracy.* Doubleday.

Gartner. (2019, Aug. 8). *Gartner magic quadrant for enterprise low-code application platforms.* Gartner. www.gartner.com/en/documents/3956079/magic-quadrant-for-enterprise-low-code-application-platf

HolonIQ. (n.d.). *Global AI strategy landscape.* www.holoniq.com/wp-content/uploads/2020/02/HolonIQ-2020-AI-Strategy-Landscape.pdf

Hürthen, H., Kerkhoff, S., Lubatschowski, J., & Möller, M. (2020, Aug. 14). *Rethinking AI talent strategy as automated machine learning comes of age.* McKinsey & Company. www.mckinsey.com/business-functions/mckinsey-analytics/our-insights/rethinking-ai-talent-strategy-as-automated-machine-learning-comes-of-age

Jasper, M. (2020, Sep. 21). *Hurd, Kelly introduce resolution to encourage governmentwide vision of artificial intelligence.* Nextgov. www.nextgov.com/emerging-tech/2020/09/hurd-kelly-introduce-resolution-encourage-governmentwide-vision-artificial-intelligence/168655

LinkedIn. (2020). *2020 emerging jobs report.* https://business.linkedin.com/content/dam/me/business/en-us/talent-solutions/emerging-jobs-report/Emerging_Jobs_Report_U.S._FINAL.pdf

Lipsey, R. G., Carlaw, K. I., & Bekar, C. T. (2005). *Economic transformations: General purpose technologies and long term economic growth.* Oxford University Press.

Merlo, F. (2019, Feb. 25). Pope on artificial intelligence: Technology is a human characteristic. *Vatican News.* www.vaticannews.va/en/pope/news/2019-02/pope-francis-address-human-technology-academy-life.html

Pearson, K. (1892). *The grammar of science.* Adam & Charles Black.

Penn, W. (1682/2001). Fruits of solitude. *The Harvard Classics (Vol. 1, Part 3).* P. F. Collier & Son. www.bartleby.com/1/3

Rymer, J., Koplowitz, R., Mines, C., Sjoblom, S., Turley, C. (2019, Mar. 13). Forester. *The Forrester wave: Low-code development platforms for AD&D professionals, Q1 2019.* www.forrester.com/report/The+Forrester+Wave+LowCode+Development+Platforms+For+ADD+Professionals+Q1+2019/-/E-RES144387

Sonnad, N. (2017, Nov. 29). *Google Translate's gender bias pairs "he" with "hardworking" and "she" with lazy, and other examples.* Quartz. https://qz.com/1141122/google-translates-gender-bias-pairs-he-with-hardworking-and-she-with-lazy-and-other-examples

The White House. (n.d.). Artificial intelligence for the American people. www.whitehouse.gov/ai

Summary

Data science and analytics is an ascendant field of practice, which will increase in scope and scale well into the future. In the near term, representation in all organizations will increase, with executive presence becoming more common as chief data and analytics officers take their seat at the table. In the long term, whether it remains a distinct function within organizations or whether it is assimilated into every function, the competitive advantage afforded to an organization that can react rapidly to its environment, make data-driven decisions, and require less knowledge labor than its peers will make it a part of the business landscape for a long time to come. Regardless of size, industry, or sector, analytics has become an organizational necessity.

Many organizations continue to struggle, however, with how to extract the most value from these teams. They have hired the most technical people, given them the best tools, and have become disappointed at the lack of a return. These failures have soured many to the practice, causing them to abandon their analytical ambitions and double down on traditional approaches.

The practice of analytics is at a transition point; as fundamental business practices and organizational maturity enter the field, those who are well prepared will see huge returns. With an explicit focus on the three key pillars discussed in this work, strategy, process, and people, teams and individuals can find success well into the future.

Through the effective development and articulation of a strategy for the analytics function, leaders are able to establish a compelling vision and have the organization and the team unite behind a common objective.

Through the establishment of productive processes, teams are enabled at each stage of the project life cycle from planning to sustainment, reducing variability and increasing efficiency.

Finally, through the thoughtful structuring of teams and establishment of appropriate conventions, leaders can engage their teams and ensure continuity for the organization.

Innovation comes from small dynamic and passionate teams. The top tech companies exist because of products and ideas that were created when they were small. Those companies in their present form struggle with true creativity; they are massive and are capable only of iterative improvement. Similarly, analytics teams, once they hit a critical mass and level of success, tend to rest in their areas of strength. People are content, operate in the physical and psychological edifice of their successes, but lack the spark of ingenuity that got them there. They have no big ideas, and even if they did there is no mechanism for them to develop an idea. The innovative people who want to, as Steve Jobs said, "make a dent in the universe," turn in their corporate badge and join a smaller firm, seeding it with the practices and swagger of the corporation they are departing.

Leaders should aspire not to simply complete projects, or to use the latest technology, but to mind the machines. It is only engaged teams, united under a compelling vision for the future and enabled by parsimonious processes, who can make a dent in the universe.

This manuscript was prepared between the latter part of 2019 and the beginning of 2021. At the start of the work, the general consensus among even moderates in the business community was that at some point in the future people would work remotely and collaborate online and that companies would become more agile. The eight-hour day, bookended by a frustrating commute, spent mostly in maintaining archaic processes and completing reports, would die out in a new brighter, more lean future.

In March 2020, the COVID-19 pandemic caused mass lockdowns, made old heuristics instantly obsolete, and made historic data all but useless. Metrics such as year over year growth quickly became meaningless. Physical processes that had always been a bottleneck were now incompatible with lockdown laws and were promptly and enthusiastically discarded. Court filings could be done online. Engineering documents could be submitted by PDF. Every industry was forced to rapidly mature and to immediately cut costs to preserve cash.

Old budgets and forecasts were no longer relevant, and neither was the normal process to generate them. Without intuition and growth projections to depend on, many organizations turned to their analytics function to create a more systematic way to navigate the new environment.

While none of this has changed the future of data science and analytics, it has certainly accelerated the pace of change. Despite significant capital constraints, several organizations continue to invest in the function, and newly laid-off people are seeking to upskill and enter the field.

There will certainly be failures because of this rush to change approaches, but without an option to change they will remain into the future. Black swan events, whether new diseases, the political landscape, or the environment, will require organizations to be able to adapt quickly and to have robust data-driven decisions to stay alive. Prospects remain bright for analytics to support and enable this less certain future.

Index

A

academic partnerships, 23
accountability
 parsimony and, 72
advisor, 47
Affective Primacy Theory, 70–71
Agile
 DevOps, 105
 Kanban, 103
 Manifesto for Agile Software
  Development, 103
 methodologies, 104–105
 Scrum, 103
 Scrumban, 103
 sprint, 103
 stand-up, 103, 162–163
AI (artificial intelligence), 107–108
 Edge AI, 199–200
Alteryx, 191
analytics
 leaders, 8
 negative uses, 201–202
 organizational role, 20–25
 overview, 1–4
 practitioner characteristics,
  124–126

shortages of practitioners,
  204–206
 for social good, 200–201
 transition point, 211–212
analytics champion, 39
architect, 48
architecture, 21
AutoML, 189–191

B

Bethlehem Steel, Frederick Taylor
 and, 11
bias, 203–220
brainstorming, 107–108
budget
 project scoping and planning,
  94–95
bureaucracy, 71–72
business advisor, 39
business analyst, 48, 129
business leaders, 5

C

capability modeling, 28–32
career transitioners, 6
 future, 206–207

Centers of Excellence, 3
change agents, 40
change management, 62–64
  AI (artificial intelligence and),
    107–108
  brainstorming, 107–108
  iterative insights, 110–111
  skeuomorphs, 106–107
closeout and delivery
  automation, 112–114
  debriefing, 114–118
  model operationalization, 111
  presentation, 112
  process operationalization, 111
  product transition, 111–112
coffee chat meetings, 164–167
cognitive bias, 152
cognitive fluency, 70–71
communication
  project execution and, 99–102
  relationship management and,
    170
  team building and, 147–149
communication gap, 9–10
compliance, 12
conflict management, 167–169
consultants, 60–62
contractors, 60–62
CoP (Community of Practice), 3,
  24, 52–55
COVID-19 pandemic, 213–214
culture
  Hofstede cultural dimension
    theory, 142
culture ambassadors, 40
culture change, 24–25
culture, teams and, 140–145
  characteristics, 142–144
current state assessment, 26–37

D
DAMA (Data Management
  Association) International, 34
data architecture, 35
data artisans, 158–159

data assets
  CoP (Community of Practice),
    53–54
data engineer, 129
data engineering, 21
data gathering, 14
Data Governance Institute, 34
data modeler, 47
data quality, 34–35
data quality owner, 39
data science
  future, 192–195
data scientist, 47, 129
  as craftspeople, 157–160
  hierarchy of needs, 139–140
data security, 35
data warehouses
  future, 195–196
Dataiku, 191
DataRobot, 191
delivery phase of project delivery
  model, 56–57
demystifying, 25
departmental sponsor, 100
dependencies, 82
developers
  front-end, 129
development objectives, 81
DevOps, 105
Diderot effect, 153–154
discovery phase, project
  pipeline, 79
Dunning-Kruger effect, 152–153

E
Edge AI, 199–200
eminence building, 23
  CoP (Community of Practice),
    53
ethics, 12, 203–220
execution phase of project delivery
  model, 56
executive sponsor, 100
exogenous data, 198–199
extensibility, 12

F

feedback
  CoP (Community of Practice), 54
front-end developer, 129
future
  analytics for evil, 201–202
  analytics for good, 200–201
  AutoML, 189–191
  bias and, 203–204
  career transitioners, 206–207
  data science, 192–195
  data warehouses, 195–196
  Edge AI, 199–200
  ethics and, 203–204
  exogenous data, 198–199
  explainability, 188–189
  no-code/low-code movement,
      189–191
  operationalization, 196–198
  process, 188
future state, 37–38
  governance model, 40–42
  mandate, 39–40
  project delivery model, 55–57
  SFA model, 38
  target operating model, 42–55

G

GDPR (General Data Protection
    Regulation), 89
governance, 22, 34–35
  project execution and, 99–102
  strategy and, 34–35
  structure, 35
governance model, 40–42
  implementing, 64–65
GPT (General Purpose
    Technology), 206

H

hiring, 129–131
Hofstede cultural dimension
    theory, 142

I

innovation, 212
inprogress phase, project pipeline,
    79
intake, project planning, 73–83
integration, 24–25
intentional relationships, 24
interaction models, 44–45
  avatars, 47–48
  mapping to function, 48
  personas, 47–48
  swimlane diagram, 46
interoperability, 11
interpretability, 12

K

KNIME, 191

L

limits
  parsimony and, 72
low-code. *See* no-code/low code
    movement

M

mandates, 30
  comprehension, 31
  roles, 39–40
Manifesto for Agile Software
    Development, 103
Maslow's hierarchy of needs,
    139–140
metadata, 35
MLaaS (machine learning as a
    service), 188, 191
models
  capability modeling, 28–32
  compliance, 12
  ethics, 12
  extensibility, 12
  interoperability, 11
  interpretability, 12
  performance metrics, 178

political implementation, 11
procedural implementation, 11
scalability, 12
stability, 12
technical implementation, 11
moonshots, 81
motivated practitioners, 6

N
narrative ownership, 175–177
no-code/low code movement,
    189–191
  data science tools, 191
  ETL tools, 191

O
OCM (organizational change
    management), 22, 63–64
OD (organizational design),
    48–49
  center of excellence, 51
  centralization, 51
  decentralized, 51–52
  enterprise level, 49
  federated, 51–52
onboarding, 129–131
operationalization
  confirmation and, 197
  human gatekeeper and, 196
  parallelism and, 196
  parsimony and, 72
  project scoping and planning,
      90–91

P
parable of the stonecutters, 158
parallel *vs.* serial projects, 81
parsimony, 4, 71
  accountability, 72
  limits definition, 72
  materials prep, 101
  operationalization, 72
  relationships and, 171

people, 9. *See also* team building;
    teams
performance metrics, 177
  defects and errors, 178
  delivery compliance, 178
  enablement, 179
  feedback, 179
  managed value, 178
  model performance, 178
  planning compliance, 178
  productionalized models, 178
  strategic alignment, 179
  Theory X, 180
  Theory Y, 180
planning phase of project delivery
    model, 56
planning phase, project pipeline,
    79
platform owner, 39
POC (proof of concept), 109
policy setter, 39
political implementation, 11
politics, 82
  relationship management and,
      173
portfolio project management
    hierarchy, 80
pre-qualification phase, project
    pipeline, 79
prioritization, project planning,
    73–83
procedural implementation, 11
process, 9
  cognitive fluency and, 70–71
  future, 188
  outsiders *versus* experts, 84
  parsimony, 71–72
  project execution, 96–98
    agile analytics, 103–106
    change management, 106–111
    closeout and delivery, 111–118
    governance, 99–102
    project kickoff, 102–103

project planning, 73–83
project scoping and planning, 83–96
Venn diagram, 182
processes, 58
product management, 22
product manager, 39, 48
product owner, 128
project delivery model
  delivery, 56–57
  execution, 56
  planning, 56
  scoping, 55–56
project execution, 96
  Agile, 103–106
  approval, 97
  change management, 106–111
  closeout and delivery, 111–118
  communication plan, 99–102
  governance, 99–102
  meetings, 101
  project kickoff, 102–103
  review, 97–98
  self-government, 98
  sprint execution, 97
project kickoff, 102–103
project lead, 100
project management, 22
project manager, 100
project manager/delivery manager, 128–129
project pipelines, 77–80
project pitching
  CoP (Community of Practice), 54
project planning, 73
  intake, 73–83
    corporate model, 75
    first in, first out model, 74
    initial questions, 75–76
    preferential model, 75
    seniority model, 74
    urgency model, 74

pipelines, 77–80
portfolio project management, 80–83
prioritization, 73–83
  alignment and, 76
  challenges and, 76
  inspiration and, 76
project scoping and planning, 83–84
  design thinking, 86–88
  operationalization, 90–92
  planning, 92
    budget, 94–95
    limitations, 95–96
    project plan, 93–94
    risks, 95–96
    statement of work, 93
  regulatory, 88–90
  stakeholders, 84–85
projects
  co-development, 25

Q
qualification phase, project pipeline, 79

R
RACI (Responsible, Accountable, Consulted, Informed) models, 45
readiness assessment, 26–28
regulatory compliance, 23
relationship management, 169–175
  intentional relationships and, 24
relationship phase, project pipeline, 78
reporting, 12–13
resources, 58
risk manager, 39
risk mitigation plan
  project scoping and planning, 95–96
roadmap, 35

S

scalability, 12
scoping phase of project delivery
  model, 55–56
scoping phase, project pipeline, 79
self-service enabler, 39
SFA (suitability, feasibility,
  acceptability) model, 38
shortages of practitioners, 204–206
solution phase, project pipeline, 79
stability, 12
stakeholders
  balancing, 81
  engagement, 35–37
  project planning and, 84–85
  project scoping and planning,
    84–85
statement of work
  project scoping and planning, 93
steering committees, 100
strategic alignment, 81
strategy, 8, 17–19
  analytics as culture change,
    24–25
  analytics roles, 20
    academic partnerships, 23
    analytics governance, 22
    architecture, 21
    change management, 22
    data engineering, 21
    data governance, 22
    eminence building, 23
    product management, 22
    project management, 22
    regulatory compliance, 23
    systems support, 23
    vendor management, 22
  capability modeling, 28–32
  change management, 62–64
  CoP (Community of Practice), 24
  current state assessment, 26–37
  data as culture change, 24–25

data governance, 34–35
data quality, 34–35
demystification, 25
goals, 19
governance model, 40–42
  implementing, 64–65
intentional relationships and, 24
mandate definition, 39–40
performance metrics, 179
project co-development, 25
project delivery model, 55–57
readiness assessment, 26–27
technology accessibility, 25
technology stack review, 32–34
Venn diagram, 182
strategy architect, 39
students, 7–8
subject matter experts, 100
synergies, 82
systems support, 23

T

talent roadmap, 59–60
target operating model
  capabilities, 43–44
  CoP (Community of Practice),
    52–55
  functions, 43–44
  interaction models, 44–48
  OD (organizational design),
    48–52
  principles, 43
  RACI models, 45
  services, 43–44
Taylor, Frederick, 11, 70
Taylorism, 10–12
team building, 122–123
  analytics practitioners, 124–126
  communication and, 147–149
  culture and, 140–145
  departing members, 137–139
  hiring, 129–131

innovation and, 145–147
member composition, 128–129
member retention, 136–137
onboarding, 129–131
pitfalls, 151
    Diderot effect, 153–154
    Dunning-Kruger effect, 152–153
professional development,
        131–135
success in, 123–128
succession planning, 149–151
teams, 30–31
coffee chats, 164–167
conflict management, 167–169
formal meetings, 162
    daily standups, 162–163
    quarterly meetings, 163–164
    weekly kickoff, 163
leadership
    data artisans, 158–159
    leader qualities, 154–155
    parable of the stonecutters, 158
    seekers, 155–156
    translators, 156–157
narrative ownership, 175–177
one-on-one meetings, 164–167

performance metrics, 177–181
relationship management,
        169–175
strategy, people, process Venn
        diagram, 182
technical implementation, 11
technology
    accessibility, 25
technology representative, 100
technology stack review, 32–34
    stakeholders, 36
Theory X, 180
Theory Y, 180
time to value, 82
trainers, 40
transition point of analytics,
        211–212

V
values, 58
vendor management, 22

W–Z
WBS (work breakdown structure),
        94
Zajonc, Robert, 70